WID

Singing Schumann

Singing Schumann

An Interpretive Guide
for Performers

RICHARD MILLER

New York   Oxford

Oxford University Press

1999

Oxford University Press

Oxford   New York
Athens   Auckland   Bangkok   Bogotá   Buenos Aires   Calcutta
Cape Town   Chennai   Dar es Salaam   Delhi   Florence   Hong Kong   Istanbul
Karachi   Kuala Lumpur   Madrid   Melbourne   Mexico City   Mumbai
Nairobi   Paris   São Paulo   Singapore   Taipei   Tokyo   Toronto   Warsaw

and associated companies in
Berlin   Ibadan

Published by Oxford University Press, Inc.
198 Madison Avenue, New York, New York 10016

Oxford is a registered trademark of Oxford University Press

Library of Congress Cataloging-in-Publication Data
Miller, Richard, 1926–
   Singing Schumann : an interpretive guide for performers / Richard
   Miller.
   p. cm.
   Includes bibliographical references and index.
   ISBN 0-19-511904-5
   1. Schumann, Robert, 1810–1856 Songs. 2. Songs, German—
   Analysis, appreciation. 3. Songs, German—History and criticism.
   4. Schumann, Robert, 1810–1856—Criticism and interpretation.
   I. Title.
   MT121.S38M55 1999
   782.42168'092 — DC21   98-31645

9 8 7 6 5 4 3 2 1

Printed in the United States of America
on acid-free paper

In loving memory of Alice Miller,
who taught me my first Lied

PREFACE

In writing this book, it has been my intention to meet the need for a comprehensive study of the Schumann solo and duet Lieder. I hope performers may be alerted to the number of magnificent Schumann songs that lie neglected and that this study will assist singers, teachers, and pianoforte collaborators in supplementing their awareness of a unique mid-nineteenth-century Lieder style.

It was tempting to include trios, quartets, and other vocal ensemble music, but I reluctantly had to conclude that those categories must be omitted in the interest of producing a manageable manual. Assembling more than two recitalists for public appearance occurs only under special circumstances; the duet recital does still exist, however, and therefore Schumann's duets are included here. (They are grouped together in the penultimate chapter because they have been collected and published as a unit apart from their original opuses.) Schumann's youthful compositions from 1827 and 1828 and the declamatory ballad (*Melodram*), in which spoken texts are wedded to descriptive or dramatic music, are mentioned only in passing because they are chiefly of musicological interest.

Although I have mostly adhered to chronological and opus sequence, for practical reasons it has not always been possible to follow that course. In considering how compositional techniques affect performance practice in the Schumann Lieder, it seemed logical at the outset to look briefly at examples from several opuses, so that the principles identified would become more apparent when applied to the remainder of the oeuvre.

My primary aims are to deal with style and interpretation, not with harmonic analysis or with musicological investigation, both of which belong in the hands of music theorists and musicologists. Yet performance goals cannot be understood without some knowledge of both structure and ambience. Style and interpretation are not superimposed on the music of any period—they result from what lies within the music itself. No one can claim to know Robert Schumann's intentions, but performers who lack information on the musical and social environment to which he reacted and on the role he assigned himself cannot expect to perform the Lieder with adequate understanding.

Without any claim to the advancement of Schumann scholarship, I have attempted to take into account both of these essential areas when considering how the songs should be performed. Accordingly, I have consulted and included in the references some scholarly studies that deal with the Schumann Lieder chiefly in terms of literary sources and the cultural milieu out of which the songs emerge, along with others that are the work of theorists whose main interest logically is in form and structure. The present work, by contrast, is concerned with the specific issues of style and performance as they arise in the entirety of the Schumann song literature. Only by examining the vast span of his Lieder with style and performance practice in mind can one make a true assessment of Schumann as a song composer.

Within the past two decades, a number of important analytical studies of the Schumann cycles have appeared, among them Barbara Turchin's *Robert Schumann's Song Cycles in the Context of the Early Nineteenth-Century "Liederkreis"* (1981), Rufus Hallmark's *The Genesis of Schumann's "Dichterliebe"* (1979), and David Ferris's *From Fragment to Cycle: Formal Organization in Schumann's Eichendorff Liederkreis* (1993). Turchin and Ferris question some assumptions proposed earlier by Arthur Komar in his seminal *Schumann: "Dichterliebe": An Authoritative Score* (1971). I have continued to rely on Komar, not because his Schenkerian analysis is infallible or his viewpoints final, but because he combines a practical study-score with an accessible analysis of the *Dichterliebe* compositional scheme.

I have avoided quotations from the large body of German-language sources, both analytical and biographical. *The Marriage Diaries of Robert and Clara Schumann*, edited by Gerd Nauhaus and translated by Peter Ostwald, and Nancy B. Reich's *Clara Schumann: The Artist and the Woman* furnish background information, but I have not felt the necessity to quote extensively from the Schumann correspondence or from biographical studies such as John Daverio's *Robert Schumann*. These more comprehensive sources should be consulted by performers who desire greater historical detail than is appropriate to this study.

Peter Ostwald's *The Inner Voices of a Musical Genius* provides factual support for my long-held conviction that it is inappropriate to assume that Schumann's health and psychological problems plagued him only in his final years and that as his condition worsened his artistic output underwent decline. It is my viewpoint that much of the negative critical comment regarding the late Schumann Lieder is the result of false notions as to how the health of his psyche determined the value of his output.

For many years I pondered why only such a small segment of Schumann Lieder (the "canon of forty" that includes op. 42, op. 48, and some two dozen selected song favorites) found its way into recital programming. With the inherent value of so many Schumann Lieder leaping out from the page, I began to question why the major reservoir of his Lieder lay dormant. I have concluded that there are several explanations for this neglect.

The Schumann criticism most accessible to the performance community has been directed largely toward the pianoforte and symphonic works. With regard to the song literature, it is mostly the "Clara Year" Lieder (1840) that have received scrutiny. They are too readily considered the consequence of a temporary exuberant emotional state brought about by the winning of Clara's hand in marriage. One of my premises is that although the copiousness of Lieder composition never again attained that of the 1840 Lieder Year, for the most part neither the historical record nor the literature itself supports the perspective that the composer's creativity thereafter fell into decline. (Of course, the illness of his final several years ended all possibility for creative work.)

In addition, adverse criticism of the late Lieder comes from the fact that Schumann, after contriving his unique lyric-declamation style in works such as *Dichterliebe* and *Frauenliebe und -leben*, was not content to restrict himself to that idiom and went on to experiment with other forms of the Lied. "Aha! His creative powers have diminished," say some critics who have examined the complete Lied oeuvre only superficially and therefore have failed to discern the developmental continuum of one of the most original songwriters of all time.

Other adverse criticism of the middle and late Lieder results from narrowly defining the structure of the Lied and from finding Schumann at fault when his Lieder are measured within arbitrary aesthetic boundaries. If it is thought that adherence to metric scanning of verse ought to dictate the musical setting of every poem (music acting chiefly as a frame for the enhancement of the poetry), the intrinsic value of much of the nineteenth-century Lied repertory, including that written by Schubert, Brahms, Wolf, and Strauss, will be found wanting. It is exactly in the liberties Schumann takes with his poetic sources during all periods of his Lied composing that he exerts considerable influence on later major Lied writers. Schumann's inventive treatment of verbal meter is one of his assets, an integral part of his declamatory lyricism and of his later more expansive Lieder style. His truncation of strophes (a habit shared by Schubert and numerous other Lied composers) does not detract from his synchronization of word and music. Even if *Dichterliebe* and *Frauenliebe und -leben*, which for the most part deal faithfully with poetic scanning, word inflection, and inclusion of the complete poem, had never been written, Schumann's stature as a superior Lied composer would remain secure.

I have often felt it essential to cite negative mainstream critical sources and to refute pejorative criticism by looking anew at the songs themselves. My purpose is to call this criticism into question, particularly with regard to the late Lieder.

The entire Schumann solo Lieder oeuvre (with the few exceptions mentioned previously) and the invaluable duet literature are organized in such a way that performers, both singers and pianists, may look for comment on a specific Lied, opus, or cycle. However, the entire study is best read as a commentary on Schumann's compositional techniques as they dictate style and interpretation.

Because of space considerations, I was faced with a serious dilemma as to which music examples to exclude; those I included had to be relatively brief and limited in number. I have made the assumption that the dedicated Lieder singer will have access to the total body of the published Schumann songs and that readers will be most familiar with the best-loved and most frequently performed of them. For those reasons, commentary on important Lieder is not always accompanied by music illustration. In other cases, music examples have been selected in order to allow the reader to judge the accuracy of conflicting critical comment.

The serious performer will possess or have available copies of the published Schumann Lieder: Band I, Band II, Band III (Volumes I, II, and III), *Duette für Zwei Singstimmen* (Duets for Two Voices), and *Spanisches Liederspiel*. The Peters edition volumes, being the most complete, are the suggested reference sources for this study. Song titles are italicized in order to avoid confusion with text quotations.

Because of the close integration of voice and keyboard skills in the Schumann Lieder (particularly in those that have suffered neglect), I have been so bold as to offer pianistic as well as vocal advice. My aim is to assist both singer and pianist to achieve greater stylistic integrity and possibly a higher degree of artistic communication.

Above all, my intention is to be an advocate, to further an assessment of Robert Schumann's impact on the Lied, with the hope of bringing a greater number of his songs to life in performance.

Oberlin, Ohio   R. M.
September 1998

ACKNOWLEDGMENTS

It is not possible to express thanks to each teacher, coach, conductor, performing colleague (singer or pianist), and author who over the years helped mold my convictions regarding style and interpretation in Lieder. What this book contains is not the result of one person's intimate experience with a significant body of literature but an amalgamation and filtering of insights gained from many professional sources, a few of which are cited in the references. Acknowledgment is due them all.

My greatest indebtedness is to the ageless Lieder themselves and to the genius that created them. I have had decades-long association with the Schumann Lieder, based on frequent personal performance of them and on a Lied performance course devised for voice majors that I taught for more than twenty years at the Oberlin Conservatory of Music. These experiences heightened my awareness of the multifacetedness of the Schumann oeuvre and the significant role played by Schumann in the evolution of the nineteenth-century song.

In more recent years, when reading studies of the Schumann Lieder written by two premier performing artists, Dietrich Fischer-Dieskau and Gerald Moore, I discovered that my own assessments, which so often had differed from the written comments of other well-respected Schumann critics, were often shared by the two artists most closely associated with that literature. Their insights strengthened my earlier convictions. They are extensively quoted and deserve my special acknowledgment. Although I find myself frequently at odds with his aesthetic conclusions, I am, nonetheless, deeply indebted to Eric Sams for his comprehensive study of the Schumann Lieder.

Don Gillespie assisted in obtaining the kind and generous permission of C. F. Peters Corporation for the reproduction of all the cited musical examples; Reinhard G. Pauly and the Amadeus Press granted permission to quote extensively from Pauly's translation of Fischer-Dieskau's *Robert Schumann, Words and Music: The Vocal Compositions*; from Jay Gress of Random House/Alfred A. Knopf (Pantheon) came permission to quote the Paul Rosenfeld translations of Schumann's *On Music and Musicians*; Jeffrey Czekaj was instrumental in arranging permission for excerpts from *Poem and Music in the German Lied* by Jack M. Stein, Copyright ©1971 by the President and Fellows of Harvard College, reprinted by permission of Harvard University Press. Taylor Hess arranged the granting of permission to extensively quote from Eric Sams's *The Songs of Robert Schumann* (Indiana University Press). The Bildarchiv Preussischer Kulturbesitz, Berlin, has kindly permitted the reproduction of the 1847 lithograph of Robert and Clara Schumann.

The most important acknowledgment I reserve for last. I would not have been able to undertake or complete this project (or any other publication in which I have been involved) without the advice, encouragement, understanding, and critical eyes, ears, and judgment of my wife, Mary. Her assistance has been indispensable.

CONTENTS

Singing Schumann

1

Robert Schumann as Song Composer

Anything that happens in the world affects me; politics, for example, literature, people; and I reflect about all of these things in my own way—and these reflections then seek to find an outlet in music. This is also the reason for which so many of my compositions are hard to understand, because they are connected with distant interest; and sometimes striking, because everything extraordinary that happens impresses me and impels me to express it in music. For this reason, too, so many other composers do not satisfy me, because—in addition to all their lack of professional skill—they enlarge on lyrical commonplaces. The highest level reached in this type of music does not come up to the point from which my kind of music starts. The former may be a flower. The latter is a poem; that is, belongs to the world of the spirit. The former comes from an impulse of crude nature; the latter stems from the consciousness of the poetic mind.

Letter to Clara Wieck, April 13, 1838

Biographical details of a composer are of secondary interest in determining how to perform the works themselves, but there is no better way to understand Schumann's orientation in his Lieder composition than by recalling his immersion in the literary world around him. His father's bookshop in Zwickau (Saxony) influenced young Schumann, surrounded as he was by classic and contemporary literature and acutely aware of the literary proclivities of his father. By age thirteen, Robert was compiling collections of poems, some of them written by himself. Beginning at age fifteen, he encountered Greek and Latin classics at the lyceum (which he had entered at ten years of age and where he stayed for eight years). The works of Schiller and Goethe were part of his early experience. But it was German Romantic novelist Jean-Paul Richter who spoke most intimately to the youthful Schumann. Here was a kindred soul, given to fantastic flights of imagination and emotional expression.

In 1833, when Schumann was twenty-three, he showed a growing sense of mission, looking to the elevation of music composition beyond mere entertainment and to the development of a standard by which to judge it. He founded the *Neue Zeitschrift für Musik*, of which he was to be editor for a period of ten years. The first edition, published in April 1834, introduced the *Davidsbündler*, a group of forward-looking contributors, some real, some fictitious. Modern Davids were needed to best the musical Philistines of the period. Aphorisms were borrowed from Goethe, Jean-Paul, and other literary figures. In an 1854 foreword to collected articles that had appeared between 1834 and 1844, Schumann (p. 25) wrote:

> The musical situation in Germany at the moment [1834] was anything but inspiring. Rossini reigned in the opera houses, and nothing was to be heard on the pianoforte save Herz and Hünten. Yet merely a few years had passed since Beethoven, C. M. von Weber, and Franz Schubert had lived among us. . . .
>
> So on a day the following idea came to these musical young hot-heads: "Let us not be mere spectators! Let us lend a hand ourselves for the glory of things! Let us bring the poetry of our art into honour once again!"

As flamboyant Florestan, Schumann declared his aggressive viewpoints; his more temperate thoughts were expressed by the gentler Eusebius. The Florestan/ Eusebius duality is of interest not only for its appearance in Schumann's written critical commentary but also as an indication of division within his psyche. This dualism is evident in his compositional techniques, especially in the Lieder. As early as July 1, 1831, Schumann's diary attests to an interest in creating the literary duality of Florestan/Eusebius: "Entirely new persons enter my diary today—two of my best friends . . . Florestan and Eusebius." By October of that year, Florestan had become "my bosom friend; actually . . . he is my real self." Later, Eusebius and other characters "have changed their roles and from real persons have become fantasy characters." Florestan and Eusebius had literary, psychological, and musical significance for their creator. In both personal and professional matters, the young Schumann displayed a strong streak of independence that alternated with an equal need for dependency. Undoubtedly, this psychological dichotomy provided profound impetus to the direction his music was to take.

Within Schumann's subliminal self, intense literary and musical interests vied for expression. His propensity for creatively fusing music and literature is apparent not only in his Lieder but also in the programmatic, extra-musical aspects of the pianoforte and orchestral works. Schumann was not alone in promoting this aspect of Romanticism; his tendencies were reinforced by prevailing attitudes within the artistic coterie to which he belonged.

Surely over the past century enough has been written and speculated about Robert Schumann's relationship to Clara Wieck (and to her father) to plead for limited further comment on the subject. Letters written by both Robert and Clara, as well as those of her father, present a detailed story of one of the stormiest courtships of all time. How closely did these personal events relate to the composer's turning to the Lied? The popular romantic viewpoint is that the impetuous outburst of song in 1839–40 stemmed from Schumann's emotional response to Clara Wieck and to their troubled courtship, but his interest in Clara had long been expressed through other musical forms. Rufus Hallmark (1996, p. 105) emphasizes this point:

One common suggestion is that the composer broke into song because he was inspired by his anticipated marriage to Clara, but the underlying reasoning is fuzzy on several accounts. Robert and Clara had been in love for years and had even made a secret pledge eventually to be wed, in spite of her father's objections. In the winter of 1839–40, when he began to write songs, their marriage was still far from certain. Furthermore, by no means all the poems Schumann set have to do with happy love, or even with love at all. Finally, and more importantly, Clara had already been a constant source of inspiration; he had composed much piano music with her in mind. His feelings toward her cannot logically be advanced to explain a change in genre, though they unquestionably continued to inspire him in whatever he did. But, although rejecting this explanation as facile and sentimental, one may still view Clara as a catalyst; she had been encouraging Robert to compose songs, for example, and he enjoyed hearing her sing.

Suffice it to say that what marked the beginning of a new phase in the composer's impulsive life, following his infatuation with Ernestine von Fricken in 1834 and the breaking off of his engagement to her the following year, was his subsequent attraction to Clara in 1835 and his expression of love for her in 1836. During the 1840 "Lieder Year" before his marriage to Clara Wieck, Robert Schumann wrote 138 of his 250 Lieder. This explosion of creativity epitomizes the essential Romantic composer. (The ensuing diaries of Robert and Clara Schumann, begun September 13, 1840, the day after their marriage, and continuing for a period of four years, have been collected by Gerd Nauhaus and translated by Peter Ostwald as *The Marriage Diaries of Robert and Clara Schumann*. The Schumanns' joint record provides much insight into both creative artists and their relationship.)

The phenomenal eruption of song includes the major cycles and many beloved single songs, as the staggering list of opus numbers from that year indicates: op. 24 (Heine *Liederkreis*), op. 25 (*Myrten*), op. 27, op. 29, op. 30, op. 31, op. 33, op. 35, op. 36, op. 39 (Eichendorff *Liederkreis*), op. 40, op. 42 (Chamisso *Frauenliebe und -leben*), op. 45, op. 48 (Heine *Dichterliebe*), op. 49, op. 53, and op. 57. Such volcanic lyric explosion recalls Schubert's Lied outpouring. The productive periods of Lieder composition by Hugo Wolf were equally intense, though briefer and more sporadic.

Bach and Beethoven were influences on the Schumann circle, as acknowledged by Schumann's essay on Robert Franz's op. 2 (p. 241), but it is to Franz Schubert that one must turn if the Schumann Lieder are to be understood within historical context. Whereas Schubert's Classicism sustains an objectivity in his Lieder even when the poetry is dramatic and/or intimate, the impact of a highly personal emotional response to literary ideas marks Schumann's songs. Yet the seeds of several aspects of the Schumann Lieder can be traced to Schubert. Through his mastery of the *Stimmungslied* (a song that creates a particular mood), Schubert provided Schumann with significant models—for example, *Frühlingsglaube, Nacht und Träume, Wanderers Nachtlied, An die Nach-*

Robert Schumann (1810–56) and his wife, the pianist Clara Wieck (1819–96). Lithograph by Eduard Kayser, 1847. Photo © Bildarchiv Preussischer Kulturbesitz, Berlin.

tigall, Die Rose, Nachtviolen, Die Liebe hat gelogen, Du liebst mich nicht, Früh-lingstraum, and *Ihr Bild.* Schubert's elevation of the *volkstümliches* or *im Volk-ston* (folklike) Lied also exercised a potent influence.

Much critical evaluation of the songs of Schumann has emphasized the in-creased role of the pianoforte as an equal or at times dominant partner of the textual and vocal components of his Lieder. There is no doubt that the demands for technical keyboard facility based on improvisatory pianism, so much in evidence in the works for pianoforte, are at times equally present in the Lieder. Kathleen Dale (p. 32) identifies some specific techniques on which Schumann depended (particularly prior to 1840) in his keyboard compositions:

> the combination of dissimilar metrical or rhythmical units; frequent series of syncopations and unaccountable accents on apparently unimportant beats, riotous chromaticisms and swift modulations, and ingenious polyphonic texture which looks rather more impressive on paper than it sounds in actual performance.

But when one considers the interplay of voice and keyboard in many Schubert Lieder, the suspicion grows that Schumann was not making such a groundbreaking departure from the past as he may have thought but rather was building extensively on Schubert's genius for combining skilled vocalism with virtuosic pianism. However, Schumann (p. 75) explains his own pianistic orientation in the Lieder as compared with that of Schubert as follows:

> Paralleling the development of poetry, the Franz Schubert epoch has already been followed by a new one which has utilized the improvements of the simultaneously developed instrument of accompaniment, the piano. . . . The voice alone cannot reproduce everything or produce every effect; together with the expression of the whole the finer details of the poem should also be emphasized; and all is well so long as the vocal line is not sacrificed.

It is true that Schumann, as he himself recognized, benefited by the technical advances in pianoforte construction, which furthered distinctive solo literature. It is not, however, the actual introduction per se of the pianoforte into the Lied that marks a major Schumann contribution. Rather, it is the heightened personal expression achieved through the developing Romantic movement that he helped bring to flower.

When the role of the pianoforte in the Schumann Lieder is stressed, the importance of the vocal melody sometimes is overlooked. A balanced assessment should include an awareness of Schumann's own written views on what constitutes melody. In campaigning for the superiority of the German musician, Schumann (p. 236) compares Germanic vocal writing with that of Rossini and Bellini:

> As though song and music were two different things! As though bad music could be covered over by a good vocal line! As though for the sake of singing one ought first to become a bad musician! I say again that not all that is easy to sing constitutes a melody! There is a difference between melody and melodies. Who possesses melody also possesses melodies, but the reverse is not always true.

Pursuing the battle to correct the notion that the land of song lay solely below the Alps, Schumann continues:

Do we Germans possess no melodic style of our own? Has not the most recent past taught us that there are minds and masters in Germany who know how to unite profundity and facility, significance and grace? Do not Spohr, Mendelssohn, and others know how to sing and how to write for singers? We must point this out to the German-Italian hybrid school, which has so many adherents in Vienna. But the union is not natural. The highest peaks of Italian art do not reach much beyond the first beginnings of the truly German. How can we stand firmly, with one foot upon an Alp, the other on a convenient meadow?

In 1827–28, the youthful Schumann composed eleven exploratory Lieder (one of which has been lost). Two were set to his own poetry, five to Kerner poems, one to a Byron translation, one to a text by J. G. Jacobi, and another to Goethe's *Der Fischer* (previously set by Schubert). Two of the Kerner songs were later incorporated into op. 11 and op. 22 for pianoforte.

For a decade, Schumann's efforts were directed almost entirely to the pianoforte. Significantly, many of these pieces were given extramusical titles, as though his literary interests were finding expression through nonverbal means. Eleven years later, aware of his neglect of the song as an outlet for creativity, Schumann became consumed by the setting of verse. He may have deliberately paused at that point in his career before attempting larger forms of composition. Up to then, some of his most successful compositions for pianoforte had been in small form; perhaps he recognized that the slighter forms of the Lied were well suited to his capabilities.

Critical opinion identifies the Schumann piano literature as his most successful genre. This can be attributed, at least in part, to Schumann's pianistic skills, particularly in the aforementioned area of improvisation, which so shaped his idiomatic writing for pianoforte. But when his total Lieder oeuvre is examined, it can be argued that Schumann actually is at his best in the song literature, where he synthesizes personal sensitivity, strong literary orientation, and fully Romantic pianistic excursions. Perhaps the most complete Schumann is to be found in Schumann the Lied composer.

In all probability, the most frequently performed songs of Robert Schumann are those of the two best-known cycles, *Frauenliebe und -leben* and *Dichterliebe*. The difficulty many females currently experience in performing *Frauenliebe und -leben* may come not only from the problematic attitude of a male poet writing about female adoration of the male but also from the musical idiom itself, which at times skirts the sentimental. Likewise, the chief peril for performers of *Dichterliebe* lies in its lure toward intemperate romantic indulgence. There is here no intent to diminish the remarkably high value of these two durable cycles as performance vehicles, but some of the most meritorious Schumann Lieder are found in other collections. In fact, both cycles may be cited as examples of works that tread the thin line that separates sentiment and sentimentality (a charge it would be difficult to level at most Schubert Lieder). Schumann's Romantic message is less compelling when his self-consciousness and internalization of the poetry become excessive. It might be thought that such criticism is unfair because it applies criteria that did not constrain the composer and that ignore the period in which the works were born. Nevertheless, for the modern listener Schumann is most effective when he avoids overripe Romanticism.

Some Compositional Devices in Schumann Lieder

A few general observations about Schumann's compositional techniques are in order. Awareness of these techniques may assist the performer to determine how best to approach the songs of Schumann, taking into account the diverse styles that exist among them. Some characteristic devices are the following:

- calculated reiterated chordal uniformity
- arpeggiated keyboard configuration
- frequent use of dotted rhythms
- offbeat rhythms and syncopation
- improvisatory-like pianistic configurations
- frequent and sometimes extensive pianistic digressions in prelude (*Vorspiel*), interlude (*Zwischenspiel*), and postlude (*Nachspiel*)
- tonality ambiguity (the avoidance of a key center until the voice establishes it)
- coherent tonality schemes for cycles and for key relationships among related Lieder
- chromaticism to enhance introspection
- overlapping of pianoforte and voice in the development of thematic material
- melody paralleled in voice and keyboard
- frequently occurring melodic nuclei
- close-intervallic melodic structure
- frequent repeated single-note (*eintönig*) melodic phrase beginnings
- motivic juxtaposition of exuberance and quietude (Florestan/Eusebius elements)
- frequent preference for word inflection over poetic meter
- poetic recall through thematic repetition

Before the Schumann Lieder are examined in a systematic way, following chronology and opus sequence, it seems appropriate to look at Lieder (from various opuses) that exemplify a few of Schumann's frequent compositional techniques.

As an introduction to how structure affects performance in the Schumann Lieder, no better example can be cited than *Widmung* (Dedication) from *Myrten*. (Most published editions, including the Peters, use the spelling *Myrten* rather than the older form *Myrthen*.) *Widmung* was appropriately the first song in the collection of Lieder that Robert presented to Clara as a wedding present. "Eine jungfräuliche Myrte" is a bridal wreath made of myrtle and other flowers.

Florestan/Eusebius duality is immediately apparent in this remarkable Lied.

Example 1.1.   *Widmung*, bars 1–4.

The rocketing dotted arpeggiated keyboard figure, which provides motion and excitement, is introduced in the very first bar by persistent sixths (Ex. 1.1). Subsequently, angular ascending vocal lines and a dotted rhythmic pattern add intensity. This musical device is one of several in which Schumann speaks as Florestan. An understanding of the propelling function of this motif offers a key to the performance of a number of favorite Schumann Lieder. Phrases built on this sort of rhythmic and melodic structure should be sung with ardent fervor, not as the deep mutterings of a lovesick soul. Here is Florestan, not Eusebius.

Performers may misunderstand *Widmung*, misled by the composer's habit of combining tempo and interpretation designations into a single marking (in this case, *innig/lebhaft* over the opening bar). The word *innig* should not be confused with *innerlich* (inwardly). *Innig*, although implying intimacy, is best translated as "ardent, fervent, hearty, sincere." In the A section of *Widmung*, both vocal and pianistic configurations illustrate the high level of impetuosity Schumann brings to the Friedrich Rückert text. At the vocally and harmonically climactic "mein Himmel du, darein ich schwebe," Florestan expression demands an exuberance and vitality from the singer best expressed through vibrant vocal sound and a well-articulated legato. Even though rhythmic incisiveness and clarity are required from the pianist, the singer should not be unduly influenced by the assertive pianoforte score. Unity comes through the balancing of voice and pianoforte (each realizing its own instrumental potential), not through each imitating the other's task. The emotional character of the poetry changes at the concluding lines of the first section with "O du mein Grab, in das hinab ich ewig meinen Kummer gab." Schumann adroitly takes this change of poetic direction into account.

The B section, beginning "Du bist die Ruh," with its obvious indebtedness to Schubert, finds Eusebius at work (bars 14–19). Gone are Florestan's dotted broken arpeggios, replaced by straightforward reiterated chords that arrest pianistic flight. While the repeated chords provide motion, they create a contrasting aura of quietude. The melody is correspondingly small-intervalled, with whole notes and half notes producing an increased sense of inner calm (Ex. 1.2). It is not necessary for performers to make an obvious tempo change at the B section, because the composer himself accomplishes the *Ruh* expressed by the text, through changing the musical figures vocally and pianistically; tempo change is thereby written in. The juxtaposition of the A♭ tonality of section A with the E tonality of section B (A♭ becomes G♯ in the new key) adds to the distinctive mood change.

A telling modulation in the final bar of the B section (C♯ turned into D♭) leads into a recapitulation of the rocket theme, with textual repetition. This serves as perfect Florestan/Eusebius bridging. The singer, who in section B must be careful to keep sound flowing through the long notes without loss of intensity, now returns to the "ardent fervor" with which the Lied began. In the

Example 1.2.   *Widmung*, bars 14–19.

postlude, the composer has Eusebius speak again by maintaining sustained B section material in the right-hand treble clef while Florestan comments in the left-hand bass clef. Here Schumann is in top form, identifying personally with the poetry yet remaining untrammeled by the self-conscious sentimentality that occasionally is apparent in some of his Lieder. Surely no bride has ever had more cause to rejoice at an expression of love than Clara when she opened the cycle of songs presented to her as a wedding gift, with *Widmung* (Dedication, Schumann's own title) its initial offering.

Segments of improvisatory arpeggiated configurations, followed by chordal reiteration, are skillfully combined to produce Lieder with a distinct Schumann flavor. These formulas are equally useful in *Er, der Herrlichste von allen*, this time directed to the opening vocal motif. The sonority of the pianoforte resounding in middle range combines richness and rhythmic exactitude to create vitality which matches that of the vocal line.

Mondnacht, perhaps the quintessential mood-evocative song (*Stimmungslied*), is a prime example of similar compositional techniques used under entirely different circumstances and with remarkably dissimilar results.

Much has just been made of Schumann's frequent practice within a single Lied of using two contrasting musical phrases in close proximity. Some critics espouse the notion that the frequent use of sustained reiterated chords and rapid broken arpeggios (of which this thematic contrasting often consists) is an indication that Schumann constructed his 1840 Lieder hurriedly, relying heavily upon "filler," in compensation for limited musical imagination. Although the songs were, indeed, composed rapidly, proof of the error of this assessment can be found in the high quality of Lieder in which one or both of these techniques can be found. As with his arpeggiated figures, Schumann made successful use of reiterated chords that outline static harmony in quite different sets of circumstances and for unrelated reasons. Compare, for example, the diverse utilization of chordal repetition in *Du bist wie eine Blume*, *Die Lotosblume*, *Stille Tränen*, *Mondnacht*, *Ich grolle nicht*, *Du Ring an meinem Finger*, and *Süsser Freund, du blickest mich verwundert an*.

Characteristic arpeggiation is tellingly used under disparate circumstances in *Der Nussbaum*, *In der Fremde*, *Helft mir, ihr Schwestern*, *An meinem Herzen, an meiner Brust*, and *Ich will meine Seele tauchen*, to cite but a few examples. As has been noted, this Florestan arpeggiation is often combined with a dotted rhythmic pattern that serves as an ostinato, as in *Helft mir, ihr Schwestern*, with its two inner keyboard voices moving in tandem. The pianoforte voices of *Helft mir, ihr Schwestern*, it could be postulated, depict the *Schwestern* to whom the young woman appeals for help. If such a reading seems too pat, it is at least safe to affirm that agitation, excitement, and forward movement are frequently engendered through the dotted arpeggio.

An meinem Herzen, an meiner Brust offers similar application of this favorite Schumann stratagem. In the more subdued *Lied der Suleika*, arpeggiation indicates quiet urgency. To portray excitement and drama, *Waldesgespräch* relies on a harmonically enriched dotted-arpeggio figure in section A. Somewhat later in *Waldesgespräch*, as the siren makes her threatening appearance,

Schumann reverts to the squareness of strong repeated arpeggiation in C major, later returning to an arpeggiation in sixths for the bewitcher's victorious cry.

In settings that express tranquillity, chromatic arpeggiation is effectively used for pianistic color. *Aus den hebräischen Gesängen* is typical; the arpeggios take on an improvisatory nature, as is the case in *Zwielicht*. This is especially true for the pianistic reveries that enhance the poetic expression. In both of these introspective Lieder, the composer's sensitive realization of textual content instructs singer and pianist on the suitable colors of sound: intimate and reflective. *Zwielicht*, one of the most remarkable compositions in the entire Lied repertoire, grows out of the changing tonalities and introspective timbres of middle-keyboard octaves. Interpolated quasi-recitative passages "was will dieses Grau'n bedeuten" and "stimmen hin und wieder wandern" momentarily arrest the flow of melody. The recitative-like conclusion is haunting and chilling. Harmonic movement throughout is closely allied to speech inflection and to word accentuation.

An example of the pianoforte singing forth a melody that the voice then concludes is found in *Im wunderschönen Monat Mai*. *Am leuchtenden Sommermorgen* makes use of the same device in less obvious fashion. *Seit ich ihn gesehen* and *Süsser Freund, du blickest mich verwundert an* put the same principle to work not as pianistic commentary but as harmonic overlapping. Other examples are: *Lied der Braut I*, *Lied der Braut II*, *Die Soldatenbraut*, *Meine Rose*, *Aus den hebräischen Gesängen*, *Waldesgespräch*, *Schöne Fremde*, and *Frühlingsnacht*. In *Der Nussbaum*, the voice does not complete the pianistic melody but is inserted into it midway. These Lieder are examples of several related compositional techniques devoted to an uncanny realization of the poetry.

Extended ambiguity of tonality, for both voice and pianoforte, another compositional scheme dear to Schumann, is illustrated in *Im wunderschönen Monat Mai*. F♯ minor is suspected to be the tonic, but cadences that introduce the voice appear to be in A major. Is the tonality A major or F♯ minor? In *Mondnacht*, for a period of time, a sense of mystical vagueness based on key uncertainty (late resolution of the dominant) catches the diffusion of moonlight and romantic dreaming.

Increased use of chromaticism, characteristic of the developing Romantic idiom, is a major ingredient of Schumann's harmonic language, contrary to criticism that says he is conservative in his use of chromaticism (Cooper, p. 121). In this regard, Schumann occupies a middle ground between Schubert and Wolf. Within a single Lied Schumann's chromatic harmonies often extend beyond the normal Schubertian idiom, yet he usually avoids the sudden contrast of chromatic and diatonic segments so typical of Wolf. As is true with most Lied composers, when Schumann is composing in the folk idiom (*Volkston*, or *volkstümlich* mode) his harmony generally remains diatonic. Chromaticism is employed by Schumann for psychological insight, uncertainty, nostalgia, longing, despair, mystical states, and the evocation of nature.

A sense of urgency and impatience characterizes a number of Schumann settings, in contrast to the soulfulness of the Brahms Lieder and the frequent ebullience of the Schubert Lieder. One is familiar with the quick tempi and effervescence that characterize many Schubert Lieder, yet Schubert's songs mostly remain within Classical dimensions of emotional control. Schumann's impetuosity and unabashed strong emotion come into focus in Florestan mode, most strikingly in contrast to Eusebian moments of rhythmic moderation and tranquillity. An inner "Eusebian" voice cries out: "Enough! Regain control over uninhibited emotion!"

For this reason, the singer who approaches the Schumann Lieder with hearts-and-flowers Romanticism parodies the eagerness that Schumann introduces into his lyrical and nondramatic poetic sources. By diminishing this innate zealousness, singer and pianist go contrary to the internal evidence of the music and to the nature of Robert Schumann the man. Mannered effects and miniaturism that pose as salon artistry are inappropriate to the Schumann Lieder. His songs demand performance in which sensitivity, youthful exuberance, and impetuosity are united.

Any consideration of Schumann's compositional techniques must take into account his fascination with riddles and enigmas. Eric Sams (pp. 23–26) draws attention to Schumann's preoccupation with "Clara themes": motivic elements consisting of five notes that correspond to the five letters of the name Clara. By allowing the note B to serve as the letter L and G as the letter R, C–B–A–G–A comes to stand for C–L–A–R–A. Sams believes that these notes, as well as related pitch combinations, become symbols, gestures, and signs in the Schumann Lieder. He finds *Dichterliebe* to have Clara themes in common with op. 24, op. 25, and the *Davidsbündler*, op. 6.

It has long been known that Schumann was given to extramusical symbolism. There is no doubt that Clara was on the composer's mind and that the unmistakable omnipresent melodic nuclei in many of the Lieder are best explained by recognizing them as variations on the Clara theme. Yet the constant search for encipherment may divert attention from other factors that distinguish the Schumann Lieder. Of greater importance than the search for symbolic meanings associated with frequently occurring melodic fragments is recognition of how the compositional techniques identified earlier actualize Schumann's personal interpretation of a poet's meaning and how that information can be used by performers to the enhancement of style and interpretation.

2

Performance Practices in the Schumann Lieder

Every Lied has its particular characteristics. Its re-creation calls for individual artistic imagination as each performer reacts to the composer's intention. Yet certain practices are common to the performance of all Schumann Lieder.

The first principle to be kept in mind is that the nature of music composition changes from one decade to another. Music is often inappropriately forced into historical periods of considerable length, sometimes as long as half a century or more. Designations such as Early Music, Early Baroque, Late Baroque, Classical, Romantic, Impressionist, Postromantic, Modern, and Postmodern, frequently are cited with beginning and terminating dates as though nothing changed until one style suddenly was surpassed or elevated to another level, like a boat progressing through a series of canal locks. In point of fact, the history of music is one not of static artistic strata but of flowing gradations of change. This is nowhere more apparent than in the literature of the nineteenth-century Lied.

As a part of the determination of stylistic considerations in the performance of Schumann Lieder, it is tempting to consider what went before Schumann and, in the process, devote a chapter to the precursors of the Schubertian Lied, an extensive topic in itself. Suffice it to say that genius though he was, Schubert, "the father of the Lied," did not spring onto the musical landscape without historical generation. But the more immediate point for this discussion is where

Schumann stands with regard to what came immediately before him and to what followed him.

Despite the contributions of Haydn, Mozart, and Zelter and his contemporaries, Franz Schubert is the progenitor of the nineteenth-century German art song. Schubert is, as Alfred Einstein describes him (p. 97), "the Romantic Classic." In the brief span of his creative life, Schubert explored a number of compositional solutions for Lieder construction, developing them as he went along, never abandoning any of them. Yet almost immediately, and subsequently within little more than a decade of intensive creativity, he revolutionized the German-language song and prepared the way for the art song in any language. Schubert is the source of nearly every Lied stream that flows through the nineteenth century and into the twentieth. It is doubtful that this source of inspiration will lessen in the twenty-first century or as long as the solo song exists.

A common mistake is not differentiating between the performance styles of Schubert and Schumann. Classical proportions of the Schubertian Lied, in both melodic and harmonic dimensions, make specific stylistic demands on the performer. Only a decade after Schubert's death, the "Romantic Classic" tradition becomes the "Romantic" in Robert Schumann. For some singers and pianists, a performance pitfall is the assumption that Robert Schumann is but an extension of Franz Schubert. The reverse performance peril, and the more common, is to sing Schubert as though Schumann had already happened.

Singing Schumann as though he were Brahms, Wolf, Strauss, or Mahler is as much in error as singing Schumann as though he were Schubert, Mozart, or Haydn. The main body of the Schumann Lieder belongs within the period 1839–52, a time during which such dissimilar composers as Franz, Loewe, Mendelssohn, Chopin, Liszt, Wagner, and Verdi were flourishing. Given the nature of the mostly subjective Romantic poetry that inspired Robert Schumann, it is tempting to approach his Lieder with the sensibilities of the full-blown Romanticism of the last half of the nineteenth century. Many excesses in the performance of Schumann Lieder come from applying late-nineteenth-century and early-twentieth-century art song performance customs to them. A rule for the performer who wishes to stay on stylistic track when performing the Schumann Lieder: *Romanticism without excess*.

Some inappropriate singer mannerisms that commonly occur are:

- scooping into important words (beginning the note slightly under pitch, with gradual arrival at the tonal center)
- starting the vocal tone straight and then letting it "wiggle" with vibrato
- introducing rubato where the composer never intended
- detailing and underscoring each long note in every musical phrase
- negating the vocal legato on notes of short duration
- removing vibrancy on notes of short duration
- changing the dynamic intensity of each note in a phrase
- using exaggerated "vocal coloration" and "word painting" to the detriment of vocal timbre

These errors stem from the late-twentieth-century habit of asking music to serve chiefly as a vehicle for self-expression and from attempts to put a contemporary personal stamp on music from every period. Some singers and pianists forget that they are *re-creators,* not *creators,* of the music, mistaking self-indulgence for sensitivity. Producing links of maudlin vocal sausage is not part of authentic Lieder performance. Artists who have elevated their art beyond self-indulgence may still need to become aware of the progressive stylistic continuum that extends throughout the history of song.

A singer's voice should remain true to its own acoustic and physical dimensions. It is not necessary to search for parameters of sound that are not an inherent part of an individual singer's voice, as though Lieder singing were the art of vocal impersonation. Nor is it appropriate to distort vocal timbre in order to heighten drama. Less-than-beautiful tone does not belong in the Lied literature any more than it does in other vocal literature; unattractive vocal sounds intended to produce expressive effects are never successful.

Great Lieder composers were acquainted with the great singers of their time, often writing for specific artists. While every attention must be paid to full realization of the meaning of the text, Lieder are to be sung, not parodied after spoken language. Dynamic levels must be relative to the dimensions of the individual instrument and to hall ambiences. Imitations of recording-studio performances do not work effectively in the concert hall. Cloying mannerisms are stylistically unacceptable.

The harmonic language of a Lied determines how the singer and pianist mold poetic language into phrase shapes. At least from Bach onward, chromatic harmonic language has been associated mostly with introspection, tragedy, deep emotion, and soulful expression. In general, chromatic harmonies require more obvious pointing up than do diatonic harmonies. In the nineteenth-century Lied, as harmonic language undergoes greater expansion, adherence to language inflection generally diminishes. Syllabic duration becomes extended, and important words are heightened by the undergirding harmonic motion.

The German language, with its short and long vowel sounds, its doubled consonants (particularly those that have pitch and intensity), and its prominent unvoiced sibilants, fricatives, and plosives, readily lends itself to the expanding chromatic/harmonic richness of mid-nineteenth-century music. The time it takes to enunciate consonantal clusters (accumulating consonants within a word or a syllable or conjoining two words to form a compound word) partly determines phrase shaping. *Zwielicht* (Twilight), from *Liederkreis,* op. 39, illustrates the integration of the German language with interpretative practice.

As is the case with most introspective Schumann Lieder, in *Zwielicht* the harmonic movement mirrors speech inflection and word accentuation. The vocal melody evolves over arpeggiated chromaticism, providing singer and pianist ample opportunity to discreetly play with the elements of speech inflection, word accentuation, and consonantal doubling and clustering (bars 6–13). Schumann's setting of "Dämm'rung will die Flügel spreiten, schaurig rühren sich die Bäume, Wolken ziehn wie schwere Träume" wonderfully combines poetic elements, musical language, and the instrumental colors of the voice and

Example 2.1.   *Zwielicht*, bars 6–13.

the pianoforte, producing a new form of synthesis, examples of which will frequently be pointed out in this study (Ex. 2.1).

A common fault in singing Lieder is overlooking the duration of short and long vowels in the German language. Elongating the vowels in words such as "Dämm'rung" and "will" or shortening vowel duration in a word such as "ziehn" is an error as glaring as an actual rhythmic mistake. Slighting doubled consonants would be equally offensive. The doubled voiced consonants of German ought to assist the legato line, not negate it. With the double consonant [m], as in the word "Dä**mm**'rung" for example, the singer must not diminish vocal intensity on the first syllable of the word as soon as the sustained voiced consonant (the nasal [m:]) appears but should fill the dot with the same decibel level used for the preceding vowel component of the syllable. (Touch-and-retreat dynamics must be avoided.) The practice of making a vocal diminuendo on every dotted note, regardless of the phrase shape or of the importance of the word found on the dot, should be strenuously avoided. The nasal [ŋ] of the second syllable ("Dämm'ru**ng**") must be kept at an even intensity if the legato is to be maintained. Another consonantal doubling occurs with the word "wi**ll**."

Skillful handling of voiced consonants permits the singer to control phrase shape through musical and linguistic factors without falling prey to speech habits. By means of an uncanny amalgamation of chromatic harmonic language and melodic direction, Schumann contours the line so as to advance to the word "Flügel," marking the first phrase peak.

The subsequent portion of the phrase, beginning with the word "schaurig," provides an example of *consonantal anticipation*, in which the consonant should occur a split second *in advance* of the changing underlying harmony. Slightly ahead of the beat, the nonpitch [∫] of the syllable "**sch**au-" must be audible without robbing from the rhythmic value of the oncoming vowel. Anticipatory consonantal technique, applicable to all nonpitch (unvoiced) consonants, brings about synchronization of vowel occurrence and harmonic digression, producing a binding vocal legato (despite the intrusion of an unvoiced consonant). Authoritative German-for-singing is the result.

Of equal importance to the singing of Schumann Lieder (humorous topics are excepted) is the avoidance of intrusive habitual speech-inflection behavior that diminishes the vocal legato through transition sounds that occur within a vowel or within the component vowels of a diphthong. Because Schumann dexterously molds the innately musical sounds of the German language (Heine's "Singen und Klingen") into a poetic/musical synthesis, the question may be raised as to how the singer who does not speak the German language may successfully perform Lieder. Most talented singers are good imitators of foreign-language sounds. While it may not be essential to be fluent in German in order to sing Lieder, no singer who does not speak the language with some ease should undertake public performance without relying on an exacting coach who is well versed in the sounds of the German language, both as spoken and as sung on the professional stage. Even native German singers must devote much time to mastering the subtle rules of sung German.

It is not a serious artistic option to sing Lieder in translation. Lieder translations belong in program notes, not in the mouths of performers.

Publishers provide transpositions that offer voices of several categories access to the traditional song literature. Unfortunately, they sometimes fail to discriminate among those Lieder that can support transposition and those that are not well served by it. Especially Schubert and Schumann search for colors associated with specific keyboard ranges. Transposing upward or downward often distorts the intended coloration. In downward transposition, what was sparkling effervescence no longer bubbles; clear running brooks become muddied rivers; nightingales become crows. In upward transposition, *Männerchor* (male chorus) harmonies become soubrette choirs, and mysterious moonlight turns into sunny midday. Serious performers should examine carefully what would happen to both vocal and keyboard sound before opting to sing Lieder in transposition. Although this is true for all Lieder, it is especially the case with those songs of Schumann (particularly the early Lieder) in which the tessitura often lies largely in middle range for both performers.

When Schumann chooses key relationships that are part of the structural design of cycles, it is a shock to the ears and to the sensibilities to hear performers leap from one unrelated tonality to another. If *Dichterliebe* is to be sung in keys lower than the original, then all of the Lieder in the cycle must be correspondingly transposed.

The Lieder of the last years of Schumann's creativity attest to the development of his artistic imagination. While it is true that not all of the songs from the late period are the result of new adventuresomeness, many are. Late Schumann Lieder often require higher levels of vocal and keyboard sound than the early songs do. It is a mistake to sing *Dichterliebe* like the Hussar songs or to turn the

Harper's expressions into the lyricism of "the poet's love." It is essential to realize that there is no one static style among the Schumann songs but rather a wide variety.

In almost all of the Lied repertory the pianist is not an accompanist but a collaborator. From Schubert through Strauss and Marx, the level of skill demanded from the keyboard artist for the performance of Lieder is equal to that required of the solo pianist. The notion that the song literature is unrewarding for the pianist, who simply accompanies the singer, is a naive one. On the contrary, the level of technical and musical skill demanded from a pianistic full partner is not less in the Lied than in the sonata and concerto literatures. A gifted keyboard performer ought to consider the limited market for the pursuance of a solo pianoforte career and become aware of the artistic satisfaction that abounds in the literature of the Lied. Public performances of the solo pianoforte and concerto literature of Robert Schumann often lack poetry because they are devoid of singing style. A pianist who wishes to perform the Schumann pianoforte works with understanding is advised to become familiar with the Schumann Lieder.

The same risks of stylistic excess that face the singer confront the pianist. Perhaps the most undesirable habit when playing Schumann Lieder is the awkward practice of striking the bass note in advance of other voices of a significant chord, as though the pianoforte were a harp. As will be noted, when Schumann wishes such an effect he writes it. Keyboard kerplunking does not increase romanticism; it destroys the phrase shape and reduces sentiment to sentimentality. Equally unacceptable is the inept sounding out of the melody note in each chord in advance of the total harmonic movement.

In the Lieder, Schumann often does not provide pedal indications. On one hand, it is up to the pianist to sustain sonority without smudging harmonic progression. On the other hand, keyboard textures of the Schumann songs ought not to be played as though written for the harpsichord. The use of una corda is partly dependent on the size of a singer's voice and the dimensions of the hall but can also be a coloration device in introspective Lieder.

In performing any song from the Schumann Lied literature, singer and pianist need to be aware of how completely harmonic design and linguistic emphases are integrated with voice and keyboard timbres. Awareness of the rhythm of the German language and its relationship to harmonic movement will also determine the tempo and the phrase pacing of each Lied.

It is time to turn to specific Lieder.

3

Liederkreis (Heine), Opus 24

Robert's letters to Clara tell her that she is the inspiration for his setting of the Heine *Liederkreis*. Schumann explicitly mentioned to his publisher that he considered this opus to constitute a performance whole. Without doubt, the songs make greater impact in their entirety than when excerpted. Perhaps one reason for neglecting to program the whole cycle comes from publishers' decisions to place the final *Mit Myrten und Rosen*, #9, in a volume apart from the rest of the opus. Because *Mit Myrten und Rosen* enjoys popularity, the Peters Max Friedländer edition includes it among the *ausgewählte Lieder* (selected songs) of volume 1. Little wonder that some singers, finding the first eight songs of the Heine *Liederkreis* in volume 2, hesitate to program the cycle, assuming it to conclude with simplistic #8, the chorale-like *Anfangs wollt' ich fast verzagen*. The Sergius Kagen International Music Company edition also places *Mit Myrten und Rosen* among other selected songs in Volume I. The Hugo Riemann older edition, published by Steingräber of Leipzig, avoids this confusion, keeping the nine songs of the opus intact.

The Heine *Liederkreis*, op. 24, from 1840, has not met with as much favor as the Eichendorff *Liederkreis*, op. 39. Op. 24 was written in Leipzig in 1840 between May 1 and 9 and is almost contemporary with *Dichterliebe*, which was begun on May 24 and finished June 1. Martin Cooper (p. 105) finds that only two of the songs (*Ich wandelte unter den Bäumen* and *Lieb' Liebchen*) of the

Heine *Liederkreis* come up to the level reached in all sixteen of *Dichterliebe* and concludes that "the difference in quality can only be connected with the choice of poems." It is true that the quality of op. 24 may not be as uniformly high as that of several of the more famous cycles, including *Dichterliebe*, but on turning to *Es treibt mich hin, Schöne Wiege meiner Leiden, Warte, warte, wilder Schiffmann*, and *Berg' und Burgen schaun herunter*, one questions the judgment that only two songs of the cycle have high merit.

However, the issue of quality brings into focus the fact that Schumann was capable of writing less-than-stellar songs in the 1840 "Clara Year" as well as later and equally capable of conceiving masterpieces in the last creative years of his life. The latter point will repeatedly be made in this survey. Critical commentary about the earlier versus the later Lieder is often based on the conviction that only so long as Schumann showed respect for poetic sources through lyric declamation was he successful and when he did not do so his output deteriorated. If this same rule regarding respect for poetic sources were to be applied to other composers, they in general would fare less well than Schumann. In addition, such criticism tends to see Robert's anticipatory love for Clara as the explanation for his outburst of lyric declamation and finds less merit in most of what was written by him after he gained Clara's hand in marriage.

It can be objectively concluded that op. 24 contains some songs of genius and some of more modest inspiration. There is a folklike character about *Morgens steh' ich auf und frage*, #1. The walking motif that harmonically underlies the simple melody recalls a device used by Schubert in *Auf dem Flusse*, here put to an entirely different emotional purpose. The joy of waking in the morning finds a firm, striding gait (allegretto) in bright D major. Such jauntiness is all well and good, but it is not the poet's intent. Heine regrets that he wakes each morning wondering *if* he will see his dearest and grieves each evening that he has *not* seen her. He lies awake, sleepless in his sorrow. By changing to minor mode Schumann may partly respond to the poet's languishing but remains almost cheerful. The postlude expresses little of actual sorrow or pain.

This conflict between Heinrich Heine the poet and Robert Schumann the musician cannot be resolved by singing *Morgens steh' ich auf und frage* with slow, mournful, solemn straight-toning. The existing dichotomy between the music and the poetry is not to be avoided by devitalizing the allegretto setting. There is, in fact, little the performers can do to assist Heine. The answer is to take not Heine's version but Schumann's, which is built on the joy of waking to thoughts of the beloved. Filled with yearning, the musical setting still dodges despair.

To give the composer his due, from bar 21 onward Schumann attempts through dynamic indications and ritardandos to accommodate the text, especially at "träumend wie im halben Schlummer wandle ich bei Tag," but his basic contentment remains unperturbed. Although the keyboard figure indicates a walking motion, it fails to depict a lover who walks about in a dreamlike state. For Schumann, the poem is an expression of love, not of depression; day and night he happily thinks of his lover. Heine suffers; Schumann enjoys! The composer writes a charming Lied and remains far more hopeful than does Heine, and so should the performers.

Es treibt mich hin, #2, retains the offbeat rhythmic patterns of *Morgens steh' ich auf und frage*, #1, but with a new vigor and impatience that fits the poetry. Both singer and pianist express rage and frustration over the hours of separation. The final eight bars of the postlude underscore those feelings. Performers should give themselves over to fierce involvement with their instruments. Sharp staccato attacks with the left hand are required from the pianist. The singer must make use of complete vocal timbre and, if at all possible, for dramatic reasons take the low B at bar 34, the low A♯ of bar 38, and the high G in bar 63, rather than the *ossia* indications. The very ranginess of the song, its angularity, its percussiveness, and its frequently changing dynamic and tempo markings prove that Florestan is at work here. Schumann tells us, with his *sehr rasch* (very quick) marking, that he wants extreme contrast with the subsequent *ziemlich langsam* (rather slow) that is indicated for #3.

Ich wandelte unter den Bäumen, #3, demands beautiful, smooth vocalism and warm pianistic colors. Cooper comments (p. 105): "Already in *Ich wandelte unter den Bäumen* we meet for the first time that astonishing blend between the simplest folk-song manner and the most subtle and highly organized psychological suggestion which is the distinguishing note of the *Dichterliebe*." Romantic questing, tonal ambiguity, and harmonic richness characterize the four opening bars of the keyboard, in contrast to the impetuosity of the just-concluded postlude of *Es treibt mich hin*, #2. Here Schumann is more melodist; he plainly owes a debt to Schubert. There is greater interest in psychological probing than in the more precise lyric declamation that abounds in *Dichterliebe* and in *Frauenliebe und -leben*. The keyboard introduction of *Ich wandelte unter den Bäumen* prepares us for the sensuous ascending melodic excursion of bars 11 and 12 at the words "und schlich mir ins Herz hinein." The pianoforte parallels that excursion in bars 13 and 14.

It is apparent from the rhythmic chordal repetitions and the frequent dynamic markings that phrase movement each time progresses to the half note of the vocal line and to the keyboard's whole note. These bars (6, 8, 10, 12, 15, 17, 19, and 21) and corresponding moments that follow the return of section A give an impression of suspended motion, through subtle tenuto strategy.

In its melodic construction, the B section is germinated from the repeated single-tone (*eintönig*) beginning, a favorite Eusebian device. Pensive and plaintive writing occurs in the last four bars of the vocal line, now approaching more nearly the lyric declamation of *Dichterliebe*. The postlude, with its recall of introductory material, should become a thoughtful, unhurried reflection on the text that has gone before.

The rhythmic patterns of #1 and #2 return with #4, *Lieb' Liebchen*, once again as part of a voice-pianoforte duet. Despite the obvious imitative beating of the heart ("hörst du, wie's pochet im Kämmerlein?"), heavy keyboard accents on strong beats should be avoided. In contrast to #2 and #3, the vocal tessitura is low; as with #1, speech inflection is closely mimicked. Because of the low vocal range, the pianist must take care to avoid dynamic imbalance. A pianoforte in-

Example 3.1.   *Schöne Wiege meiner Leiden*, bars 1–6.

terruption at bar 15 just before the completion of "einen Totensarg" and again in bar 35 before "schlafen kann" produces intimate dialoguing between the two instruments. The effect is that momentarily the performers simply cannot continue directly on to the completion of the poet's text, both being halted by its intensity. Sams (p. 40) finds this "one of the most original songs ever written." Integration of pianoforte and voice, in interjectory nature, is imaginatively handled.

In *Schöne Wiege meiner Leiden,* #5, we encounter a mood-evocative Lied (*Stimmungslied*) that only a genius could have written (Ex. 3.1). Gently rocking pianistic motion outlines harmonies over which a vocal melody with a bel canto contour is developed. It may be plausible to suggest that Schumann does not completely catch Heine's rebuking of the city of Hamburg for his lost love; yet the composer offers a graciously shaped vocal line. Memories of Franz Schubert are not far away. This is grateful vocalism. Amiable pianistic articulation moves the vocal melody forward.

Schumann turns to his device of reiterated eighth-note chords for forceful pianistic commentary at "Hätt ich dich doch nie geseh'n," briefly bringing in the intensity he will later use with frequency in many other Lieder. These chords momentarily replace the pulsating eighth notes of the previous and subsequent sections. The passage should be firmly played as well as sturdily sung.

In addition to its engaging vocal cantilena, *Schöne Wiege meiner Leiden* offers a rich pianistic idiom concentrated in the lower-middle keyboard. A unifying rhythmic contrivance in syncopated octave doublings begins at "Wahnsinn wühlt in meinen Sinnen und mein Herz ist krank und wund" and continues until two bars before the text repetition at "Schöne Wiege."

The mounting semitone line at "und die Glieder, matt und träge, schlepp' ich" and its descent that follows (occurring above insistent pianoforte syncopations) produce an emotive fervor that defies description. A subsequent adagio of "ferne in ein kühles Grab" presses onward to an eventual point of relaxation at the ritardando; this brings one of the most moving moments in all of Lieder repertoire. The return to the initial line of poetry takes us back to the musical quietude of the opening bars. The concluding fourteen bars of the Lied provide the pianist an opportunity to sing out in an expansive Romantic fashion.

Like *Mit Myrten und Rosen*, this beautifully constructed song is frequently excerpted for performance. Indeed, because of its grateful writing for both voice and piano and its communicative possibilities, a singer may find it tempting to perform this magnificent Lied apart from the cycle. Only a purist would forbid doing so, yet much of the impact of the song depends on what immediately precedes and follows it within the opus.

Warte, warte, wilder Schiffmann, #6, is a song of large proportions and high performance demands for both singer and pianist. The driving staccato octave pattern, developing into sixths and thirds, rushes forward in forceful mounting-scale statements matched by energetic vocalism above it (Ex. 3.2). The arresting of motion with the half-note chords that begin in bar 12 adds additional emphasis to the passion embodied in the Heine verses. These rhythmic contrasts are text-oriented, and despite pianistic independence from the voice, this Lied could only have been conceived as a result of Schumann's understanding of Heine's ironic sentiment, expressed so well in the vocal line. The song requires skillful pianism and high-level vocalism. Schumann had in mind a professionally viable singer (not an amateur miniaturist) and an accomplished pianist as purveyors of this song. The dramatic climaxes indicated by the *ossia* notes at "sahst mich bleich und herzeblutend lange Jahre vor dir stehn!" (bars 45–52) and at "Tod" (bar 98) must be taken; otherwise excitement is dissipated.

It is just this kind of dramatic vocal and keyboard writing that makes some critics rate the Heine *Liederkreis* as inferior to Schumann's Heine settings of *Dichterliebe*. Once again: wrong conclusions from an incorrectly applied aesthetic. While the cycle itself may not maintain uniform artistic level throughout, *Warte, warte, wilder Schiffmann* is a great song and huge in scope, mounting to a climactic high A at "Tod."

When turning to the frequently excerpted *Berg' und Burgen, schaun herunter*, #7, we should recall the composer's own statement to his publisher that he had conceived of this group of songs as an entity. With #7 we are in a mood-evoking world, an atmosphere that only Eusebius could have created (in opposition to Florestan's wild outbursts in #6). It would be difficult to find more shades of instrumental colors and dramatic and intimate lyricism in the sequential progression of the songs of any other Schumann cycle (Ex. 3.3).

Example 3.2.   *Warte, warte, wilder Schiffmann*, bars 1–5.

Example 3.3. *Berg' und Burgen schaun herunter*, bars 1–6.

Using the undulating figures of right and left hand the pianist should depict the ship's movement on the Rhine. As with strophic settings from all composers in which changing poetic sentiments develop, the music of this Lied does not suit each of the four verses equally well. It is up to the singer and pianist to make interpretive differentiations among the strophes; in this case the peacefulness of strophe 1 is replaced by the awakening of suppressed longing in strophe 2, by an awareness of night and death in strophe 3, and by a recognition of the treacherousness of both the river and the beloved in strophe 4. As has been mentioned earlier, it appears that Schumann either misses or wants to ignore the perennial worm in the apple that in this case peeks out from the concluding final verse of the brief Heine poem. In its overall atmosphere, there is in *Berg' und Burgen schaun herunter* a Brahmsian forecast.

An inexorable bel canto legato is called for, given shape not through vocal moaning and sighing but through a graduated and controlled *messa di voce* spread out over the contour of the melodic line. The melodic discourse here is not unlike that of *Schöne Wiege*. *Berg' und Burgen schaun herunter* is splendid writing for voice and pianoforte.

It might at first appear that *Anfangs wollt' ich fast verzagen* is lodged between #7 and #9 chiefly to provide contrasting thematic material. But could the composer have had a profounder intent in his appropriation of a familiar Bach chorale melody? In the first phrase of *Anfangs wollt' ich fast verzagen* Schumann quotes the beginning harmonic texture of *Wer nur den lieben Gott lässt walten*, which in its various permutations appears in six Bach cantatas. (The tune is found in the Joh. Phil. Kirnberger collection of Bach chorale preludes for organ, 1707–1717.) "If you earn God's blessing, then it is every morning new!", which stems from an interpolation by Bach, probably was known to Schumann. Before terminating the cycle with the surging vocalism and pianism of *Mit Myrten und Rosen*, might this have been the composer's way of expressing thankfulness about his relationship with Clara?

Although brief, *Anfangs wollt' ich fast verzagen* has a grandeur that may draw on extramusical implications. By no means is it a miniature in its emotional message; this Lied requires intense expression from both performers.

Sams (p. 45) and Gerald Moore (p. 127) see in this "Liedchen" direct corre-spondence to Chopin's prelude, Op. 28, no. 20, which had only recently been published.

Mit Myrten und Rosen, #9, the final Lied in op. 24, with little alteration could have been published as a piano etude. Its keyboard dominance is gradu-ally mitigated through a central melodic nucleus for the voice. Following the in-troductory keyboard excursion, the voice joins the sweeping figure of the pi-anoforte. For the new section, at *schneller*, Schumann returns to the pianistic offbeat rhythmic scheme that gives unity to the progression of songs from #1 through #9. The final fourteen bars surrender to Eusebian instincts. Singers like to sing this Lied, and pianists like to play it. It fits both instruments well and is one of the most popular of all Schumann Lieder. There is a certain expository quality about it that differentiates it from other songs in the cycle. Its presence diversifies the opus.

Within the cycle, a recurrent melodic nucleus (with B as the core note in several of the songs) parallels the one so prominently found in *Dichterliebe*. A look at *Es treibt mich hin, Ich wandelte unter den Bäumen, Lieb' Liebchen*, and *Schöne Wiege meiner Leiden* quickly confirms this. *Berg' und Burgen schaun herunter* also plays with a small C♯–D–B motivic seed group.

Largely neglected, op. 24 is excellent recital material. The nine songs offer the singer and pianist a full range of power and interpretive subtlety. This gar-land of songs deserves a higher evaluation than it generally has been given.

4

Myrten, Opus 25

It would be an unusual experience to hear all twenty-six *Myrten* Lieder performed as a cycle, yet there may be a good argument for an ambitious recitalist to perform them as a unit. A sequential pass through the collection shows convincingly that, despite the random choice of poet and the wide diversity of subject matter, the composer aimed at variety among the songs with an eye to their performance as a whole. They achieve a unity because they were intended to express many facets of love, specifically that of Robert Schumann for his prospective bride.

The musical fabric of Schumann's treatment of Rückert's *Widmung*, op. 25, #1, already discussed in chapter 1, stands in sharp contrast to the neighboring Goethe *Freisinn*, #2.

Freisinn is characterized by harmonic directness, showing none of the psychological involvement of *Widmung*. There is an openness of musical expression in accord with the *frisch* marking. Motivic squareness is accentuated through the repetitive sixteenth rest and later by the introduction of strong quarter-note chordal marching at the text "Er hat euch die Gestirne gesetzt." Harmonic structure remains tonic/dominant, in major and relative minor juxtapositions. Unremarkable in itself and of limited performance value when excerpted from the cycle, this song provides an exuberant mood change from the two songs that lie on either side of it. Its neighbors thus lend it a value that the Lied does not have when standing alone.

Der Nussbaum, #3, is an example of nearly perfect synthesis among literary and musical elements—a model resolution of the age-old aesthetic debate *prima la parola, dopo la musica* versus *prima la musica, dopo la parola*. Composers from Mozart to Strauss were actively intrigued by the relationship of word and music, spawning innumerable pages of critical comment, from the Goethe/Reichardt correspondence onward. The favorable opinion regarding the successful achievement of synthesis in *Der Nussbaum* is not universally held by critics, who sometimes lament the inherent quality of the poetry (which they find not to be of high merit) and Schumann's somewhat cavalier treatment of the poem's metrical form.

Jack M. Stein, Harvard University professor of German, describes (p. 126) *Der Nussbaum* as "unfortunately a gorgeous song to a bad poem by Julius Mosen." Sams (p. 53), perhaps momentarily forgetting many of Schubert's poetic sources, not to mention those adopted by Brahms, writes:

> Perhaps only Schumann among the great song-writers would have countenanced so inept a lyric as the German text of this song. Then having chosen it, only Schumann would have so chopped and changed its rhyme scheme as to prune away such small interest and merit as it had. But then only Schumann could have persuaded this cutting to flower into a unique masterpiece of charm and tenderness, which has entranced the whole world ever since.

For an objective evaluation of this Lied, a restricted view of synthesis between word and music must be discarded. In general, in Lieder the traditional word/music synthesis needs to be expanded to include another highly important factor: the instrumental relationship of the voice and the pianoforte. Major Lied composers adopt differing philosophies for finding solutions to these problems. *Der Nussbaum* illustrates a Schumann solution: subject the poem to musical enrichment by taking into account the inherent sonorities of the two instruments involved, coalesce each of the four elements—poetry, musical construction, voice, and pianoforte—into an amalgamated artistic whole. In short, it is not chiefly the value of the poetry that dictates the merit of a Lied but the accomplishment of its musical realization through the sensitive use of idiomatic vocal and keyboard sonorities. Strikingly, Robert Schumann, the nineteenth-century composer with the deepest immersion in German literature, is the one who most emphatically decides that poetry is there for the musician to remold into new forms of artistic synthesis.

One might assume that synthesis can take place only when all elements are equal, yet even when considering the works of the great synthesizer himself, Richard Wagner, who can support the viewpoint that texts are on an equal footing with music? This point needs to be taken into account when the wedding of word and music is examined in the Lieder repertory or in any other musico-literary form.

In *Der Nussbaum*, the "song" has been given not to the voice with its text but to the instrumental timbres of the keyboard, yet the voice does not lose its role of equality. The pianoforte improvises a melodious figure above a fragmentary, folklike vocal line. The arpeggiated "accompaniment" could well be an excerpt

Example 4.1. *Der Nussbaum*, bars 1–6.

from a *Fantasiestück* or an etude. The broken-arpeggio figure provides an atmosphere of airiness and dreamy contemplation, enhanced by downward harmonic progressions, beginning with "flüstern von einem Mägdlein, das dächte,
die Nächte und Tage lang," transcending the folklike vocal line that lulled the listener in the earlier strophe. The setting unfolds in a melodic folk manner around
which an intriguing pianistic web of sound is spun. Schumann's intent behind his
commentary regarding Rossini as vocal composer—"take away the artificial
lighting and the illusion of the theater, and see what remains!"—becomes manifest with *Der Nussbaum*. Here Schumann's vocal foot rests upon his Germanic
"convenient meadow"; he avoids placing the other foot on the "Alp" of Italianate
vocalism and instead stakes out a location where balance is maintained between
text and music, voice and pianoforte. Sung inflection is masterfully patterned syllabically after speech inflection, not poetic meter. Using the keyboard as the initial "singer" is a favorite Schumann technique for the furtherance of synthesis.
The keyboard not only introduces the melody but also completes the musical
phrase that had been only minimally suggested by the voice (Ex. 4.1).

 A recurrent keyboard figure here elevates to new importance an aspect of
early Romantic style borrowed from Schubert: *poetic recall*. This is a major
means by which Schumann accomplishes synthesis. Because of the association
of musical figuration with poetic expression, the composer echoes and thereby
augments the poet's sentiment each time the thematic material reappears. It
may be disproportionate to term this technique a leitmotiv, yet Schumann
through his repetition of the initial soaring pianistic arpeggio before and after
subsequent poetic ideas distinctly induces *textual recall*. He has invented a poetic as well as a musical duet between voice and piano. The poet's expression

has become expanded beyond his original intention. *The composer has also become poet.*

The conclusion of the Lied, at "Das Mägdlein horchet," with its almost recitative-like one-note melodic contour, vividly depicts the young girl's falling into dreamland, while the pianoforte comments on the reasons why. Surely this Lied must represent the highest level of the combining of keyboard, voice, literary elements, and musical style. It is foolish to complain that Schumann has gone beyond the bounds of respect for the poet (especially after critical denigration of the worth of the poetry) and that he has obliterated the significance of the singing voice.

Dietrich Fischer-Dieskau (p. 53) suggests that "the coquettish quality to which interpreters of this song occasionally resort is entirely out of place." *Der Nussbaum* is no more lacking in drama than is a small Vermeer domestic scene and should be portrayed as the delightful vignette it is.

The fourth song, *Jemand*, to a Wilhelm Gerhard translation of a Robert Burns poem, is a disjunct composition. Its segmented nature gives a curious sense of formal disquietude heightened by the contiguous eighth-note and triplet figures, by a sudden shift from minor to major, and above all by the change in meter from $\frac{2}{4}$ to $\frac{6}{8}$ for the concluding eight bars. It is not without charm, but its insufficient musical weight requires the juxtaposition of contrasting miniatures.

Sitz' ich allein, #5, is a delightful miniature in which Schumann captures the spirit of Goethe's appealing verse. The last twelve bars illustrate the ramifications of drinking alone. Could it be possible that Schumann, who frequently experienced the effects of strong spirits, was indulging in a little humorful keyboard hiccuping? The singer and the pianist must be willing to enter into the playful spirit of this mischievous setting.

As with *Sitz' ich allein*, #5, *Setze mir nicht*, #6, is selected from Goethe's *Schenkenbuch im Westöstlichen Divan*. It is a gay song, a companion drinking piece to #5. Schumann admirably characterizes the changing circumstances of the two strophes; the postlude offers a happy commentary on the poetic images. Both #5 and #6 may be humorous answers from Schumann to the accusation of drunkenness leveled at him by Wieck. It is true that these songs do not measurably expand the Lied idiom, but they prove that Schumann, not unlike the architectonic Beethoven, can write engagingly humorous Lieder. Their lilting pianistic figures give relief from the arpeggiated and chordal techniques so prominent within this large opus. In #6 the vocal line charms through folklike writing, then is developed pianistically in the eight-bar postlude. If Lied #5 and Lied #6 are excerpted from *Myrten*, they should be performed together.

With *Die Lotosblume*, #7, performers turn to one of the most frequently performed of all Lieder. Its "calculated rhythmic monotony" indicates indebtedness to a Schubertian principle pointed out by Richard Capell (p. 52), although here differently realized. The device propels the harmonic movement of dominating bass octaves. Superimposed insistent $\frac{6}{4}$ quarter-note/half-note patterns of the vocal part, in a range of close intervals, produce a feeling of compactness and serenity un-victimized by the intentional mechanical monotony of

Example 4.2. *Die Lotosblume*, bars 1–3.

the keyboard (Ex. 4.2). The vocal line mounts in short sequences, arriving at "sie duftet und weinet und zittert," to which emotional peak the harmonic rhythm leads the performers. This moment of heightened emotion falls away quickly at the repetition of "vor Liebe und Liebesweh." Schumann in his sweet amorousness either is unaware of or chooses to ignore any irony that may be present in the poet's conclusion.

In this Lied, an inexorable vocal legato is essential for fullest musical and poetic realization. Each note must be completely filled with sound. No *messa di voce* treatment of each syllable should interrupt the close-intervallic melodic structure. Vocal intensity—not volume—must match the relentless nature of emotional expression achieved by never-ceasing quarter-note chords that undergird the vocal legato. In the closing measures, pianistic commentary intertwines with the now intervallically expanded vocal conclusion. Schumann avoids his usual concluding pianistic commentary, no doubt recognizing that the high level of concentration he has achieved requires nothing more. The final "vor Liebe und Liebesweh" says everything the composer needs to say about himself and his longing for the betrothed.

The pain of being apart from the beloved is a frequent theme in Romantic poetry. No composer has ever more successfully caught that sentiment than Schumann. Whereas some composers depict how phenomena of Nature recall the beloved, Schumann seems to lament that they are not the beloved herself. *Die Lotosblume* has that feeling. Such a viewpoint is not shared by Stein, who has this to say (p. 110):

> The popular setting of "Die Lotosblume" . . . misses the real character of the poem. The cool, exotic narrative of the lotus flower, which avoids the sun and yields itself to the moon, is set to a warm flowing melody, typical of Schumann, which toward the end becomes impassioned just where Heine's poem becomes enigmatic.

Moore's assessment (p. 73) differs from that of Stein:

Innocence, and the depth of chaste love are so marvelously expressed in Heine's allegory that it took the genius of a Schumann to embrace the poet at this exalted level. *Die Lotosblume* is universally loved. It shares a virtue which many memorable creations have in common, utter simplicity. Also it is a mirror, exposing with a clarity that cannot be disguised, the stature of the singer. Beauty of voice is essential, but not enough in itself.

Sams (p. 57) gives qualified approval by suggesting that "the sheer depths of devotion revealed in this song are almost frightening." By Heine's last verse, "the relevance has faded from Schumann's inspiration; all that is left is the idea of humility in repeated chords."

Fischer-Dieskau (p. 54) offers this perceptive evaluation:

The sultriness of the poem led Schumann to previously unheard musical effects and harmonic tensions, reflecting the poem's twin poles of tenderness and passion. . . . Schumann slavishly honored the length of the lines in Heine's poem, charging the singer to support the line to the end, sustaining it dynamically and avoiding a pause. The criticism that these rests mar the work is unfounded when it is understood that we are not dealing with caesuras in the traditional sense.

The $\frac{4}{4}$ square setting of Goethe's *Talismane,* #8, with its strong arpeggiated vocal statement on the C major descending/ascending broken chord and its detached pianistic chords, makes a stark change from the $\frac{6}{4}$ lyrical legato of *Die Lotosblume*. The dotted-quarter/eighth-note rhythmic trademark is joined to the arpeggiated melodic pattern. Section B provides welcome variety. A duet of keyboard voices in thirds, with the upper pianistic voice doubling the vocal line, marches along in relentless eighth notes. The singer must be aware that the vocal statement mirrors the underlying chordal orientation. However, vocal percussiveness should not substitute for forthrightness and vigor. Sams finds that the humanistic piety of the words elicits a small-scale secular oratorio (p. 58). Despite the quasi-contrapuntal voices of the B section in G major, there is little of piety here. The "Amen!" pair is conclusive but not devotional. The Lied deals with the omnipotence of God, not with his grace.

Lied der Suleika, #9 (to a poem attributed to Goethe but probably from the hand of Marianne von Willemer), makes use of a vocal melody that parallels expressive speech inflection by using interjectory phrases such as "Liebevoll du scheinst zu sagen" and "Dass er ewig mein gedenket." These broken poetic fragments are superimposed over a pianistic matting, largely in four-voice harmony moving in equal eighth notes. The keyboard scarcely needs the vocal line; the pianoforte "sings" the melody, in which from time to time the singer joins. The voice is doubled in the keyboard, not in the Schubertian manner and not, as so often is the case with Schumann himself, where singer and pianist mutually sustain the melody that comprises the "soprano" voice. Here is a melodic integration of pianism and vocalism that calls for complete ensemble unity (Ex. 4.3).

A version of the "Clara" melodic nucleus (here C♯–D–B–A–G♯–B–A) must have been meant for Clara's eyes and ears. It is uncanny how the expansion of

Example 4.3.   *Lied der Suleika*, bars 1–3.

the vocal line from this melodic kernel perfectly matches the sentiment of the poetry. Such writing cannot help eliciting warm timbres from singer and pianist.

The *nach und nach schneller* marking, beginning in bar 11, initiates a reiterated chordal passage, with a ritardando effectively supporting the unresolved melodic cadence. Schumann, as he ties together formal compositional elements, contrary to the Goethean aesthetic repeats the poet's verse.

The text of *Lied der Suleika* spurs Schumann to one of his most penetrating realizations of musical and poetic synthesis. A case could be made, as with *Frauenliebe und -leben*, that Schumann's masculine response to feminine expression reveals sensitivity akin to reverence. His idealization of Clara clearly permeates his emotional answer to such poetic sources. The gracious melody, through meandering excursions, catches to perfection the intimate Romanticism of the poetry. The pianistic commentary of the postlude recalls the song's earlier poetic expressions. Again the composer becomes poet. This composition could almost exist as a piano etude, but once one has encountered the vocal melody that is so closely wedded to both the poetry and the keyboard the thought becomes untenable. *Lied der Suleika* is equally grateful for keyboard and voice.

Die Hochländer-Witwe, #10, another Burns translation by Gerhard, is idiomatically far removed from *Lied der Suleika*. Notated in $\frac{6}{16}$, the detached rhythmic motif produces inquietude. The syllabically set text moves within narrow limits in folk-song manner, seldom venturing beyond the range of a fifth. Schumann catches the urgency of despair and pain expressed by the widowed Highlander. Though not a remarkable song, it is a decided departure from the Lieder lodged on either side of it. Schumann purposely does not place *Die Hochländer-Witwe* with two other Burns texts (the Rückert *Brautlieder* being interpolated between the Burns poems). Nor does Schumann include it among later Burns texts. Clearly, the composer's aim is variation of musical idioms among the Lieder in an opus, not continuity of poetic sources. (It is possible that he also wanted to contrast several kinds of female emotional states.)

Language patterns are carefully followed, and the tessitura within the individual phrase is often limited. The fast tempo and the syllabic setting of the text rush the singer onward until she reaches a dramatic *f* with the explosive "O

Weh, o Weh!" in the final vocal passage. The pianoforte epilogue continues the wild despair of *Die Hochländer-Witwe*.

Only Robert Schumann could have written the two brief Rückert *Lieder der Braut*, #11 and #12. They present a woman's (presumed) adoration of the male with a sensitivity that verges on the sentimental. The *sehr innig* marking of #11, however, as with *Widmung*, should not be taken as morbid internalization but as emergent fervor. The andantino further indicates that the singer should not indulge in subjective emotion but ought to outwardly communicate the joy of new love. Today's performers cannot approach these two Lieder with any lesser interpretative concept and still retain artistic honesty.

The keyboard first "sings" the approaching melody in *Lied der Braut I*; then the voice repeats the keyboard melody over a languid broken arpeggiated figure (Ex. 4.4). The embellishing turn in the vocal line is a favorite Schumann expressive device (a Bellini/Chopin influence?). It occurs here in bars 9, 13, 22, and 33. The way the melody is suspended at the F♯ of "er" (bars 25–26) evokes wonderment. Without losing the simple grace of the young girl's happiness, Schumann extends the vocal range at the climactic "das mir ward zu solchem, solchem Glanz." As is his frequent practice (later to be seen in its fullest development with *Er ist's*), Schumann, by repeating the text at increasing levels of vocal and harmonic strength, heightens poetic sentiment. His weaving of text and music into one cloth is not bound by the aesthetic rule that music should act as a frame to the poetry without disturbing its metric nature.

The postlude is a thoughtful commentary that combines previously treated musical and poetic elements—a summation of the synthesis of literary and musical events already encountered in the body of the Lied. The last three adagio bars form an exquisite pianoforte reverie of recollecting, accomplished through harmonic transformation of thematic material.

This reverie is extended further in #12, *Lied der Braut II*. The suspended harmonic hymnlike structure depicts "hanging" on the beloved's breast: "Lass mich ihm am Busen hangen." The simplicity of Schumann's setting of this small drama matches that of the poetry. Schumann follows the penultimate "lass mich" with a brief pianoforte episode. The young woman's confused emotions are thereby captured through harmonic indecisiveness, resolved only by the

Example 4.4. *Lied der Braut I*, bars 1–5.

Example 4.5.   *Lied der Braut II*, bars 28–36.

final "lass mich," which should be sung as an affirmation and not simply an afterthought (Ex. 4.5). In this small pearl of a song, the composer has assumed duties of the poet in recalling thematic material that previously grew out of the text. If excerpted from *Myrten*, these two miniature masterpieces ought to be performed as a unit. (One marvels at Sams's description of them as "two fascinating failures" [p. 62].)

The lines of the subsequent Burns poem, *Hochländers Abschied*, #13, are recited in folk-song fashion following a four-bar keyboard motif in ⅜ meter. The folk element that Schumann associated with the Burns sources is accomplished through a modified strophic AABA. In the first several measures of the B section, the composer moves to his arpeggiated-pianoforte trademark but does not venture long from the ⅜ rhythmic pattern of the A segments. The Lied must be sung and played freshly and directly, without pretension.

Number 14 of *Myrten*, *Hochländisches Wiegenlied*, to a translation by Gerhard of a Burns source, is a strophic Lied in traditional manner, the voice doubling the pianoforte melody. It is an effective cradle song. (Benjamin Britten engagingly set the original-language version of this endearing poem in his *A Charm of Lullabies*.) The opening melodic contour of *Hochländisches Wiegenlied* bears some relationship to *Schöne Wiege meiner Leiden* of the Heine *Liederkreis*. However, *Hochländlisches Wiegenlied* displays no distinctive marks of genius. Its gentle rocking presents both rhythmic interest and yet another facet of womanhood. Within the three strophes performers will need to vary textual accentuations and dynamic levels.

Sams (p. 64) is particularly fond of this *Wiegenlied*:

Something of the original's homely [homey] tenderness has got into the German text and thence into the music, making this a worthy successor of Schubert's cradle-song, and a worthy forerunner of Brahms's. Indeed, in one respect it surpasses theirs, for all their beauty. Schumann has fashioned his rhythm from the rock and return of a rough cradle; and inside his music (as in Wolf's *Wiegenlied im Sommer*) lies the idea of a sleeping child.

Every listener is entitled to choose favorites, but most will probably not find that this *Wiegenlied* surpasses the Schubert and Brahms cradle songs.

In his splendid setting of the Byron poem (translation by Theodor Körner) that follows, *Aus den hebräischen Gesängen*, #15, Schumann reaches a high level of creativity. At the very opening bar, the progression of descending semitones in the keyboard compels the listener to enter a world of introspective pondering. Stylized harp arpeggiations produce chromatic harmonies (bars 1–7). This chromatic language transcends the etudelike pianoforte writing, transporting us psychologically into a world of longing and nostalgia. The semitone "warp" is incorporated into the harmonic "woof" to produce a compositional garment of rich fabric (Ex. 4.6).

The improvisatory keyboard texture achieves a uniquely Schumann introspection; vocally, it results in extended melodic declamation where phrases rise and fall in correspondence to word inflection and emotional power. Voice and pianoforte combine the pain and longing that are inherent in the original English-language poem. In its *Myrten* context, the poem reveals no relationship to Saul and David. That does not take away from the composer's success at music/word synthesis. He takes an existing text and welds it into a new form of personalized expression.

In bar 5, the serpentine intervallic pattern of the right hand should be shaped dynamically so as to point out the significance of the changing chords stretched over a tenth. These chords must be struck as a harmonic unit, not rolled. They afford proper preparation for the entering vocal line at "Mein Herz ist schwer!" (If the pianist's left-hand reach falls short of the intervallic tenth

Example 4.6.   *Aus den hebräischen Gesängen*, bars 1–7.

stretches of bars 5 and 6, the upper notes of the bass clef may be transferred to the right hand.)

With the opening line of poetry, what compelling musical commentary emerges from the rich colors of the chromatic palette! The vocal entrance begins in lower-middle voice with a ritardando; the next four melodic phrases commence on long notes (dotted half, half, quarter, half-note/quarter-note tie) in upper-middle voice. These phrases subsequently turn downward, summoning up a sense of despair. Not bound by exact word inflection, Schumann becomes almost Brahmsian in giving more importance to melodic sweep than to metric accent. The singer should take full advantage of the melodic peaking and falling that come after the initial *sf* at "Auf!" (bar 9), by giving each phrase a similar shape through energized vocal onset and subtle dynamic tapering at every phrase termination.

At the new key, the four-bar pianoforte interlude creates a calm that will prevail for the next sixteen bars. The melodic contour now derives from a move to diatonic harmonies that replace the chromatic colors and avoid the wrenching melodic peaks and valleys of the first section. The subsequent nine bars of the interlude recall the plaintiveness of the opening harp arpeggios and momentarily lead to a new but neighboring tonality (almost always the case with Schumann when key changes occur within a Lied). Insertion of C major achieves a momentary emotional plateau on which the chromatic tuggings appear assuaged. But this is denied by the oncoming vocal melody in its descending ninths and its mounting octaves. Then back again to the opening quest, to harmonic indecision, to melodic meandering. It is difficult in all of the Lieder repertoire to find a page that surpasses the final one of this Lied with regard to its translation of poetry into music. It is clear that Brahms drank fully at this artistic spring.

Schumann's melodic conception may not permit every singer to program this exceptional Lied. The composer descends with "Nur tief sei, wild der Töne Fluss, und von der Freude weg gekehret!" to a vocal range strongly dependent upon rich timbre (increased acoustic strength in the lower portion of the voice spectrum). The tessitura of the rest of *Myrten* implies that it is aimed at "High Voice." Yet for many "hohe Stimmen" (tenors and sopranos) insufficient depth of vocal sound for negotiating the low passages makes *Aus den hebräischen Gesängen* patently impossible; in addition, the remainder of the Lied lies uncomfortably high for most baritones and contraltos. Despite its tremendous beauty, this may be, because of its possible register difficulties, a problematic Lied for the person who wishes to perform the entire opus. However, *Aus den hebräischen Gesängen* remains ideal as an excerpted item for the appropriate singer. The most successful performer would be a mezzo-soprano or a dramatic soprano with strong chest voice and chest-mixture possibilities. In transposition to higher keys, the pianoforte color becomes thin and inappropriate to the original rich pianistic tapestry.

This song should enjoy major standing within the total Lied literature. Fischer-Dieskau, the scholarly performer who has immersed himself more completely in Lieder than has any other singing artist, gives a pertinent critical assessment (pp. 57–59) of *Aus den hebräischen Gesängen*:

> Clarity of expression and melodic beauty give *Aus den hebräischen Gesängen* a significant place in Schumann's work. He attempted to recreate a romantic, dreamlike sense of "foreign lands and peoples," and succeeded in creating a vision of Oriental melancholy. Although the music is conceived on a large, sweeping scale, it retains a sense of both inscrutability and sorrow. The arpeggios which accompany the lamentation do not simply weep to and fro, as in the popular "background music" of the period, but are used harmonically so that each note contributes to the expressiveness of the piece. Such complicated figures closely approximate those used by Chopin. The magic circles in which the accompaniment swirls, seemingly without beginning or end, assures its independence, yet allows the piano to join the voice as if in a duet—each with its own role while pursuing an independent course. By suppressing the traditional use of the caesura as it had been used in strophic song, an unending melody is achieved, which provides new freedom of expression giving direction from the beginning with merely a sigh.

An interjectory comment may be in order regarding whether members of both sexes may sing cycles or individual Lieder that include male and female poetic expressions. (In this case, Saul and David are the presumed protagonists.) Artistic communication transcends the boundaries of male and female experience. In any event, it is questionable that a great divide actually exists between them. There is no reason that a singer of either gender may not be the medium through which universally experienced emotion is expressed. There are, of course, some clear examples of restrictions: A male cannot sing *Frauenliebe und -leben* under nonparodistic circumstances. It would also be inappropriate for him to perform Mignon's songs, except for *Nur wer die Sehnsucht kennt*, with its universal sentiment. Perhaps it would be equally pointless for a female to attempt to perform Goethe's *Harfenspieler Lieder*, many settings of which are actually written in bass clef.

Returning to the songs of op. 25, we find that Schumann's interpretive note (which he characteristically places at the beginning of each Lied instead of a tempo indication) for *Rätsel*, #16, provides the performance clue: *gut zu deklamieren*. Clean declamation and crystal clear diction are essentials. A playful ostinato of alternating left-hand quarter note, right-hand eighth note, prevails through most of the song. The rhythmic element remains routine until the final three bars, at which point the performers encounter in quick succession a ritardando, an adagio, and a concluding presto. At the terminating adagio comes an interpolated "was ist's?" The syncopated presto, on a single pitch, crescendos to the surprising conclusion "Es ist nur ein ____," the word "Hauch" being omitted. A publication note from Schumann reads: "Der Musiker glaubt durch Verschweigen der letzten Silbe sich deutlich genug ausgesprochen zu haben." (The musician believes that by omitting the last syllable he has made his mean-

Example 4.7.   *Zwei Venetianische Lieder I*, bars 1–10.

ing clear enough.) The poem, attributed to Byron but actually from the pen of Catherine Fanshawe (translated by Karl Kannegiesser), is a lighthearted play on the phoneme [h], which in onomatopoeic fashion commences the German word "Hauch," here best translated as "breath." Schumann is adding his own joke to that of the poet. (H in German stands for the pitch B♮, the tonality and final pitch.) He wrote to Clara that the Lied was written in "a sense of fun." It can be highly effective when performed in the same spirit.

In *Zwei Venetianische Lieder*, to Ferdinand Freiligrath's German translations of texts by Thomas Moore, Schumann moves to a lyrical pianistic idiom that could have come from his *Albumblätter* pages. In *Leis' rudern hier*, #17, a lilting keyboard tune (bars 1–10) introduces a gracious vocal melody that does not follow poetic inflection (Ex. 4.7). This motif and its later repetitions surely represent the gondola's motion; the right-hand pianoforte triplet motif imitates the rippling of canal water in response to the left hand's dotted-eighth/sixteenth moving oar. This is another example of Schumann's use of a descriptive mechanical figure for the realization of poetic images (which it is generally claimed he does not do). Subsequently, word inflection dictates the settings of "reden," "traun," and "er spräche vieles wohl von dem, was nachts die Sterne schau'n." These are followed by four interjectory statements of "Leis', leis', leis', leis'!" (bars 29–32). At the conclusion of the Lied, the same musical pattern occurs with "Sacht, sacht, sacht, sacht!" Schumann ignores the meter to great advantage.

Sams (p. 68) comments: "The form of Schumann's setting destroys most of what is left of the rhymes; performances tend to destroy all that is left of the rhythm." That Schumann violates the meter is of little moment when one recognizes his genius for capturing the poetic essence through musical means, not simply by metric verse framing. Sams (p. 68) concedes: "But with only a modicum of [Thomas] Moore's light laughter as a leaven this song will rise as appetizing as any ever written in this genre."

Each text repetition must be sung with the intimacy carefully created by Schumann as he depicts the lovers keeping tryst in a gondola. At bar 33, the pianoforte resumes the dotted-quarter/sixteenth-note ostinato figure of the opening bars.

The second song in this cameo duo, *Wenn durch die Piazzetta*, #18, leaves no musical doubt regarding the "Abendluft" blowing across the *piazzetta*. The pianoforte motif is full of a charm and grace all its own (Ex. 4.8). Even more than *Leis' rudern hier, mein Gondolier*, this pianistic arabesque could have come out of the *Albumblätter* or the *Bunte Blätter*. Pianist and singer share in a moment of lightheartedness (despite more attention to the pianoforte than to the voice) as the two lovers flee across the lagoons. It may be useful to excerpt the two songs from the cycle for inclusion in a potpourri Schumann group, but neither of these delightful Lieder, suggestive of canals sparkling in moonlight, should be performed without the other. Their very brevity and their fleeting quality evoke stolen moments of pleasure.

In *Hauptmanns Weib*, #19, and *Weit, weit*, #20, Schumann returns to Burns (translations by Gerhard) as a poetic source. The contrast between the two poems seems the reason for their pairing. The first is marked *keck* (bold, pert), the second *ziemlich langsam*. The heroic squareness of *Hauptmanns Weib* has a forthright character that relies heavily on dotted rhythms and reiterated marching chords.

The musical simplicity of *Weit, weit* matches the poetic sentiment. Schumann's license with poetic integrity is apparent in his omission of a strophe that would not have made a suitable part of a wedding offering to Clara. The opening bars and the interludes after each of the three strophes of *Weit, weit* offer refreshing but not spectacular pianoforte activity. These Burns Lieder are pleasant but not outstanding songs from the same period of inspiration in which Schumann created masterpieces. His output, even in this period, is uneven; op. 25 attests to that fact. (This should be kept in mind when the late Lieder are evaluated.)

Was will die einsame Träne, #21, to a Heine text, shows Schumann again in

Example 4.8.   *Zwei Venetianische Lieder II*, bars 1–5.

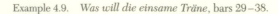

Example 4.9. *Was will die einsame Träne*, bars 29–38.

splendid form. The song is worthy of inclusion in *Dichterliebe* but finds its home in *Myrten*. The opening chords (which keep tonality momentarily secret) introduce a harmonic frame for the poetry out of which the melody develops. Schumann's melodic phrase shaping, with rising and falling contours that mirror the poetic meter, admirably catches Heine's mood. The Lied consists of a series of musical and poetic questions and answers. Of more than passing interest is the structure of the last ten measures, based on initial harmonic and melodic motifs that point to late Romantic harmonic idioms (Ex. 4.9). It should be recalled that Schumann frequently marks a ritardando at phrase and section terminations without indicating a subsequent a tempo for the phrases in a new section that must move forward (bars 4 and 8, for example).

Schumann again calls on Burns (and Gerhard) for *Niemand*, #22, and *Im Westen*, #23. His search for lilting Scottish directness succeeds in *Niemand*. *Niemand* has inventiveness in its sprightly postlude, which displays Schumann's distinctive keyboard hand. As a folk song with pianistic embellishment, *Niemand* has considerable value.

Niemand was originally the poetic companion to *Jemand*, #4. The separation of the two closely related Burns poems within the opus supports the assumption that Schumann was looking for variety appropriate to a performance of the complete collection.

Im Westen's hymnlike chordal harmonies of the first eight bars give way to alternating bars of arpeggiation in the remaining eight measures. The two contrasting sections are so brief that they yield a sense of disunity in this small Lied.

The Schumann Burns settings (#4, #10, #13, #14, #19, #20, #22, and #23) are examples of how a mid-nineteenth-century Lied composer continues to make use of the folk-song idiom. Perhaps these Burns Lieder might benefit from being grouped together as a performance set. Conceivably, they could make an interesting group of songs in circumstances where limited vocal and pianistic skills are available. Their dispersal throughout *Myrten* indicates another intention on the part of the composer.

The twenty measures of *Du bist wie eine Blume*, #24, comprise a sublime page of vocal literature. Once again it is Heine who ignites high-level creativity in Schumann. As mentioned earlier, this Lied illustrates Schumann's compositional device of reiterated chords for harmonic stability and forward movement, combined with a sustained vocal line that mostly follows language inflection. Equally well, the song demonstrates Schumann's use of initial close-intervallic melodic structures that progressively expand, which is fully apparent in the *Dichterliebe* settings (Ex. 4.10). At the risk of Romantic subjectivism, it might be suggested that each melodic phrase of *Du bist wie eine Blume* opens out from bud to full flower, from close intervals to extended leaps of fifths and sevenths: phrase beginnings such as "ich schau dich an," "schleicht mir ins Herz hinein," and "Mir ist als ob ich die Hände" are initially close-intervalled but then evolve into phrases of melodic expansion. This gives *Du bist wie eine Blume* a tight construction and emotional intensity that elevate music and poetry to equal importance.

Such technique does not result in memorable melody but produces something of far greater value: synthesis of word and music, voice and pianoforte. A lover's fervent hope that innocence and beauty not be corrupted is treated through modest musical means yet with profound psychological penetration. As is often the case with Heine, the pessimist's ability to find the proverbial fly in the ointment clouds his expression of love. If there is irony in Heine's words, there is none in Schumann's music. Schumann's expression is one of devotion and reverence for the beloved. (Little wonder that so many brides and grooms have listened to this Lied while waiting to exchange vows!)

The compact reiterated keyboard chordal figure is interrupted at bar 14 ("betend, dass Gott dich erhalte"), with the vocal melody then undergoing pianistic metamorphosis in bar 15. Octave doubling, embellishments, and grace notes point up the resultant harmonies. The postlude skillfuly develops previous motivic material, offering textual recall through thematic association.

Example 4.10.   *Du bist wie eine Blume*, bars 1–4.

How can performers accomplish the inherent musical and poetic values of this Lied? The vocal line demands a constant legato even though important words need to be stressed, each phrase being given an arching dynamic trajectory. Sentimental crooning is foreign to the musical and emotional depth of this monumental miniature. Because the modern ear has become jaded by familiarity with the rich harmonic progressions on which this small song is constructed, performers may be tempted to nudge the listener at each enriched harmonic moment through exaggerated rubato and accentuation. Self-indulgence is not suitable to *Du bist wie eine Blume*. There is a refinement about this page of music which lifts it to a level of artistry that must be matched in performance by elegance, not by sentimentality.

The setting of the Rückert poem *Aus den östlichen Rosen*, #25, constructs a duet between the vocal melody and the descending and ascending bass line, the latter to be executed with solid sonority despite the preponderance of eighth and dotted-eighth notes. A marginal note in the manuscript indicates that *Aus den östlichen Rosen* represents Robert's anticipation of his approaching union with Clara. That may explain the greater polarity between the outer two voices (vocal melody/keyboard bass line) than is usual for Schumann. The sixteenth notes between the bass line and the vocal line act as harmonic filler for the two outer voices and should not be conspicuous. In this fashion, the two prominent voices are wedded. *Aus den östlichen Rosen* needs to be quietly and tenderly sung, with neither vocal display nor a loss of urgency.

From the Rückert poem *Zum Schluss*, #26, the verse "hab' ich dir den unvollkomm'nen Kranz geflochten, Schwester, Braut!" is a fitting conclusion for a wedding offering, an affirmation that marriage will complete the braiding of the proffered myrtle wreath. Hymnlike in its harmonic structure and in its somewhat static melody, the song exemplifies simplicity. Perhaps this Lied is more fitting as the conclusion of Schumann's personal gift to his bride than it is as the completion of a long performance journey through the twenty-six Lieder of *Myrten*.

Within op. 25 are housed a number of great songs. Quality may not be uniform, yet all are performance-worthy. *Myrten* is a fine source of individual songs for a composite recital group, such as the Burns songs. It may be useful to select out the Heine or the Rückert Lieder, or to combine the two poetic sources into one recital set. The Goethe Lieder work less successfully as a unit but could be included with the Heine and Rückert songs in an extended group. As mentioned previously, if performance time permits, the complete cycle ought to be considered. However, this observer has never personally experienced a public performance of the entire opus.

Several poetic settings originally slated for inclusion in *Myrten* were omitted from the published version, apparently because they were considered to be of lesser merit, not sufficiently varied, or inappropriate to a wedding gift.

Since some of the opuses between op. 25 and op. 35 are brief and contain material not intended for solo voice or are nonchronological insertions, strict opus chronology will now be abandoned in favor of cycles and opuses with larger groupings of songs.

5

Kerner Lieder, Opus 35

In spite of the variety of dramatic situations within op. 35, there is a unity among the Kerner songs (*Zwölf Gedichte von Justinus Kerner*) that suggests the group could well be programmed in its entirety (or at least ten of the songs, omitting the last two). The opus contains some of the most successful Lieder written by Schumann.

Lust der Sturmnacht, #1, through rapid right-hand and left-hand eighth-note splashings, over which an extended melody arches and falls, depicts a storm. Rhythmic disquietude never ceases, regardless of the gradual change from minor to major beginning at "ruht es sich so süss hier innen." In contrasting the moods of the poem, Schumann plays between the opening E♭ minor tonality, which he often uses to paint dark and foreboding musical landscapes, and major tonality, which he usually reserves for expressions of exuberance. This modal variance produces affirmation that life and love can triumph over all, a concept inherent in the poetry.

At the thought of love and peace, a less excursive melody is introduced, later joined by the pianoforte at the lower tenth. Although inner peace answers outward storm, the initial syncopated driving force continues. Robert Schumann's psyche was itself composed of light and shadow—Eusebius and Florestan. In these few brief bars, an outward-raging storm and inner joy at the richness of life mirror that divided self. Depicting the subtle interplay of

dark environment and internal satisfaction offers a challenge to both performers.

In the opening bars, energy should be unbounded (the first marking is
kräftig) and somber shades of both voice and pianoforte are called upon. Then
a change of timbres ought to occur, but the performance must continue to be
leidenschaftlich, with passion from both singer and pianist. The pianist will want
to accent slightly the opening rhythmic pattern and make much of the interpolated *sf* crashes of the chords on the dominant. Beginning at bar 11, the melodic
theme in the left hand should ring out lyrically, soon to join in loving duet with
the voice. This can be accomplished through extreme legato, in contrast to the
earlier descriptive pounding of the rain, although the alternating eighth-note
pattern remains. The concluding syncopations catch the wild night of the storm
through which heavenly radiance shines.

Kerner's poem *Stirb, Lieb und Freud!*, #2, is an intense drama filled with
religious sentiment and admiration for the devout young maiden who is about
to become a nun, yet equally full of the pain felt by the would-be lover who
pines for her. Schumann has good success in liturgical, organlike assertions, and
this example is no exception. A moving inner voice of the keyboard is firmly an-
chored over dotted whole-note and half-note bass octaves. A chorale prelude
ensues, over which the singer (Schumann suggests a tenor, despite the relatively
low range and tessitura) intones a description of the cathedral scene. The spirit
of J. S. Bach hovers above *Stirb, Lieb und Freud!*

At the end of bar 22, the prayer of the young woman begins on a theme that
may have been a conscious quotation from the *Saint John Passion*. (Fischer-
Dieskau [p. 109] and Sams [p. 69] believe so.) Schumann achieves an aura of
melancholy through the Baroque keyboard configurations by which he moves
the vocal line. Deep emotion must be expressed with conscious restraint. Only
beginning at the outcry "Zur Nonne weiht mich arme Maid!" can this studied
emotional control be abandoned; even then, a *p* dynamic level must be maintained. The concluding painful tone of the man who loves and swears eternal fi-
delity should be devoid of vocal vitality and vibrancy. The long sustained chords
in the keyboard underscore the death of love and light. Schumann's further
liturgical ending is completely fitting.

Wanderlied, #3 of the Kerner songs, is published outside the opus among
other selected Lieder in several editions because it is one of Schumann's most
popular songs. Percy M. Young, in his *Tragic Muse: The Life and Works of
Robert Schumann*, joins the traditional, generally negative, British criticism for
all but the Schumann lyrical-declamation compositional style of 1840. He cites
Wanderlied (pp. 120–21) as an example of numerous songs "which demonstrate how effectively Schumann represented the comfortable tastelessness of
his compatriots. Armchair music—music that is, to which the bourgeois parent
would listen approvingly, and nostalgically." He goes on to excoriate Schumann:

> Pathetically one recalls Schumann's schoolboy and student attempts to adjust
> himself to the ways of fencing fraternities and drinking parties. So the self-
> conscious opening of *Wanderlied*. At the end of one stanza Schumann had had

Example 5.1. *Wanderlied*, bars 1–4.

quite enough. With a quite incongruous enharmonic turn to E major he stood still on a dactyllic [*sic*] framework until the time came for a brazen explosion of the dominant of the original key. Then one more glass all round.

Young (pp. 124–25) states that "Schumann's posthumous reputation as a song-writer largely depends on, say, some twenty or so songs."

Although aware of the popular appeal of *Wanderlied*, Sams (p. 169) similarly suggests that in this song from December 1840 "the music itself testifies that Schumann's creative powers are slowing down." On the contrary, there is no evidence here of diminishing creativity. Sams does grant that even "second order music from 1840 has a quality of invention that preserves it against criticism and against time." The poetry is swashbuckling, and Schumann finds the proper bravura for setting it. There is no failure of creative power here. Florestan is responding with youthful vitality to an adventure conceived in folk manner. *Wanderlied* is excellent for a singer capable of delivering free, energetic vocalism. Both pianist and singer should bring to *Wanderlied* a sense of joyous abandonment (Ex. 5.1).

The more relaxed tempo of the middle section in G♭ major offers relief from the upward-sweeping arpeggiated opening vocal figure of section A, a frequent event in Schumann Lieder, as has been previously noted. The new material, germinating from a single-note melodic beginning (another favorite maneuver), permits the singer to express tender feelings for birds, flowers, and the meadow. The blustering of the A section is now varied by warm, lyric timbre. (Florestan and Eusebius, while always retaining distinct individuality, are comfortable companions in *Wanderlied*.) The return to the A section offers strong contrast; one welcomes hearing "the tune" once again. This is a big song, requiring collaboration from a large voice and a sonorous pianoforte; it is an aggressive male expression.

Erstes Grün, #4, has completely different goals from *Wanderlied*. It is a wonderful miniature, whose three stanzas are set strophically. How ill-advised to complain that, because of strophic form, words and music are at odds with each other! Though assessing the setting as effective, Sams (p. 170) finds that "Schumann contrasts a melancholy minor song-music with a joyous vision of springtime in the major piano interludes. In the result the words and their

Example 5.2. *Erstes Grün*, bars 8–14.

music are at different stages of recuperation. Thus the ecstatic second verse is sung to the same tune as the first." This judgment would seem to diminish *all* strophic Lieder, including much of the output of Schubert and Brahms. Besides, the musical concept here is so engaging, so completely appropriate to the strophic simplicity of the poetry (it is marked *einfach*), that negative assessments are difficult to comprehend.

The lilting syncopated figure, with its change to G major, is pure delight. The pianist's assignment is to match vocal color through a singing legato in the right hand (bars 10–13) and a discreet semistaccato commentary in the left. Schumann's return to the G minor chord at bars 13–14 is enchanting. The keyboard digressions have about them a freshness and oneness with Nature that makes *Erstes Grün* an eternally youthful expression. One is tempted to ask, "Is three times really too much to be subjected to such pleasure?" As in all strophic Lieder, it is the task of the singer and pianist to interpretatively vary the strophes. Yet vocal timbre should remain quietly vibrant; restrained, intimate excitement must be projected (Ex. 5.2).

There could be no greater contrast in style and interpretation than that between *Wanderlied*, #3, and *Erstes Grün*, #4, of the Kerner Lieder. Side by side, they attest to the scope of Schumann's ability to successfully set widely ranging poetic stimuli. Publishers do the composer a disservice by taking these popular songs out of their opus locations for publication elsewhere. *Wanderlied* is best heard in contrast to *Stirb, Lieb und Freud!* and to *Erstes Grün*. *Wanderlied's* impact and that of the subsequent Lieder in the opus can only be properly considered "der Reihe nach" (all in a row). Schumann himself called these Kerner songs a "Liederreihe."

It is a pleasure to sing the lines of *Sehnsucht nach der Waldgegend*, #5, and to play the gracious pianoforte score. The indication *phantastisch* is combined with *innig*. (*Innig*, it will be recalled, has a variety of meanings: ardent; cordial; fervent; intimate; heartfelt; hearty; sincere.) Keyboard sonority is almost Brahmsian (bars 1–6). Fischer-Dieskau (p. 110), Sams (p. 172), and Moore (p. 148) all mention the relationship of *Sehnsucht nach der Waldgegend* to Brahms's *Alte Liebe*. It is not just the key relationship between the two pieces nor the pianoforte figure itself that foreshadows what lies ahead with Brahms; it is the general sweep of the vocal line, so apparent in this opus and in some later Schumann Lieder. The breadth of the vocal melody and the pianoforte texture capture the longing expressed by the title. Dynamic markings and tempo alterations appear with great frequency (Ex. 5.3). (It is well to again remember that Schumann seldom places a written *a tempo* following a ritardando indication. At bar 7, the performers must return to *a tempo* and not continue to retard up to the *etwas bewegter* section.) The syncopated harmonies of bars 8–11 further capture longing; they also anticipate Brahms's use of syncopation.

For the singer, the danger in *Sehnsucht nach der Waldgegend* is to slight the short notes (especially the eighths and, to some extent, the less frequent sixteenths) as they occur in the $\frac{6}{4}$ rhythm, thereby losing the linear character of the vocal line. The briefer notes should not be de-timbred or lose intensity. For the pianist, it is essential to maintain clear differentiation between triplet figures and quadruplet figures (bar 12 and following), yet to combine them in flexible, flowing improvisatory support for the broad melody. The singer, having long wandered through the forest in G minor, with "regt sich selten nur das Lied" appears to arrive at B♭ major and will linger there until the sustained final word

Example 5.3.   *Sehnsucht nach der Waldgegend*, bars 1–6.

"schied," on what feels like the fifth of the relative major. But we are mistaken; the cadential pianoforte figure leads the singer back to G minor by way of a descending scale passage that reestablishes minor tonality. The two concluding keyboard measures, still in search of a solution for longing, beautifully sum up the inherent subtlety of this neglected Lied.

Auf das Trinkglas eines verstorbenen Freundes, #6, is one of the most difficult of all Schumann Lieder to bring to successful performance. Its phrase units of four bars (each concluding with a fermata) and octave chords give a hymnlike sobriety and stateliness to the song. They also predispose to a sectionalization further accentuated by sudden brief changes of tonality. Unless care is taken, what was intended as elegiac tends to become ponderously disjunct. The almost spectral illusions of the poetry, describing the chalice full of memory and mystery, its meaning still veiled, are admirably reflected in Schumann's musical imagery. At "Still geht der Mond das Tal entlang. Ernst tönt die mitternächt'ge Stunde. Leer steht das Glas!" Schumann repeats octave chordal harmonies in lower-middle and upper-middle ranges that evoke midnight, achieving an eerie, otherworldly effect. The pianist must give full rhythmic value to semistaccato articulation, appropriately "tapping" the sostenuto pedal so as to avoid harmonic smudging. The Lied concludes with a choralelike commentary that must not be rushed. Vocal timbre should be cool and restrained, without manufactured ethereal coloration. It is easy to make this Lied parodistically spooky, belying the dignity of hallowed remembrance. Better to sing it with straightforward solemnity than to emulate ectoplasmic spirituality.

The subsequent Kerner song, *Wanderung,* #7, has a distinct freshness about it, especially if the pianist adheres to Schumann's *die Begleitung leicht und zart* admonition. A folk tune centers around one of Schumann's favorite melodic nuclei, B♭–C–D–E♭, which here simply may mean that he favors scale pitches 1, 2, 3, and 4 for melodic contouring. The keyboard's B♭ harmonies imitate a horn call within trotting rhythm, another example of Schumann's use of imitative musical figures. At the risk of turning tune detective, it could be mentioned that bars 6 through 11 are close relatives of the horn call in Schumann's *Der Knabe mit dem Wunderhorn.*

Schumann's farewell to home with its shrines, trees, and hills is more concerned with the loved one than with Kerner's piety. It is the song of a young man who faces a new day and new occasions. The poem in Schumann's hands takes on adventuresome delight as the melody bounces along above the staccato keyboard figure. The voice lifts to a rangy *f* climax at "denn ach! auf meinem Herzen trag ich ihr teures Pfand." There appears to be little regret at departing from the homeland.

The *haut-relief* of *Wanderung,* while creating an atmospheric turnabout from the lugubrious colors of *Auf das Trinkglas eines verstorbenen Freundes,* is placed next to the *bas-relief* of *Stille Liebe,* #8, which follows it. Perhaps that is why Schumann treated the poetry of *Wanderung* in such lighthearted fashion.

With *Stille Liebe* we meet a musical language different from what has been encountered thus far in the Kerner opus. That there are formal and harmonic

Example 5.4.   *Stille Liebe*, bars 1–6.

relationships between the opening measures (bars 1–6) of *Stille Liebe* and
Schubert's *Dass sie hier gewesen* has occurred to several observers, as it has to
Sams (p. 174). (It is somewhat more difficult to support the suggestion that influences from Beethoven's *An die ferne Geliebte* are evident in the melodic
structure and piano interludes of *Stille Liebe*.) *Stille Liebe* recalls Wolf's *Herr,
was trägt der Boden hier*, which also owes a distinct debt to Schubert's *Dass sie
hier gewesen* (Ex. 5.4). Despite strong indebtedness to Schubert, *Stille Liebe* is
a remarkably original song. Contrary to some assessments, its appeal lies not in
that "the music is all melody" but rather in that its pianistic motifs built on rich
harmonies ring true as expressions of unrequited love.

The three fermata indications of the first four bars and the rocking keyboard motion that begins at bar 7 produce uncertainty—rhythmic hesitance—
as do the unexpected chord progressions of the ritardando at bars 5 and 6 that
establish E♭ major. Similarly, bars 14–18 conclude with an emotive keyboard
embellishment that leads to the unanticipated tonality of G♭ major. Here the
harmonic alterations are especially telling as they propel the vocal line to a climactic A♭ on "Herz."

The return to E♭ major causes a striking change in tonal color. Schumann's
inevitable keyboard arpeggiations (bars 31–33) move the melody along with a
purposely misleading air of pleasant lyricism that masks a deep expression of
bitter pain. This subtlety may be the reason that some commentators think
Schumann misunderstood the poet's intention. It is not true that "instead of bitter sorrow here is a sweet melancholy"; the pianoforte tells of something quite
other than mere sweet melancholy. The small rhythmic semistaccato stabbings
of the right hand and the brief, enriched chordal harmonies develop a distraught emotional ambience. For the limited melodic excursion of the opening
bars the singer must use the most sustained legato possible. This is particularly
necessary because of the nervous broken rhythms in the keyboard that reveal
the true sentiment that lies behind the simplistic melody.

The concluding bars restate the opening chordal motif and lead to a whole-
note dominant-seventh chord in E♭ (which should endure forever!), out of
which winds a hesitant semidetached chromatic scale, arriving at a melodic suspension that resolves on the tonic note. However, before achieving this resolu-

Example 5.5.   *Frage*, bars 8–16.

tion the pianist has an improvisatory measure that must be thoughtfully, almost prayerfully, played.

There is more need for the singer and the pianist to take a keen look at performance solutions to *Stille Liebe* than is the case with many Schumann Lieder. *Stille Liebe* offers a rich lode of possible vocal and pianistic colors. Perhaps the only probable fault with the song is that so much happens within such a short span of time. Schumann's setting disturbs some purists because the composer omitted the third strophe of the poem.

Frage, #9, exists chiefly to separate the remarkable *Stille Liebe* from *Stille Tränen* (an even more extraordinary undertaking, as shall be seen). In *Frage*, pianoforte and voice double in a modest melodic beginning that rises to high Ab for a momentary climax, after which the melody tapers off to close in an unexpected G major, not yet a musical conclusion. The melodic material of this composition of only sixteen bars relates to what went immediately before in *Stille Liebe*, and the G-major termination acts as the dominant chord of *Stille Tränen*, into which it leads (Ex. 5.5).

It is eminently plain that Schumann conceived of *Stille Liebe*, *Frage*, and *Stille Tränen* as a distinct unit within the opus. Moore (p. 152) expresses the hope that performers will program the entire opus, an ideal suggestion. But if there is to be excerpting, these three Lieder (#8, #9, and #10), because of their impact when taken together, make a separate brief grouping within a larger set of songs.

Stille Tränen, #10, requires consummate vocalism and pianism. Although not technically difficult for the pianist, it demands a profound understanding of how best to point up harmonic progressions, achieve overall phrase direction, and elicit ensemble perfection. For the singer, *Stille Tränen* requires the ultimate level of technical vocalism in the maintenance of sustained middle-range and upper-range *tessitura* while retaining resonance balance (the classic chiaroscuro tone). The song must display beautiful and effortless timbre and a monumental legato.

Stille Tränen is Wagnerian in proportions. Indeed, with regard to its linear aspects and the unfolding of its long vocal lines, it is interesting to compare *Stille Tränen* with the *Wesendonk Lieder* or the *Tristan* studies. The initial quietude of *Stille Tränen* eventually leads to the highest of emotional peaks. This Lied is the quintessential exemplar of the need for levelheaded emotion when performing challenging vocalism. The exquisitely molded melodies must slowly unfurl in a world of quietude that becomes profoundly dramatic because of the cool governance of emotion. There is no room for obvious dramatic histrionics or verismo vocalism. But there is ample opportunity for fully vibrant singing, at both low and high dynamic levels.

The pianist must accommodate the harmonies at significant chord changes through subtle rhythmic flexibility that involves very slight, nearly imperceptible hesitation before each new level is reached. Then the reiterated pattern again moves forward. In this way, the pianist will be matching the singer's taking time to savor the consonants of important words with their German-language consonantal clustering. Yet there should be no loss of forward phrase motion from either of the performers.

The skill of anticipatory consonantal formation and subsequent synchronization of chordal change with vowel arrivals (a performance technique previously mentioned and universally important for Romantic Lieder) is particularly crucial to *Stille Tränen*. This practice is especially necessary in the almost painful harmonic change to A♭ major that occurs at bar 19 with the text "So lang du ohne Sorgen geschlummert schmerzenlos." In this verse, Kerner plays on heavy Germanic sibilant clusters; temporal space is required to pronounce them in such words as "geschlummert schmerzenlos." This poetic and harmonic pointing up of the sounds of the German language finds its apogee (bar 41) at the *f* B♭ on the word "Schmerz" (Ex. 5.6). One appreciates Moore's personal confession regarding this passage (158): "When accompanying this song I became so excited for the singer's B♭ that I gave everything I had in support. Now, even in writing about it, my blood tingles and in consequence I have called it 'the mightiest note' of all." The sonority of the long stabilizing keyboard bass notes is soon supplemented by octaves that add even more intensity and grandeur. Schumann never used his reiterated-chord formula with greater success. *Sehr langsam*, built into the phrase movement itself, is Schumann's marking. Rhythm should be experienced in $\frac{6}{4}$, not in 2. Yet for each phrase there must be an evolving trajectory, a mounting and an arching. This motion not only extends through each individual phrase but also propels the entire Lied onward as it soars to ec-

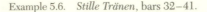

Example 5.6. *Stille Tränen*, bars 32–41.

static emotional heights. To be avoided at all costs is the tasteless habit of striking the hands unevenly to underscore harmonic progressions—in this or in any other Schumann Lied (the "pa-*tum*" that sounds parodistically Romantic).

The keyboard interlude (bars 49–56) is magnificent. It could be Wagner sketching for strings, winds, and brasses. The bass-line triplet/trill figure (bar 52), terminating in a sixteenth-note embellishment, ought to be prominently sounded without impeding forward motion. The corresponding right-hand figure should begin directly on the downbeat of bar 54. Bar 55 displays an emotive moment that ought to last and last, crescendoing to the aproaching harmonic elevation at bar 56. "Und morgens dann ihr meinet" (bars 56–60) may regain forward momentum. At "stets fröhlich sei sein Herz," the singer's fullest *voce completa* timbre and the undergirding triumphant *ff* chords conclude one of the most exciting vocal climaxes in literature for voice (bars 57–66). The postlude is sheer joy for the gifted and sensitive pianist. Only the indicated anticipatory embellishments are to be struck in advance of the chordal progressions. Orchestral Wagner joins keyboard Chopin. Here is reverie coupled to grandeur, energy to lyricism, poetry to music. In *Stille Tränen* Florestan and Eusebius are united as equal partners; Schumann achieves a completely unified personality (Ex. 5.7).

Perhaps the chief problem in programming the Kerner Lieder as a unit is that anything that comes after *Stille Tränen* is bound to be devastatingly anti-climactic. If the opus is performed in its entirety, an extended silence must occur before the performers continue with #11 and #12. Performers

Example 5.7. *Stille Tränen*, bars 57–66.

and listeners need time to reflect on and recover from what has just taken place.

The two songs (#11 and #12) share the same melody, despite texts that would seem to cry out for distinct treatment. *Wer machte dich so krank?* and *Alte Laute* are melodically linked by Schumann, becoming substantially a single Lied. What could have prompted him to tack these two poems together? One might conclude that his genius for the Kerner verses spent itself with *Stille Tränen*. Moore suggests that it may be possible to place #11 and #12 elsewhere in the opus. However, wedging them in between *Frage* and *Stille Tränen*, as Moore suggests (p. 160), overlooks the fact that *Stille Liebe*, *Frage*, and *Stille Tränen* comprise a compositional unit. Better options would seem to be either omitting #11 and #12 altogether (although sweet, they belong to the category of less distinguished Schumann Lieder) or pausing appropriately after *Stille Tränen*, then concluding with them.

6

Reinick Lieder, Opus 36

Opus 36, settings of poems by Robert Reinick, begins with *Sonntags am Rhein*, which the Peters edition places among the *Sämtliche Lieder* in Volume I. For Friedländer, *Sonntags am Rhein* was significant enough to lodge among popular Lieder. Sams (p. 149) makes a different assessment: "[Schumann's] superiority over this fourth-rate poem does not amount to more than second-hand music." Sams expands his comments by mentioning that the second half of the melody sounds like a discarded sketch for *Im wunderschönen Monat Mai*. The relationship between *Sonntags am Rhein* and *Im wunderschönen Monat Mai* is no greater than that found among many Schumann Lieder, a number of which use common melodic formulas. It is equally hard to find elements of *Süsser Freund, du blickest mich verwundert an* (as Sams does) in this straightforward Lied. Regarding the linking of *Sonntags am Rhein* to *Der Page,* an occasional similar melodic snippet may be discovered, but there is no integral relationship. It is wisest not to examine *Sonntags am Rhein* for ties to distant relatives but to look at it for its own value.

Sonntags am Rhein is a prime example of Schumann's intentional reiterated chordal monotony, present in nearly every bar of the composition. There is no arpeggiated improvisatory figuration, no tonal ambiguity, nor any of the questing lyricism of *Im wunderschönen Monat Mai*. The song is charmingly unpretentious and eminently performable.

The noble rangy melody catches the *Gemütlichkeit* (geniality) experienced while taking a Sunday-morning stroll along the Rhine. The poem itself (Reinick's verse is *not* fourth-rate [Sams, p. 149]) is typical of a genre of nineteenth-century German poetry that equates pious devotion and respect of Nature with love of fatherland. The reiterated chords move forward sturdily (*mässigge-schwind* is indicated), depicting a brisk walk and an inexorably swift-flowing Rhine. The ostinato figure, often in thirds and sixths, which the pianist should sing out forcefully, provides a supportive counterbalance to the vocal melody, to be delivered with vigor and joy. Schumann seems to be distancing us from the town as the ostinato and the bouncing eighths drop off to *pp* level, concluding (as in *Stirb, Lieb und Freud!*) with a plagal cadence.

Sonntags am Rhein is an excellent song for introducing the world of the Lied to young performers who possess considerable technical control over their instruments but are not yet comfortable in achieving dynamic subtlety in either the more pacific or the more energetic Lieder. This song accomplishes that purpose well because it does not demand great depth of musical or emotional involvement. It is direct and lies easily for pianist and singer. Florestan enjoys himself, as must the performers. His happiness continues through the joyful postlude, as the plagal cadence is approached.

Ständchen, #2, with its grace and charm, looks deceptively simple. It requires performers who can deliver these few bars with subtle nuances of color. The keyboard introduces the serenader with a triplet embellishment in the left hand that, although in low register, is reminiscent of the nightingale's trilling; in the right hand a guitar strums. These two succinct motifs permeate the song. They are most tellingly used in the third strophe, where more fervor is required by the nature of the poetry. (Schumann omits two strophes of the Reinick poem.)

An elegant little serenade, *Ständchen* is ideal for the singer who can manage a beautiful legato and execute it within limited dynamic dimensions. Despite octave leaps and falling intervals, there must be no sudden vocal outbursts at the high pitches; the entire phrase shape ought to follow Schumann's dynamic markings religiously. The singer's enjoyable task is to serenade with flowing vocal timbre while remaining at the indicated dynamic levels.

To the pianist is given the distinct duty of summoning up the evocative atmosphere basic to every nocturnal serenade. In *Ständchen*, he or she ought to emphasize qualities of improvisation and spontaneity and must be willing to imitate guitar strumming. This is yet another example of Schumann's use of descriptive mechanical keyboard motifs as a unifying factor (a Schubertian heritage, as we have repeatedly seen). Though not so well known as some other serenades, Schumann's *Ständchen* deserves a place among those of Schubert, Brahms, Wolf, and Strauss.

Nichts Schöneres, #3 of the Reinick Lieder, is a pleasant, rollicking song that lends itself to joyous singing. The text's reference to becoming one, body and soul, with one's spouse would have had personal attraction for Schumann. The poem is an exuberant but somewhat coy expression of love. (Sams's typical assessment [p. 150]: "The music has not enough leverage to budge the dead weight of the poet's ineptitude.") This Lied is far removed from lyric declamation, from psychological penetration, and from synthesis of word and music, because Schumann is interested in catching the lover's straightforward joy, not in expressing depth of emotion. *Nichts Schöneres* should be performed in fun-loving fashion, in accordance with the poet's playful attitude.

Schumann's interest in the Lied form *im Volkston* (in the manner of a folk song) is evident in *An den Sonnenschein*, #4, composed in August 1840. Folk elements are achieved through forthright simplicity, yet the hymnlike squareness of its overall structure seems academic and not entirely expressive of the poetic source. There is nothing to distinguish *An den Sonnenschein* from other folklike Lieder coming from any number of hands. It is skillfully composed and worthy of performance, but it does not occupy a foremost place among the Schumann Lieder.

Dichters Genesung, #5, is a long narrative poem with several sections. In the first part, drawn to the poet's evocation of Nature, Schumann begins with a reiterated-chord motif. Sams (p. 152) believes "the opening bars for the piano say to Clara with unobtrusive tenderness 'Du bist wie eine Blume.'" Because of the composer's penchant for using a small group of melodic nuclei and reiterated chordal progressions in a great number of his songs, it is probably precarious practice to search for close relationships among songs by discovering analogous melodic and accompanimental fragments among them. Compositional mechanisms, such as pitch conglomerates, calculated reiterated-chord monotony, arpeggiated figurations, and chromatically winding scale passages, do not imply hidden relationships among diverse Lieder. Schumann relied on these tools with great frequency. *Dichters Genesung* is otherwise not related to *Du bist wie eine Blume* in style, mood, proportion, or merit.

The pianistic figure of "Da rauschten zusammen zur Tanzmelodei der Strom und die Winde mit Klingen und Zischen" must be delivered with clarity and with light accents on dissonant harmonies. Sams (p. 152) is correct that this elfin music sounds a bit Mendelssohnian. There is as well, in the pianoforte, some indebtedness to Zumsteg and to the late-eighteenth-century *Melodram* form. Keyboard sprightliness will achieve an invigorating airiness for this charming music.

The singer is narrator and should play up the drama through characterization of the changing scene, which is seldom reflected directly in the vocal score. One will be excused for not including this Lied among masterpieces of Robert Schumann. However, it is certainly as worthy as many other highly praised ballad types by other composers. Nevertheless, there are better Schumann Lieder from which to choose.

With *Liebesbotschaft*, #6 of the Reinick Lieder, we encounter a melody comparable to those that in the same period originated below the Alps. The thematic interweaving of the melody, often doubled in voice and pianoforte, grows into gracious keyboard writing, but the melodies are long and sustained, not unlike the cavatina writing of bel canto composers. The pianoforte score takes its development from the sweeping vocal line, not the reverse. *Liebesbotschaft* is an underrated song. Later Lied composers, including Max Reger, are indebted to this kind of Schumann composition, with its melodiousness supported by a rich, harmonically varied keyboard web.

The musical figure that begins in bar 9, characterized by frequent distinctive intervallic leaps, undergoes both pianistic and vocal mutations which contribute to an intriguing interplay between voice and piano without any attempt at synthesis. On the contrary, each instrument is allowed to solo in alternating duet-partner fashion. Schumann recognizes the charm of his tune, and he gives us a number of chances to enjoy it.

Liebesbotschaft allows the singer who has a substantial instrument to display virtuosic control of long phrases; the tessitura is higher than in most Schumann Lieder, and the *ossia* line, rising through the high B♭, should be mandatory (it is present in the identical mounting line of the keyboard) for a climactic expression just before the conclusion of the song. The pianoforte postlude is anticlimactic, the climax having been assigned to the singing voice. There is no concern here for lyric declamation, cautious attention to word accent, or speech inflection; the aim, clearly, is unmitigated expressive vocalism.

We have already seen a number of Schumann Lieder (and there are many more to come) that require professional vocalism and high levels of technical skill. Mostly, these songs are ignored by critics who are convinced that Schumann was less interested in the singing voice than in the pianoforte and the poetry. The unfortunate result is that a major portion of Schumann's contribution to the Lied literature goes unrecognized. Rather than demand that singers who are natively endowed with sizable voices try to turn themselves into vocal miniaturists for the production of salon sound, teachers and coaches should introduce those performers to the more vocally exacting Schumann Lieder, of which *Liebesbotschaft* is an example. In this setting, free-flowing vocal and pianistic lines unite in a warm expression of love. Schumann catches the poet's sentiment in the same way that Brahms frequently does later, through commitment to mood, not to word painting.

7

Rückert Lieder (*Zwölf Gedichte aus "Liebesfrühling"*), Opus 37

In letters to his publisher, Schumann states: "We have written a number of Rückert songs together," which he says he would like to have in print by Clara's birthday. These are the songs of op. 37, eventually published as *Zwölf Gedichte aus F. Rückert's "Liebesfrühling," für Gesang und Pianoforte, von Robert und Clara Schumann*. Critics repeatedly have tried to determine what might have been from the hand of Robert, what from Clara, and what from their collaboration. Lieder #2, #4, and #11 are generally conceded to be by Clara. (Songs #7 and #12, which are duets, will be considered later.) Nancy B. Reich (p. 249) reports:

> Clara presented four songs to Robert on his thirty-first birthday, and they chose three for the joint publication. The songs were sold to Breitkopf & Härtel . . . and Clara received the first printed copy on her birthday in 1841, just thirteen days after the birth of her first child. The title page of the collection, which lists them as op. 37/12, gives no inkling as to the authorship of each song, and reviewers were confused—probably to Schumann's amusement. He identified Clara's songs on the flyleaf of his copy of the first edition, and the extant autograph manuscripts in Zwickau and Berlin confirm her authorship of no. 2, "Er ist gekommen"; no. 4, "Liebst du um Schönheit"; and no. 11, "Warum willst du and're fragen."

With regard to the authorship of the songs of op. 37, it is probably best to accept Robert's written verification.

For Fischer-Dieskau (p. 114): "Among the *Liebesfrühling* songs, Nos. 2, 4, and 11 sound so much like those of Robert that one might think he provided some help. On the other hand, the statement that they were 'written jointly' could also mean that Clara contributed her share of ideas to songs written by her husband." Sams (p. 179) offers the following opinion regarding the Clara songs #2, #4, and #11: "They have an occasional master touch which is not hers." (Ignored are the other beautiful Lieder known to have been written by Clara Schumann.)

According to Sams (p. 180), *Der Himmel hat eine Träne geweint*, #1 of op. 37 (composed in January 1841), is "thick bland music [that] makes the verse only a little more palatable." This judgment is difficult to accept. Although not at the level of Goethe, the poetic premise is not unimaginative, and the setting by Robert and Clara deserves a higher evaluation than Sams affords it. Moore (p. 162) assesses *Der Himmel hat eine Träne geweint* quite favorably: "I found after studying it and hearing it sung that it haunted me. It is beautiful and we can be grateful to Schumann."

In *Der Himmel hat eine Träne geweint*, the singer must enhance the offbeat keyboard figure by moving the melody ever forward. Schumann's harmonic treatment at "Die Muschel kam and schloss sie ein" adds a color change that the pianist can nurture by synchronizing the harmonic movement and the singer's consonantal articulation. The postlude is traditional in its motivic development and, even if not particularly distinctive, provides musical commentary on the poetic sentiments. The brevity of this song makes it difficult to excerpt, but it is clearly of sufficient merit to warrant performance. It is not "thick bland music." Six typically improvisatory bars make up the postlude.

O ihr Herren, #3, dating from January 1841, is folklike. It does not excite accolades, but it is a respectable example of a Lied in folk manner. The postlude is full of charm.

Ich hab in mich gesogen, #5, deserves more performance than it gets. The opening bars present a motif (first in thirds, later expanded to sixths) that lends itself to canonic treatment and provides unity and cohesion to the composition. The song proceeds in a somewhat predictable manner, but it need not become perfunctory if phrases are tapered in musical fashion. Says Sams: "Perhaps the opening bars with their prim sequences derived from an idea of Clara's." The sequences are no more prim than many a canonic figure from many a celebrated composer, including Robert Schumann. The Lied does not present itself as an example of lyric declamation, nor does the composer (or composers) search for psychological depth. Of course, Hugo Wolf would not have set the poem in this way. If Clara's hand is present here, there is reason to praise her conception. This song is gratefully written for both voice and pianoforte.

Liebste, was kann denn uns scheiden?, #6, with its musical questions and its longer and more vocally demanding answers, produces a special flavor of intimacy. There is an indication that the questions and answers could be performed in duet fashion (part of a duet recital?). The poetic sentiment is sweet and heartfelt. Queries and their replies should be built at differing dynamic levels, as should the four strophes. There is game playing between the lovers (the marking is *heiter*). Fermatas (occurring over rests as well as over the longer climactic notes) should be exaggerated and silences fully observed. As a solo Lied, *Liebste, was kann denn uns scheiden?* acts as a foil to other expressions of less cheerful love.

Of *Flügel! Flügel!*, #8, Sams (p. 182) says: "The opening page is uninspired and tentative." Fischer-Dieskau (p. 115) reports: "Clara may indeed have supplied the opening phrase of *Flügel! Flügel!* . . . as has been claimed. But for the rest, Robert, inspired by the poem that is a cut above the others, composed a scherzo of great originality." The opening questioning chords are intriguing, the subsequent melodies expansive and grateful to sing. Sams (p. 183) asks: "Is the first page by Clara?" (Is it objective criticism that assigns perceived "good" things to Robert, "bad" things to Clara?) No matter who wrote it, this song achieves the intended poetic sentiment. It is a pleasure to think that Clara and Robert collaborated on this and on other songs of the opus.

Flügel! Flügel! is vocally demanding and has a much higher *tessitura* than that found in many Schumann Lieder. Its dramatically ascending lines develop as Icarus mounts upward to the stars (the last five bars of the *sehr langsam* section). There is also substantial keyboard writing that involves descending thirds and sixths and harmonic diversity. Admittedly, the postlude may seem a bit pat when compared with the urgency of the rest of the song, but it accomplishes an appropriate treatment of Icarus's plunge to the sea. This is not a simple Lied but a composition that takes on the proportions of an operatic scena, worthy of well-schooled performers who can make much of the drama. There is an inherent energy about the song that is the antithesis of Schumann's introspective Lieder.

In turning to *Rose, Meer und Sonne,* #9, we encounter in both pianism and vocalism a distinct change of direction from song #8. Broken arpeggiation provides momentum and contrast to the "ruhig" character of the melody. Enhancement by thirds and sixths, especially on seventh-chord sequences, intensifies expression. Schumann (perhaps the Schumanns) later repeats "fasst mein ganzes Leben ein" for a climactic vocal conclusion. *Rose, Meer und Sonne* is vocally gratifying; *voce completa* (complete voice) timbre that will match the sonorities of the pianoforte is required. The postlude (final twelve bars) offers the pianist an opportunity to engage in sumptuous pianism. Fischer-Dieskau (p. 115) describes it thus: "The instrumental conclusion is independent (recalling *Dichterliebe*), introducing a new theme, set off from the song with all its splendor."

O Sonn, o Meer, o Rose, #10, is a poetic continuation of *Rose, Meer und Sonne,* #9. In its musical construction, however, it is not a near relative. Sams (p. 185) states: "Though the theme is the same, the treatment is depressingly dull in the first few bars." For Fischer-Dieskau (pp. 115–16) "the song opens with a somewhat banal musical idea, possibly by Clara, which tends to weaken the impact of the entire piece." (Clara's husband was fully capable of writing banal as well as exalted music!) The squareness of the melody recalls many Schumann Lieder cast in folk mold. The conclusion develops into a pianistic digression typical of Schumann postludes. There is a certain justice in purposely underscoring in performance differences between the angularity of the vocal setting and the subsequent Romantic pianoforte commentary.

8

Liederkreis (Eichendorff), Opus 39

Composed in May of 1840, the Eichendorff *Liederkreis* was first published in Vienna in September 1842 by Tobias Haslinger Verlag. Schumann made revisions for the 1850 publication by F. Whistling Verlag of Leipzig.

The cycle is remarkable for its stylistic unity. Integration comes through reliance on kindred thematic material between songs and on melodies based on familiar close-intervalled pitch nuclei and, further, by an overall adherence to closely related keys. In the 1850 version, Schumann tightened the key relationship of the cycle by replacing the original D major *Der frohe Wandersmann* (see op. 77, #1) with the F♯ minor *In der Fremde*. (The only extant manuscript copy of *In der Fremde* is in Clara Schumann's handwriting, but there is no other substantiation for speculation that she may have written it.) In the revision, *Liederkreis* begins in F♯ minor and concludes in F♯ major; the key relationships within the cycle are significant.

The pianoforte's preludes, interludes, and postludes are compactly integrated into one weave with the vocal scoring. Though in a number of Schumann Lieder the vocal melody merely echoes that of the pianoforte, in op. 39 the pianoforte and the voice are mostly kept in equal partnership. The pianistic idiom relies on familiar Schumann techniques, but in imaginative ways that elevate them to new heights. Contrary to some critical comment, a high degree of voice and pianoforte synthesis is consistently maintained.

In *Liederkreis*, psychologic and emotional intensity are evenly sustained. Personifications of Nature and of emotional states linked to Nature (the pathetic fallacy) permeate the Eichendorff text. Schumann the Romanticist catches the human pathos of diverse aspects of Nature through musical devices both descriptive and nonrepresentational. Motifs intended as imitative of Nature sounds (in the graphic manner ingeniously devised by Schubert—mechanical figurations) serve descriptive purposes. For example: the first eight measures of *Waldesgespräch*, #3, simulate the waldhorn; in *Schöne Fremde*, #6, fast-moving sixteenth notes suggest the rustling of treetops; a rushing brook impels forward motion in *In der Fremde*, #8; horn motifs resound again in *Im Walde*, #11; quickly moving triplet figures portray flying birds passing through the breeze above the garden in *Frühlingsnacht*, #12.

In the nonrepresentational instances, it is the melodic contour, the rhythmic pattern, and the harmonic language by which Schumann catches the events of Nature. Specific means include the arpeggiation of *In der Fremde*, #1; the syncopation and countermelodies of *Intermezzo*, #2; the contrast of quasi-recitative and lyrical motifs in *Die Stille*, #4; the minimal harmonic and melodic excursions of *Auf einer Burg*, #7; the chorale-like harmonies of *Wehmut*, #9; and the slow arpeggios constructed on chromatic harmonies of *Zwielicht*, #10.

Barbara Turchin's assessment (p. 283) is perceptive:

> This *Liederkreis* proves Schumann to be a man of superior poetic judgment and exceptional poetic insight. Eichendorff's evocative and potent imagery offered him the perfect material to achieve both coherence of style and language, and beauty of thought. It was Schumann's sensitivity to meaning and design which enabled him to shape these poems into a cycle that offers not only balance and clarity in structure, but also compelling and increasing tension in expression.

Were the opening melodic phrases of *In der Fremde*, #1, detached from the pianoforte accompaniment, it could be assumed that Schumann had set the poem in folk manner. While retaining the folk aspects, the composer transcends them by artfully combining potentials of voice and keyboard that extend far beyond a folk idiom. Schumann's arpeggios move forward to harmonic pivotal points that underscore emotional peaks. Melancholy and longing result. The developing melody, with an accompaniment that recalls the guitar, is close-intervalled, in keeping with the intimacy of poetic expression.

Despite the long phrases required of the singer, Schumann's *nicht schnell* marking must be carefully observed. No hurrying is appropriate to this evocation of loneliness that reflects the transitory nature of existence. The singer will need to choose an intimate vocal timbre and the pianist a pensive, nonpercussive arpeggiated sonority *mit Pedal*. Even in slow tempo, there must be continuous forward movement. Nevertheless, the phrase "Wie bald, ach wie bald kommt die stille Zeit" should show no perceptible change in tempo, nor should either the more expansive "da ruhe ich auch" or its repetition. Total calm, and consistently low dynamic levels, from both performers is essential.

Example 8.1.   *In der Fremde*, bars 15–20.

The subsequent phrase, "und über mir rauscht die schöne Waldeinsam-keit," is to be accomplished in a single breath. The extensive phrase duration and the harmonic motion suggest increased forward movement; the repetition of "die schöne Waldeinsamkeit" should be given increased time to compensate for the slight accelerando of the previous phrase. An alternate but less favorable solution is for the singer to take an imperceptible breath following "und über mir" (bar 16), then complete the rest of the phrase without interruption. For both textual and harmonic reasons, taking a breath after "schöne" (bar 17) be-fore "Waldeinsamkeit" must be avoided (Ex. 8.1). In the brief postlude, the key-board color should be rich and warm, played reverently, without hurry.

The keyboard figures of *Intermezzo*, #2, begin in bass clef in the lower-middle pianoforte octave. Soon thereafter a countermelody sings out in the fifth octave. This register change is in striking contrast to the low-registration texture of *In der Fremde*, #1. Whereas in *In der Fremde* Schumann achieves a mood of resignation, in the A section of *Intermezzo* he translates the exuberance of love into musical terms. Syncopation, combined with the *nach und nach schneller* marking beginning at section B, effectively directs the melody to pivotal har-monic points. Singer and pianist must be religiously exact in anticipating to-gether the precise degree of accelerando. Completion of the accelerando at the conclusion of section B with "und zu dir eilig zieht" and its relaxation into a ri-tardando engender one of the most memorable manifestations of movement, relaxation, and emotional recovery in all the Lied literature.

With the addition of a countermelody in the bass register of the pianoforte, the change of mood at the return to the A section becomes particularly poi-gnant. A six-bar keyboard development of the opening melodic matter con-cludes the song, repeating the "Dein Bildnis wunderselig" vocal motif, thereby augmenting what had been expressed earlier by the poetry. A pianistic reverie

Example 8.2.   *Intermezzo*, bars 26–30.

evolves, as gracious as anything to be found in the Schumann Lieder. What the voice and the pianoforte presented is sculpted into a miniature of great beauty. Eusebius and Florestan are both at work in this brief Lied (Ex. 8.2).

Waldesgespräch, #3, is a ballad inserted into a cycle mostly introspective in character. However, this dramatic narrative integrates well because its events take place within the world of Nature. Coming between *Intermezzo* and *Die Stille,* *Waldesgespräch* produces striking contrasts. When the song is excerpted for performance outside the cycle (as it often is), much of its dramatic impact is lost.

A heroic hunting-horn keyboard theme that develops from sixths and thirds peals forth, introducing the vocal interjections that the pianoforte already has harmonically outlined; the initial vocal line consists of melodic fragments that reflect the keyboard motif. This interplay of voice and pianoforte unites the two instruments (Ex. 8.3).

Example 8.3.   *Waldesgespräch*, bars 1–8.

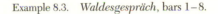

Schumann turns to reiterated-chord movement and subsequently to an arpeggiated figuration at the key change. The abrupt jump from E major to C major that introduces the second character—the dangerous siren—is high drama. A lyrical return to E major, with warm sixths and thirds, reaffirms the unsuspecting nature of the rider who is about to be entrapped by the Lorelei. This idyllic mood is suddenly shattered by a recitative-like chordal announcement sonorously delivered by the pianist, together with a tonality change to a marchlike G major at "Jetzt kenn' ich dich, Gott steh' mir bei!" The terrified exclamation "du bist die Hexe Loreley!" should not be parlando but fully sung, with complete resonant vocal balance. Surprise and disbelief ought to be paramount. It is true that in his Lieder Schumann rarely marks any passage as quasi recitativo (he does do so in *Die Kartenlegerin*), but he often interrupts his melodies with recitativelike insertions, as in this case. They are to be sung, not recited as *recitativo secco* (dry recitative).

At the *im Tempo*, the pianoforte's repeated B is taken up by the Lorelei warning, "Du kennst mich wohl." The single-note repetition permits speech-inflection imitation and the accomplishment of vocal and pianistic synchronization. From this one-note statement the vocal line ascends to a high tessitura and a dramatic climax: "Es ist schon spät, es ist schon kalt." Excitement is promoted by arpeggiation and completed by shifting chordal harmonic progressions. The last six bars of the vocal line are emphatically and victoriously declaimed over thick, strongly struck chords in the keyboard.

To close this ballad-like Lied (in spirit, not in actual form), Schumann repeats the opening horn theme, reminding the listener of the hapless rider's progression from infatuation with the beautiful siren to destruction through her wiles. The singer needs to portray the evolution of the plot by beginning with exuberant male vocalism and concluding with the Lorelei's triumphant "Kommst nimmer mehr aus diesem Wald!" The protagonists are best defined vocally through changes in dynamic levels, timbre alteration, and precise enunciation, without parodying male or female vocalism. *Waldesgespräch* proves Schumann to be a topflight ballad composer (as will become increasingly evident).

That the rhythms and melodies of *Die Stille*, #4, are patterned on language inflection is evident when the poetry itself is recited; this is an example of Schumann's famed *lyric declamation*. Recitative-like interjections mirror speech rhythms, as with "So still ist's nicht draussen im Schnee" and "so stumm und verschwiegen sind die Sterne nicht in der Höh'" (Ex. 8.4).

Staccatos of the keyboard in section A, at both their initial appearance and their reprise, should be easily but crisply struck; over them the voice cleanly but softly enunciates. The *immer sehr leise* marking over the opening bars calls for intimacy of expression from both performers. The contrasting B section introduces a melody that lifts into flight with "Ich wünscht', ich wär' ein Vöglein." The brief soaring motif should be quietly but melodiously played and sung. Speech inflection in section A and vocal lyricism in section B offer the singer (and the pianist) opportunities for varying colors.

Although there is no tempo marking, the short postlude should return to

Example 8.4. *Die Stille*, bars 8–14.

erstes Tempo following the final vocal ritardando, because the pianoforte imitates the opening "Es weiss and rät es doch keiner," tying up musically and poetically the two ends of this brief Lied. Subtle vocalism and pianism bring us into a world remote from the narrative *Waldesgespräch* that preceded *Die Stille*.

Synthesis of poetry, musical construction, voice, and keyboard is stunningly realized in *Mondnacht*, #5, one of the greatest song creations of the nineteenth century. This is the mood-evocative Lied (*Stimmungslied*) par excellence, a conception of genius. Only Schumann, with his poetic sensibilities, his idiomatic pianism, his improvisatory skills, his sensitivity to vocal color, and his artistic imagination, could have constructed such a Lied (Ex. 8.5).

The opening five bars sit on the dominant, producing tonal ambiguity that can be heightened by the pianist through subtle rhythmic exploration, as though in search of a tonal center. Harmonic changes should be played unhurriedly; bars 1–4 comprise two parallel phrases of an improvisatory nature out of which emerge the reiterated Bs of bar 5. The initial repetitions of this persistent note require a restless rubato; in its first appearance, B should be uncertain of its destination, becoming rhythmically more stable only as it is joined by seconds and thirds. Relentless repetition permeates nearly every bar of the composition and serves as anchor regardless of the shape of the vocal melody or of adjoining harmonies. Through its omnipresence, incessant B acts as an emotive unifier. Resolution of the dominant is constantly delayed; tonality hovers tenuously without definition.

Five of the six vocal phrases that grow almost imperceptibly out of the repeated B of the keyboard have an identical shape. In the sixth, the ascent of the vocal line from C♯ to F♯ (bars 8 and 9) by way of an E♯—in contradiction

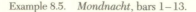

Example 8.5.   *Mondnacht*, bars 1–13.

to the E♮ of the descending keyboard melody—adds an element of disso-
nance that increases the distinctive mystical ambience. (This sudden contrasting of E♮ and E♯ must be clearly delineated by both performers.) The pitch B
provides the focal point for the accumulating harmonies from which evolves
the dissonant second that creates close-intervallic texture and delays harmonic
resolution. An eerie feeling of the suspension of time is created, an other-
worldliness that goes far beyond the poetry of Eichendorff and the mechan-
ics of harmonic structure. Here are ultimate Schumann transcendence and
synthesis. The resulting diffused harmonic atmosphere seems to evoke moonlight itself.

Of course, it is not possible through motivic configuration to literally depict moonlight or any other feature of Nature. Nor did Schubert, who often
used mechanical keyboard figures to reflect dramatic action, do so in his superb *An den Mond* ("Geuss, lieber Mond"), in which the slow F minor arpeggios remind the listener of the C♯ minor first movement of Beethoven's
Sonata quasi una Fantasia, op. 27, #2, which in the popular imagination is associated with moonlight (the "Moonlight" Sonata). It is by nondescriptive musical means that Schumann's *Mondnacht* paints the very essence of a moonlit
night.

Voice and keyboard tranquillity are essential to the realization of *Mondnacht*. To match the pianistic color, the singer would be wise to produce a *voce
finta* (feigned voice) color at a mezza voce dynamic level that never opens out to
voce completa (complete voice) even at the emotive "Und meine Seele spannte
weit ihre Flügel aus." The embellishment marked "crescendo" on "Seele" needs
adequate time and an increase in intensity that should be matched in the pi-

anoforte. The pianoforte crescendo at the word "aus" must be executed by the voice as well, while the subsequent "flog durch die stillen Lande," although ascending melodically, remains in a state of serenity. Resolution of harmonic ambiguity and of poetic question comes for the singer only with the concluding vocal line; for the pianist such resolution is reached following a thoughtful improvisation (bars 61–68) on the opening thematic material. Evocative and ethereal, the eight-bar postlude offers the pianist an opportunity to complete the spell, now through use of a sonorous region of the pianoforte (Ex. 8.6).

Kenneth Whitton (p. 140) well describes the function of Schumann postludes and their influence on later composers:

> a piano postlude of great beauty which, as in this case, not only sums up the mood and atmosphere, but gives the accompaniment the importance which it was increasingly to have in the 19th century, until, eventually, composers felt that the piano was not enough and turned to the resources of the full orchestra.

Una corda is advisable throughout the song, together with discreet use of the sostenuto pedal adjusted by occasional "tapping" so as to sustain sound without blurring harmonic changes. The rich harmonic idiom is uniquely structured to the poetic source, and instrumental and vocal colorations never should exceed a palette of pastels. Simplicity emerges out of complexity to produce synthesis that transcends the materials of word and music, of vocalism and pianism.

The temptation to excerpt *Mondnacht* from the cycle should be resisted. *Mondnacht* represents an important part of the totality of Nature images that Schumann has captured in the Eichendorff *Liederkreis*, arguably his *capolavoro*.

It is fitting that *Schöne Fremde*, #6, should follow *Mondnacht*. Both filter the phenomena of Nature through human emotion—a characteristic of the Romantic movement given strong impetus by Goethe and his contemporaries. The musical material, in its ambiguous tonal beginning, is improvisatory (bars 1–5). Once again, word inflection shapes melodic line. Offbeat sixteenths and repeated eighths create a composite rhythm that generates excitement descriptive of the rustling of trees, the summoning of nocturnal fantasy. Reiterated eighth notes of the left hand, although interrupted rhythmically, serve as harmonic anchoring, somewhat like the function of the constant B of *Mondnacht* (Ex. 8.7).

In typical fashion, the vocal melody begins in restricted range, then lyrically

Example 8.6.   *Mondnacht*, bars 61–68.

Example 8.7. *Schöne Fremde*, bars 1–5.

soars to climactic points, creating alternating Eusebius/Florestan textures in six-bar units. The keyboard offers exciting commentary on poetic images. The vocal line and the pianoforte figurations can best be described as ecstatic. Pianistic transformation of the intervallic and syncopated figures concluding over a stabilizing pedal point is remarkable. Johannes Brahms would later make much use of both pedal point and syncopation in his Lieder. *Schöne Fremde* may have directly influenced Brahms's *Meine Liebe ist grün.*

After such display of heightened emotion and vocal and pianistic skill comes *Auf einer Burg,* #7. This uncomplicated-appearing Lied may be the most difficult in the cycle to perform (Ex. 8.8). Its inherent inertia, its barren harmony that remains within E minor and C major, its limited melodic con-

Example 8.8. *Auf einer Burg*, bars 1–4.

tour, and its reiterated dotted-quarter/eighth-note rhythmic ostinato vocal line call on both performers to arrest motion without becoming static. The tumbling waterfall of rapid notes and the sweeping phrases encountered in *Schöne Fremde* now are abandoned; all lies motionless and still. The stone statue of "der alte Ritter" (Frederick Barbarossa), with his beard and hair matted together, sits for hundreds of years in his silent castle cell surrounded by peace, solitude, and falling rain; the lonely forest birds sing in the empty window arches. His stationary presence heightens the events taking place below on the sunlit Rhine, where a wedding party passes with musicians playing. For Schumann (for Eichendorff as well?) there is a sense of foreboding in that event, which begins with "eine Hochzeit fährt da unten" in low vocal range on a single pitch. Recalling the musical means used in the first strophe to describe the long-dead knight, the voice now moves three times from single-pitch intoning by intervals of a sixth and presses harmonically forward to the word "munter," after which the downward progression of harmonic strata leads to "und die schöne Braut, die weinet." By making use of identical musical comment, Schumann underscores the contrast in Eichendorff's verses between what is occurring at the castle perched above the valley and what is taking place below as the wedding party floats down the Rhine. Schumann thus draws attention to the brevity of human existence, suggesting that even a young bride will not long endure. What a different composition this would be had the rain, the wind in the trees, the birds, and the wedding music been presented in descriptive fashion. Schumann's understatement produces more than an imitation of the events of Nature; he establishes stillness and desolation through minimal musical means.

How should performers interpret the final line of poetry, "und die schöne Braut, die weinet"? Eichendorff's meaning may remain enigmatic. Schumann's does not. The composer pushes us harmonically forward to "Musikanten spielen munter," yet his subsequent harmonic and melodic handling tells us that all is not well with the young bride. Despite the playing of the musicians for the festive occasion, this bride's weeping is not for joy. Is it an arranged marriage? Does she love someone else? This may be Schumann's viewpoint, expressed with the three and a half concluding ritardando bars and the lack of harmonic resolution at the final chord, which keeps us suspended and requires us to continue to ponder events. The performance pair can make much of the suspended harmony at "munter"; despite the festive surface trappings, the singer must give the word "munter" (merry, blithe) a vocal color that belies its normal meaning. The concluding phrase should be sung with hopelessness, in a detimbred, non-vibrant voice. A final dominant chord serves as springboard for the A minor tonality of *In der Fremde*.

Performers are to proceed without interruption to *In der Fremde*, #8. The quiet excitement of the introductory keyboard figure and the speechlike pattern of the vocal line (bars 1–4) are a complete change from the preceding song. Yet the key relationship and the retention of the dotted rhythm (notated as dotted quarter/eighth in *Auf einer Burg*, dotted eighth/sixteenth in *In der Fremde)* make a pair of the two songs. The melodic shape, based on the descending in-

Example 8.9.   *In der Fremde*, bars 1–4.

tervals of a fifth, points back to *Auf einer Burg*. Even the opening melodic line of #7, "Eingeschlafen auf der Lauer oben," resembles that of #8, "Ich hör' die Bächlein rauschen" (Ex. 8.9).

In *In der Fremde*, Eusebius and Florestan are both well occupied. It is the pianoforte that provides subdued excitation by describing the voices of Nature that speak "von der alten schönen Zeit." The rippling of the brook, the murmuring of the forest, and the flickering of moonlight recall a place and time now far removed. At "und ist doch so weit von hier!" the singer and pianist should make much of the ritardando, because at this point comes recognition that the vision Nature has summoned up is a painful one. The downward leap of the fifth found in the melodic construction of *Auf einer Burg* is reintroduced here (it occurred in the first strophe as well), to become a cry of longing and despair made increasingly touching through textual and musical repetition of "und ist doch lange tot."

Wehmut, #9, uses the region of the keyboard beloved by both Schubert and Schumann for pensive collaboration with the singing voice. The octave doubling of voice and upper keyboard line and even the lyricism of the vocal writing have a Schubertian cast. Eichendorff in this poem, as in several others selected by Schumann for inclusion in op. 39, follows (as we have previously seen) a popular Romantic theme of personal pain mirrored in the events of Nature. Spring breezes and a nightingale's song gladden most hearts, but the poet, who only pretends to be happy, is hiding deep grief through his singing.

The poet's play with the voiced phoneme [l] in "im **L**ied das tiefe **L**eid" should be emphasized by the singer's momentarily lingering on the pitch consonant [l]. Certainly, legato sostenuto is the performance key for both pianist and vocalist. (*Sehr gebunden* is Schumann's marking.) Despite the *sehr langsam* indication, each vocal phrase should correspond to the crescendo-decrescendo scoring of the keyboard and to the harmonic movement that leads each time to melodic phrase peaking. Pacific lyricism expresses hidden grief.

With *Zwielicht*, #10, we enter a world of exalted creativity: a remarkable combining of vocal lyricism and language intoning. (*Zwielicht* earlier made its appearance as an example of the relationship of sung German to harmonic movement.) The vocal line shimmers above a canvas of pianistic colors built on a wandering improvisatory figure that outlines a tortured seventh-chord harmonic progression. Chromatic harmonies, tonal indecision, and cadential hesitation give birth to a mystical world. Twilight spreading its wings, trees shuddering, clouds hovering like heavy dreams—all are evoked without mechanical keyboard imitation. The seven opening bars of questing harmony in the prelude avoid cadencing; only measure 8, at which point the voice enters on the third of the prime chord, provides the first moment of harmonic rest. The single-note vocal beginning ("Dämm'rung will") progresses through the harmonically unsettling interval of an augmented fourth by means of limited melodic movement that turns downward in conjuction with accumulating dominant-seventh chord harmonies. The motif is characteristic of Schumann's use of brief melodic segments that, through repetition, bring about structural unity and emotional intensity, in part because they occur so frequently within the limited time span of a short composition. The rhythm of the vocal melody, through the favorite dotted/undotted sequence, recalls that of *Auf einer Burg*.

This opening four-bar melodic motif of *Zwielicht* is soon relieved by phrases that begin with single-note intonation, as with "Wolken ziehn wie schwere Träume . . . was will dieses Grau'n bedeuten?" in recitative-like questioning. One-note intoning occurs over consecutive seventh-chord harmonies outlined by improvisatory arpeggiation. The singer delivers those words with introspective foreboding by means of the darkest possible vocal timbre; the pianist makes use of the coloristic opportunities of the ritardando on the arpeggio of bar 13. Keyboard motion is halted at bar 14. The ritardando of bar 15 echoes the question raised by the singer; the two performers become one voice.

The next phrase, beginning "Hast ein Reh du," correlates with the opening vocal motif and, as in the previous eight bars, retains the combination of ascending melody and single-note intoning. This melodic questioning comes four times within the two brief pages of *Zwielicht*, but the third and fourth occurrences take decisively different directions. "Jäger zieh'n im Wald und blasen, stimmen hin und wieder wandern" again uses single-note recitative intoning. At the return of the original melody and continuing onward through the penultimate phrase, a relentless vocal legato is called for, while the pianoforte restlessly alters the harmonic base. At bar 26 there is a modulation that heightens the sense of warning ("trau' ihm nicht zu dieser Stunde"). This momentary harmonic departure produces an unsettling effect that allows Schumann to bring to Eichendorff's poetic expression greater intensity than is inherently present. The syncopated chromatic octaves in the keyboard, coupled to the dotted rhythms of the vocal line (reinforced by the top voice of the keyboard), weave a remarkable texture of harmony, rhythm, and melody.

An almost fretful back-and-forth occurrence of seconds and minor thirds with "freundlich wohl mit Aug' und Munde, sinnt er Krieg im tück'schen Frieden"

Example 8.10.   *Zwielicht*, bars 34–41.

leads to an integrating dominant-seventh arpeggiation that prepares the fourth occurrence of the initial vocal motif. All of this over chords that drive (even at *p* dynamic) the ascending octaves as they approach a point of harmonic and rhythmic suspension for the deliverance of the final statement (bars 34–41).

The singer, although not so instructed by the composer, needs to follow carefully the dynamics indicated for the keyboard by crescendoing the phrase to the word "hebt," then tapering off at "neugeboren." The concluding "Manches geht in Nacht verloren—hüte dich, sei wach und munter!" must be sung quietly with clean enunciation, not spoken. (It is not merely an inserted recitative passage, despite its appearance.) Depth of vocal sound and completeness of timbre in this range are needed for augmentation of lower-voice harmonic partials. The phrase is delivered not as a whisper but as a serious admonition; the concluding staccato chords should be sharply struck in exact rhythm, without rubato. As in *Mondnacht*, the genius of Robert Schumann is fully revealed here (Ex. 8.10).

The musician stands in awe of Schumann's uncanny ability to combine his musical devices with poetic content. Those who claim that Schumann has less regard for textual meaning than Wolf has are applying the wrong criteria to Schumann. Here is true realization of literary stimulus without placing the music in bondage to the poetry. Once again, by himself becoming a poet, Schumann goes beyond the poet's intention.

The emotional contrast between Lieder #10 (*Zwielicht*) and #11 (*Im Walde*) could scarcely be greater. The sprightly $\frac{6}{8}$ chordal pattern of *Im Walde* begins in carefree fashion, joined by the voice on a single-pitch melody (as has frequently been the case) that does not depart far from its tonic center. Phrase direction is more dependent on rhythmic alteration—here a ritardando—than on melodic contour. In *Im Walde*, the alternation of ritardando and *im Tempo* must be exaggerated. A momentary leap at bar 13 from persistent A major to sudden G major harmonies, en route to the tonality of D major, changes keyboard colors to correspond with the narrative poetic tesserae. These harmonies, the repetitive rhythmic progressions that propel them in exact tempo, and the imitative horn calls vividly depict the waldhorn and "ein lustiges Jagen!" (Ex. 8.11).

There comes an immediate foreboding intrusion into this wedding party gaiety. Schumann jumps to a new tonality, clearly establishing F♯ major for three bars. The upper keyboard voice at C♯ retains the somber third-octave keyboard hue, while the voice, beginning "und eh' ich's gedacht, war alles verhallt," once more intones—not recites—on the F♯ major prime. This is reminiscent of the opening vocal line, but now with a complete change of mood. The brief lilting keyboard melodic figure that was introduced in bar 6, with repetitions in bars 12, 15, and 20, leads to G♯ minor tonality. "Die Nacht bedecket die Runde," again in *ritardando* fashion, expresses fear. There follows a jump back into the A major tonality by which the wedding party was initially introduced. Still unrelenting is the ⁶⁄₈ rhythmic concept. The vocal line is built on a pattern of incrementally rising intervallic leaps that match the increasing tension of the drama: (bars 33–38) first a fourth, then a fifth, then a sixth, all catapulted from a single-pitch foundation. Once more, this is an example of Schumann's declamatory style, purposely neither distinctly recitative-like nor strikingly lyrical. (Rossini and Bellini seem distantly transalpine at this moment.)

The harmonic inventiveness of these two brief pages is exceptional. Schumann takes a technique that Schubert (in *Pause*, for example) introduced into the Lied: the sudden jump to the dramatic color of a new key without traditional modulation, bringing stark changes in mood. Singer and pianist should match those diverse tonality colors through dynamic levels, altered degrees of legato, and heightened response to the emotive character of such words as "blitzen," "lustiges," "verhallt," "bedecket," "rauschet," and "schauert's." Use of strong anticipatory German consonants is here essential for the singer.

Schumann makes the poet repeat "und mich schauert's im Herzensgrunde."

Example 8.11.   *Im Walde*, bars 15–19.

Example 8.12.   *Frühlingsnacht*, bars 1–5.

Example 8.13.   *Frühlingsnacht*, bars 24–31.

The bass line descends ominously, rhythmic motion modified, only hinting at the dotted $\frac{6}{8}$ rhythm. The long note (dotted half) on the first syllable of "**schau-ert's**" (bar 44) is a prolonged shudder, full of pain and disquiet. There is no descriptive pianistic fluttering as might have tempted a lesser composer. A sense of heartfelt anxiety due to the threatening portents of Nature has been caught, expressed by the singer with vocal color filled with pathos. This is best achieved by a *messa di voce* on the sustained D. The singer should take the low A, unless it is technically impossible, on the final syllables, with as much depth of timbre as can be mustered. These pitches ought to be treated not as throwaways or as afterthoughts, but as warnings full of anxiety and mistrust.

From this emerges, in *Frühlingsnacht*, #12, one of the most rapturous flights ever conceived for vocal and keyboard collaboration. The charge is sometimes made that in this affirmation of triumphant love the pianoforte dominates. This is by no means the case. Schumann constructs a vocal line that develops organically out of the improvisatory pianoforte triplet figure (Ex. 8.12). With its mountings and tumblings (some on seventh chords) the voice line is of equal importance to the keyboard. Together voice and pianoforte weave a vivid tapestry through musical translation of Eichendorff's colorful Nature images, piling them up in quick succession. Exuberant, triumphant, ecstatic love builds to the final affirmation "Sie ist deine, sie ist dein!" (bars 24–31). Dark aspects of Nature's events and previous questionings of the lover are transcended through the promise of a Spring night and the assurance of finally winning the beloved (Ex. 8.13). (Clara is certainly the object.)

What a treasure for singer and pianist is this cycle! Only Robert Schumann could have written the Eichendorff *Liederkreis*, a work that stands as a monument to genius and at the pinnacle of Lied composition.

9

Fünf Lieder (Andersen and Chamisso), Opus 40

The five Lieder of op. 40 include four on Adelbert von Chamisso's translations of Hans Christian Andersen poems and an anonymous poem in modern Greek, also translated by Chamisso.

Märzveilchen, #1, is an amiable song that exudes charm. It is sweet Schumann, verging on the coy and the sentimental, and fits well into a group dealing with such topics as flowers and butterflies. A miniature, *Märzveilchen* illustrates Schumann's Romantic search for musical language to capture the small things of Nature. This is a genre in which Robert Schumann excels and by which he is frequently best remembered, albeit not always to his advantage, because it fails to represent the complete Schumann.

The sixteenth-note staccato pattern in the right hand gives a touch of instability and a lack of certainty that engagingly catch the young man looking at the flowery pattern on the frozen windowpane, behind which he spies two laughing blue eyes. Pianists should treat the offbeat rhythmic figure with clarity and brevity, enunciating it precisely over the more sustained motif in the left hand. The singer ought to imitate the pianist's bass-clef legato. In a brief keyboard interjection following the initial appearance of "und Gott sei gnädig dem jungen Mann" Schumann devises a two-bar corresponding keyboard blessing. Following the textual repetition, this brief benediction develops at the *etwas schneller* into a loving, reassuring, yet gently humorous commentary on the young man's dilemma.

One cannot play the opening bars of *Muttertraum*, #2, with their slow arpeggiated keyboard figure that outlines an evolving melody, without remembering *Zwielicht*. Both *Muttertraum* and *Zwielicht* deal with darkness and introspection. That is the extent of the resemblance. Unlike the improvisatory figure of *Zwielicht*, here is a Bach-like two-part partita cast in Romantic garb. Whereas *Zwielicht* engulfs us with its Romanticism, *Muttertraum* speaks through its quasi-Baroque insistence on continuous motion. The left hand's descending syncopated sostenuto enlists a rhythmic ostinato over which groups of sixteenth notes in the right hand slowly wind by means of seventh-chord progressions. The pianist must create a sinister atmosphere by an inexorable right-hand rhythmic precision and by an insistent bass melody, foreshadowing the eventual adult tragedy that will beset the child. At this low dynamic level, the singer should use as dark a timbre as is native to his or her instrument and avoid both word and rhythmic accents. There is indeed a folk element to the melody, but the Lied must be sung subtly, not simplistically. *Muttertraum* demonstrates a facet of Schumann's wide-ranging musical genius that is light-years removed from its neighbor, *Märzveilchen*.

The reiterated chords that interrupt the arpeggiated figure at the key change (bar 28) seem jarring. This is exactly the composer's purpose. Somber qualities inherent in this octave of the keyboard must be brought out; the descending octave leaps should be strongly marked. Without resorting to the melodramatic, the singer needs to assume a tone of horror. The one-pitch intoning at the text repetition of "der Räuber dient uns zur Speise" casts an emotional chill, especially as it occurs over Schumann's skillful return to the original Baroque figuration. The dream goes on, but we now know what the mother does not: tragic reality will end that dream. *Muttertraum* is an interpretively challenging song for both singer and pianist.

With *Der Soldat*, #3, Schumann jerks us suddenly into yet another experience of horror. In these Andersen poems we are at the mercy of fate. In *Der Soldat*, both singer and pianist are balladeers, describing tragedy. The march must not be too fast; the sextolets should be allowed to give the drumroll—a call to execution—its true character. There is a stateliness about the march that might at first seem to belie the terror in the heart of the soldier who must participate in the execution of his comrade. But the unrelenting march speaks of inexorable duty over private emotion, of helplessness without recourse. The pianist must literally hammer out the repeated accented notes. Unmitigated *sf* thundering in the interlude should sound like a descent into despair, an entrance into a personal hell.

At the G minor section, the triplets of the right hand are to be exact in their relationships to the dotted-eighth/quarter-note pattern of the left hand. The singer must call on a narrative tone, reserving the ultimate horror for the recitativo passage, beginning with "ich aber, ich traf, ich traf ihn mitten in das Herz!" by using a nonvibrant timbre at almost stage-whisper level. The four bars of the concluding postlude state that nothing more can be said. They display hymnlike solemnity; the fermata (with sostenuto pedal employed) should stretch the out-of-key harmonic resolution endlessly, allowing it to die away from its own energy loss. By this means the differences between the musical ideas of *Der Soldat* and *Der Spielmann*, which follows, will be properly delineated.

Commentators have noted relationships among *Der Spielmann, Das ist ein Flöten und Geigen, Der Arme Peter,* and *Auf einer Burg* and *Im Walde* from the Eichendorff *Liederkreis*. These similarities are, however, not significant. *Der Spielmann*, #4, offers the large-voiced singer a fine opportunity. (Tessitura is something of a problem in several of the Andersen songs, because much of the drama occurs in low range. *Der Spielmann* seems to fit mezzos and *robusto* tenors best.) Florestan here has gone mad; that madness must be portrayed by both performers. The pianist needs to waltz wildly with his "fiddle" as it sweeps through anguished diminished fifths; the singer must do what the performer often has to do — portray personal suffering while singing skillfully. In this case, the performers must simulate the grief that drives the protagonist to madness. *Der Spielmann*, a first-rate ballad, is a remarkable piece of theatrical writing.

Fortissimo musical and narrative climaxes occur at "Wer heisst euch mit Fingern zeigen auf mich?" together with high octaves and thick *sf* chords in the keyboard. At the same time, the singer is held to lower-middle range. This proves problematic for many performers; it is the pianist's task to ensure through altered dynamic levels that the singer can have an effective moment in a less-than-favorable range. At *langsamer*, intensity drops to *pp*, and the singing voice must bring pathos and despair to the slow waltz. Madness is now resolved into hopelessness. Once again, it is given to the pianist to conclude the events with a true *valse triste*.

The Andersen songs ideally belong together in performance.

Schumann may have intended that #5, *Verratene Liebe*, should follow the Andersen Lieder, but it seems an unfavorable move. There has been too much drama and pain to conclude the performance with this slight vignette. A listener can endure being whirled from sweet violets to death, but returning to this little valentine seems too much to ask. *Verratene Liebe* is a good song, of equal merit with *Märzveilchen*, with which it shares a genre designation, although the two Lieder are not musically related. *Verratene Liebe* must be sung as an engaging miniature. One would like to think that a skillful artist can portray any mood and sing music of any emotional requirement, but it may be unrealistic to expect a dramatic singer to do equal justice to the delicate sketches that frame the vigorous ballads in this opus. An alternative argument could be made that Schumann does not want to leave us in a world of despair. Fischer-Dieskau (pp. 96–97) discusses that viewpoint: "*Verratene Liebe* (The Tell-Tales, Opus 49, No. 5) is a surprisingly amiable conclusion, following such an emotionally stormy series of songs. With its playful, jolly finish, including the coquettish flourish in the piano, it was no doubt intended to restore emotional balance." Perhaps it does that, but it might be more at home in a group of Schumann miniatures.

10

Frauenliebe und -leben (Chamisso), Opus 42

Female singers probably give more performances of *Frauenliebe und -leben* than of all other Schumann Lieder. There is an enduring appeal about the progression from bride to mother to widow, because it speaks directly to the joys and sorrows of several aspects of womanhood. Schumann omitted (for which we are grateful) the final Chamisso poem, wherein the now-grandmotherly protagonist confides the joys and sorrows of her life to her betrothed granddaughter. The suggestion that the lengthy postlude was Schumann's way of substituting music for the ninth poem is far-fetched; the postlude is there for musical and narrative summation.

Whatever the intrinsic literary value of the poetry, good marks are in order for the originality of a dramatic scheme that presents through brief vignettes the personal life of a woman in love. As was previously mentioned, today's performer may find it difficult to accept a male view of deeply feminine experiences that are most properly understood by a woman. But once past that hurdle, a singer will find the cycle of great musical and communicative merit. It cannot be gainsaid that *Frauenliebe und -leben* verges on the sentimental, a charge leveled at both the poet and the composer. Stein (p. 120) recognizes the dilemma, suggesting that Schumann "responded fully to the unembarrassed emotionalism, the sentimentality bordering on bathos, the Biedermeier glorification of the homely [homey] and the domestic." Nonetheless, Stein (p. 119) calls *Frauenliebe*

Example 10.1.   *Seit ich ihn gesehen*, bars 1–7.

und -leben Schumann's greatest achievement in song, a viewpoint embraced by many critics and performers. In general, those who look with disfavor on a composer's tampering with the poetry are more comfortable with the setting of this cycle than with several other cycles, in part because they stand less in awe of Chamisso than of Heine or Goethe and in part because in *Frauenliebe und -leben* Schumann makes extensive use of his much-acclaimed lyric declamation (for example, in #1, #3, #6, and #8). Melodic digressions that upset meter and accent (and professors of German literature!) are less frequent in this cycle than in many other Schumann settings. Yet text repetitions, generally thought to disrupt poetic structure, abound.

Seit ich ihn gesehen opens the cycle in an atmosphere of adoration, created by detached chords in the lower-middle keyboard register (bars 1–7); Schumann builds on the Schubertian example (Ex. 10.1). As in many early Schumann Lieder, the melody and the rhythm of the vocal line are structured on word inflection within a limited vocal range. In this melodically less adventuresome expression of love, Eusebius and Florestan share responsibilities. Because of the narrow pitch excursions of the opening motif, the leap of a major seventh on the word "tiefstem" is heartrending. Here Schumann again successfully uses rich Schubertian male-chorus keyboard harmonies that call for the use of somber vocal color.

It is difficult to erase from consciousness the many performances of this song a listener has encountered. However, if a fresh ear can be brought, blotting out memories of the near-parodistic mooings and moanings often associated with live and recorded performances, the genius of *Seit ich ihn gesehen* is evident. Vocal and pianistic technical demands are kept within modest boundaries, as befits the tenderness of the poetry. Schumann's uncanny understanding of the use of vocal and instrumental timbres for introspective mood evocation is surpassed only by Schubert himself.

In *Seit ich ihn gesehen*, as on many occasions during the cycle (#3, #4, #5, and #7), phrase movement is accomplished through chromatic harmonies that enrich the simplistic texture. The piano commentary between the strophes already evinces vintage Schumann. The false beginning over again in the postlude, through insertion of the opening chordal measures, conjures up the text that has previously overlain them. Such poetic and musical recall brings remarkable cohesion to this brief Lied. In the miniature portrayal of a young woman's love and devotion, Schumann creates a monumental emotional experience. Performers who attempt to put a personal stamp on *Seit ich ihn gesehen* by tearing it into sentimental bits and pieces destroy its inherent dignity. Sausaging of the vocal line, with diminuendos on each note (lamentably, often heard), violates the inherent musical structure. Honest vocal timbre and a good legato provide the most expressive performance mode for this Lied.

In #2, *Er, der Herrlichste von allen*, as was mentioned earlier, Florestan and Eusebius play at alternating emotional peaks and valleys. Strong semistaccato block-chordal octaves establish a stabilizing anchor from which the vocal line swings forward. Schumann's *innig* marking should be carefully noted. (An aside may be in order, to reiterate that it is the same *innig* indication found at the beginning of *Widmung*. Performance exuberance is warranted in both Lieder.)

The two brief opening melodic phrases that comprise the first four bars require rapid changes in mood and vocal quality. "Er, der Herrlichste" rockets upward with its energetic dotted rhythm and its strong statement regarding the most wonderful of men, while "wie so milde, wie so gut!" expresses the lover's tenderness and kindness. There follows a quick return to extroversion with "Holde Lippen, klares Auge, heller Sinn und fester Mut"; the latter portion of this line of poetry is filled with energy and fervor. Schumann retains for "**fes**ter Mut," "**jener**," "**hehr**," "**nur**," and "**Herr**lichkeit" the emotive turn he so effectively first uses on "**wie** so gut!" Singer and pianist should relieve the relentlessness of the reiterated blocks of chords by at those moments accommodating the expressive turns with slight rubato, immediately thereafter returning to the basic tempo.

A pianistic upward winging, imitating the initial vocal theme, bursts out again as a splash of uncontained joy at bar 17 (Ex. 10.2).

Its later appearance following "brich, O Herz, was liegt daran?" before the text repetition "Er, der Herrlichste von allen" (bars 52–59) offers an example of Schumann's skill in taking a striking motif through progressions of shifting harmonies. Singer and pianist must strongly mark the rhythmic elements without losing the melodic sweep inherent in this figure (Ex. 10.3).

Florestan/Eusebius touches are characteristically alternated in the pianoforte interlude and in the vocal line beginning at bar 21, "Wandle, wandle deine Bahnen." In bar 24, keyboard recall of "nur betrachten deinen Schein" is an example of Schumann's propensity for using small mosaic-like melodic

Example 10.2.   *Er, der Herrlichste von allen*, bars 16–25.

tesserae as integrating, emotionally evocative devices. The slight rhythmic relaxation that has just occurred in the voice part on the embellishment at "deinen"
should be echoed by the pianoforte in a momentary hesitation of the driving
chords.

One of the most effective moments in the entire cycle ensues at "nur in
Demut": the crescendo to a sudden *p* dynamic and the suspension of harmonic
certitude indicate the need for pointing up the word "Demut." The singer
should deliver these syllables with a slight emphasis on the initial consonant [d];
the subsequent vowels ought to be sung in a voice distinguished by the warmest,
most tender timbre possible.

It is exactly at this moment in the text that the contemporary woman has
most problem dealing with Chamisso's poetry, since lowliness and humility, sub-
missiveness and meekness, are clear implications. There is little doubt that
Chamisso (whose family origin was French) was giving expression to the pre-
dominant Germanic male attitude of the time toward women. In German literature, the ideal woman was associated with motherhood, domesticity, and providing comfort to her male companion. Even viewpoints about a woman's role

in the field of musical composition were part of societal perspective regarding the place of women. One has only to recall how Felix Mendelssohn felt it unseemly for sister Fanny to write and publish her songs, some of which were published as his own in order to avoid embarrassment over such wrongly directed female activity. The worthy Lieder of Clara Schumann herself were received with little enthusiasm. (Some current critics, as has been seen, attempt to associate Clara's hand with what they consider to be the less-than-successful Lieder attributed to Robert.)

It is also documented that Robert Schumann later experienced emotional stress over Clara's triumphs as a performer at a time when his own efforts as conductor were not successful. It is not possible to read the text and listen to the music of *Frauenliebe und -leben* today without looking in hindsight at subsequent events in the lives of Clara and Robert. How telling that it is she, Clara, who will furnish stability and sustain her emotionally exhausted partner, at least until his final years of withdrawal. Knowing this makes the closing Lied, *Nun hast du mir den ersten Schmerz getan*, even more meaningful for performers and listeners.

If the modern performer decides to sing the cycle—and she should—she must embrace the role played by her nineteenth-century predecessors, most of whom, at least outwardly, accepted the humble female part assigned to them. There is no more reason not to sing this cycle than for a soprano not to sing Cio-Cio-San because of the subservient female/male relationship in the *Madama Butterfly* libretto. The cycle is not a social statement but an artistic expression that portrays a young, vital, innocent woman. The decision to perform *Frauen-*

Example 10.3.   *Er, der Herrlichste von allen*, bars 52–59.

liebe und -leben must include willingness to understand the social milieu out of which this poetry and music come, and to momentarily enter into it.

Er, der Herrlichste von allen is representative of this ambience. Beginning at the middle section ("Nur die Würdigste von allen"), the leaps of sevenths bring new assertions of devotion, leading to emotional peaking at the word "Wahl." The young woman continues her effusive adoration of the male, which she vows will never end even if her heart should be broken. Schumann does not leave her there but returns to the poet's original lines, reminding us of the initial expression of love.

The musical construction of *Er, der Herrlichste von allen* presents Schumann as a highly skilled craftsman, at his best when he uses his favorite formulas: reiterated block chords, strong octave doubling, soaring vocal and pianistic dotted arpeggiated themes, and sensitive use of embellishment.

Emotional mountaintops and valleys are combined into one whole by brief musical figures. Florestan's rocketing breaks out in two pianoforte registers (bars 54–56), to be played with exuberance. The keyboard conclusion is built on earlier motivic fragments and reflects on the devotional attitudes the singer has expressed. What a burst of love and joy is this Lied!

In *Ich kann's nicht fassen, nicht glauben*, #3, Schumann is in declamatory mode, with a single-note melodic inauguration interrupted only now and again by the underscoring of important words through intervallic leaping. (But the unimportant word "unter" is also highlighted.) Chamisso's male attitudes come to the fore with "mich Arme erhöht und beglückt," which attests to the young woman's astonishment that a male has "honored and made happy poor me." (Perhaps it is of interest that at the somewhat mature age of thirty-eight, Chamisso married an eighteen-year-old woman.) It has to be confessed that it is not just the female performer who must be willing to view this kind of expression within its sociological context; today's male members of her audience also may otherwise feel squeamish.

The opening fifteen bars are not to be spoken but delivered with passion, vehemence, violent emotion—*mit Leidenschaft!* This Lied is often incorrectly interpreted. For example, the text "Ich kann's nicht fassen" should not become an internalized whisper; the composer's marking is *f*, with an additional crescendo indicated in the keyboard. Vehement emotion is what he has asked for, and that is what he should be given. To turn this Lied into a kind of introspective, intimately whispered recitative (which is what comes out of some recording studios) is to distort the composer's intent. Joy, wonderment, and excitement are the sources of this Lied.

"Mir war's, er habe gesprochen" is slower and more sustained (bars 16–24) than are the previous lyrically declaimed bars. This requires full legato to contrast with the forceful language-inflection movement of the first fifteen bars (Ex. 10.4).

The closely knit melodic line, with its opening low-lying contour, leads to the word "ewig" by way of a ritardando. By repetition of "es kann ja nimmer so sein" Schumann stretches out poetic meter for musical and emotive reasons. As with most text repetitions, the singer must give the second appear-

Example 10.4. *Ich kann's nicht fassen, nicht glauben*, bars 16–24.

ance increased emphasis, in this case through the crescendo and the ritardando marked by the composer, but also through directing special attention to the sonority of the nasal phonemes [n] and [m], particularly in the consonantal doubling of the latter ("ni*mm*er"). There is always a danger that intensity will fade on sustained German double consonants, especially in mounting phrases, thereby breaking the line. Given the underlying harmonic movement and the structural importance of the phrase as it concludes the strophe, that fault would be musically disastrous.

Heightened emotion is asked of the pianist in the eight-bar interlude before Schumann's text repetition that concludes the song. This material is built on increasingly larger intervallic leaps imitative of those already sung during the body of the Lied, now including the fourth, the sixth, and finally (after being joined by the singer) the octave (or even the twelfth, if one counts the proper accent on the embellishment that builds to the *sf* climax).

Emotional outpouring is recapitulated by the closing deceptive dream episode on which the last four keyboard bars offer comment: "Es hat ein Traum mich berückt." In defiance of poetic structure, Schumann repeats the text. Here Schumann again is not content only to compose; he takes for himself the role of poet, bringing more to the poem than Chamisso intended. (Or, as some have thought, detracting from Chamisso's poetry by distorting it. Musicians are convinced that the gains far outweigh the losses.) The final ascending and descending pianoforte arpeggio on the tenth should be unhurried and must conclude in repose.

It is difficult to look at #4, *Du Ring an meinem Finger*, without hearing wedding marches and remembering past saccharine vocal interpretations. One needs to recall that *innig* means "fervent, ardent, hearty," not "teary, internalized, sentimental." *Du Ring an meinem Finger* is not a funereal hymn. It puts forth a straightforward melody that expresses joy at the thought of betrothal. It is generally performed more slowly than Handel's famed *Xerxes* Largo (which should be "broad" but is often deadly), and Schumann, like Handel, thereby comes off the loser. *Du Ring an meinem Finger* must move joyfully (Ex. 10.5).

Structurally, this famous song consists of a traditional vocal melody frequently doubled by the pianoforte upper voice. In joining the melody, the pi-

Example 10.5. *Du Ring an meinem Finger*, bars 1–4.

anoforte should sing along with the singer but must also bring out the alto keyboard voice in duet fashion. Schumann does not remain long removed from his
reiterated block-chordal system: it forms the harmonic and rhythmic foundation
for the climactic poetic statement "ich will ihm dienen, ihm leben, ihm ange-
hören ganz" and for the subsequent surrendering, a conception that must have
set Chamisso's masculinity atingle. This song has to be convincingly sung and
played in the manner in which Chamisso and Schumann conceived the words
and the music—with enthusiasm and in joyful anticipation, not as though sub-
mitting to spousal abuse. Not of deep psychological probing, as are some
Schumann songs, *Du Ring an meinem Finger* is an honest and direct expression.
For the performer to put on it a veneer of superficial sentiment alters both poetry and music.

The "tune" returns for its third excursion and is so gracious that even the
final repetition is still a pleasure to hear.

If one wishes to judge success in the setting of poetry by the degree to
which a composer adheres to meter and accent, Schumann's marks must be
lowered for giving false inflection to unaccented syllables, as for example with
the intervallic leaps on "Du Ring **an** meinem Finger," "schön**en** Traum," "un-
end**lichen**" (the second time), "hast mein**em** Blick," "und find**en** verklärt
mich," and "an die Lipp**en**" (the last time). In performance, the singer must
help the composer by taking care to minimize false syllabic accents that otherwise (because of the melodic contour) might prominently jump out from the
text. Also to be questioned from the point of awkward melodic accent are "ich
drücke **dich** fromm," "Ich **hatt'** ihn," and "**hin** selber."

In *Du Ring an meinem Finger*, Schumann's interest lay in realizing the poetry through the flow of melody. Much critical attention has been given to
Schumann's commitment to lyric declamation, with the result that his capabilities as a first-class melodist (when he so chooses) are often overlooked. *Du Ring
an meinem Finger* is an example in which synthesis of word and music is not the
aim; music—especially melody to be sung by both instruments—is here undis-
puted master.

The use of arpeggiation for whipping up excitement in *Helft mir, ihr*

Schwestern, #5, bears a strong resemblance to the events of *Widmung* (Ex. 10.6). Cumulative phrases rush headlong without pause; there are but three fast quarter-note rests in the first twenty-two vocal bars. Vocal line and text are uninterrupted by pianoforte interludes. This gives a sense of breathlessness, an urgency well suited to the text; such urgency can be conveyed by the singer through vocal energy and clear diction. *Helft mir, ihr Schwestern* is not an exercise in parlando singing.

In the B section, Schumann moves from arpeggiation to repeated block chords, a compositional technique that, as has been seen, he uses with great frequency. His system of constructing a melody by beginning on a single note, then introducing increasingly expanded intervallic leaps (fifths and sixths) is illustrated with the questioning "Bist, mein Geliebter, du mir erschienen, gibst du mir, Sonne, deinen Schein?" and in related phrases. This is an effective way to build anticipation; it catches the sentiment of the young woman's farewell to girlhood as she puts on her wedding attire. Chamisso cannot resist reminding us how grateful a female should be for having found a man who loves her, and expresses it with his "Let me, in devotion and humility, bow to my lord."

Schumann's awareness of the need for contrast among neighboring songs is proven by the location of *Helft mir, ihr Schwestern* within the cycle. The flowing vocal line and supportive pianism of *Du Ring an meinem Finger* are now replaced by angular vocal bursts and rapid fingers. Schumann begins the last strophe as he commenced the first, but after four vocal bars he selects another direction as the bride-to-be takes leave of her female companions. He introduces four bars of melody based on a mutation of previous material and skillfully transforms his chordal-arpeggiated harmonic (and dotted-rhythmic) figure into a wedding march whose squarish melody and harmony remind tune sleuths of the *Lohengrin* wedding march.

Such diatonic directness is not to be found in the A section of #6, *Süsser Freund, du blickest mich verwundert an*. Whereas *Du Ring an meinem Finger* and *Helft mir, ihr Schwestern* are open expressions of emotion, *Süsser Freund, du blickest mich verwundert an* shows Schumann probing the psychological depths of poetic language. Initial key ambiguity (another Schumann trade-

Example 10.6.   *Helft mir, ihr Schwestern*, bars 1–4.

Example 10.7.   *Süsser Freund, du blickest mich verwundert an*, bars 1–4.

mark for the development of penetrating psychological searching) sets the stage for emotional complexity (Ex. 10.7). The vocal writing can be classified neither as recitative nor as arioso, yet it is both. The composer's lyric declamation is compelling here. It is based on word inflection and noble speech pacing. There should be no hurrying of the melody as it enters several times directly over suspended harmonies that underlie the words "süsser," "kannst," "wie," and "wüsst'." Bars 7 through 11 move forward again, imitative of language inflection and pacing. Then, at "Wie so bang" the singer should again discreetly linger over the suspended harmony before returning to the original melodic movement.

The twenty-four bars of section A display a firm grasp of the emotive possibilities of vocal and pianistic timbres. For example, "will ins Ohr dir flüstern" demands a color imitative of whispered secret joy. As is often the case with Schubert when in retrospective mood, Schumann makes use of organlike (almost male-chorus) harmonies in keyboard octaves 2 and 3. With its inserted reverie on harmonic suspension (bars 21–24) in the upper-middle keyboard octave, the pianoforte recalls the emotion expressed in the poetry.

Now Eusebius rests. With the diatonic, reiterated chordal C major tonality, a modified Florestan moves into the impassioned text of "Weisst du nun die Tränen, die ich weinen kann, sollst du nicht sie sehen, du geliebter Mann?" Individual word painting on the part of the singer, to which the pianist must respond carefully, is essential. Schumann reverts to his never-long-forgotten chordal device. The bass line of the pianoforte must join in duo with the singer, bringing out the cantilena to offset the chromatic writing of the first section. Despite the squareness of the melody, a cantabile element for both voice and piano calls for smooth vocalism and pianism. The return to the harmonic and melodic colors of the opening phrase ideally suits the mood of the text.

The piano postlude begins with recall of the opening bar, subsequently musically transformed to arrive at the penultimate adagio bar. This sets up a perfect cadential situation for the pensive repetition of the words "dein Bildnis!" Schumann the poet is here at work. Reflective text repetition, a stroke of genial creativity, is the same stratagem he uses in equally effective manner with the repeated words "lass mich!" at the close of the Rückert *Lied der Braut II*.

Florestan begins *An meinem Herzen, an meiner Brust*, #7, on exuberant seventh chords. These should be struck cleanly, not rolled (Ex. 10.8). They introduce a vocal theme built on the interval of a fourth, which Schumann often uses to present happy sentiment. The jaunty arpeggiated keyboard figurations should be clearly and energetically executed; the harmonic movement of the bass notes ought to be forceful, not smudged by excessive pedaling. The singer must be *fröhlich, innig* (frolicsome, fervent) as she sings of the bliss of holding and nursing her infant.

For Chamisso the male, motherhood is idealized in a setting of unmitigated joy far removed from the real world of abrupt regurgitation and other exasperating infant behavior. He allows the protagonist to find a deficiency in his projected male hero: "Oh, how sorry I am for a man who cannot feel a mother's bliss!" An almost stretto five-bar recitative-like passage, reminiscent of *Ich kann's nicht fassen, nicht glauben*, appears at the *noch schneller* marking. Tapering off the final poetic verse, Schumann's rhapsodizing in the postlude has an engaging *Phantasie* chromatic improvisatory nature, which is characteristic of his pianoforte compositions.

The concluding song of this cycle, *Nun hast du mir den ersten Schmerz getan*, #8, brings a moment to the Lied literature where critiquing becomes superfluous. To make any attempt at analysis is to tread on ground best left untrod. Never has Schumann more effectively put to use his lyric-declamatory style. The opening and subsequent phrases, with their repeated single-note centering and close-intervalled structure, are declaimed over a static keyboard. Schumann, by minimal musical means, deftly catches the woman's effort to control her grief. The subsequent outcry of "die Welt ist leer" is surely one of the most poignant moments in all of music. While avoiding melodramatic excess the singer and the pianist must manifest dignified anguish (Ex. 10.9).

The postlude could well have become merely contrived, a potpourri of thematic material found in the cycle's opening Lied. Instead, it transcends the previous musical and poetic expressions through combined recall of both; twenty-one bars of musical notation produce a synthesis of word and music *in the*

Example 10.8.   *An meinem Herzen, an meiner Brust*, bars 1–3.

Example 10.9.   *Nun hast du mir den ersten Schmerz getan*, bars 1–10.

absence of words. The singer and pianist are still singing, although it is the pianist who now does so for both performers. Deep sostenuto keyboard "touch" will offer warmth of timbre, to be delivered in measured, thoughtful fashion, without rhythmic torturing.

No vocal literature, with the exception of *Dichterliebe*, has experienced more distortion from self-indulgent performance than has *Frauenliebe und -leben*. Being mawkish and maudlin has no relationship to emotional truth. Misuse of the re-creative act is not art but egocentricity. Just as much as does *Dichterliebe*, this cycle requires a singer, not a *diseuse*. Its construction demands legato phrases, not musical *Würstli*.

Most critical comment places *Frauenliebe und -leben* and *Dichterliebe* at the pinnacle of Schumann's creativity. For others, *Liederkreis*, op. 39, occupies a prime position, partly because it avoids intemperate emotion. Discriminatory judgment as to the relative value of these three awe-inspiring works is trifling and purposeless. Each has its own unique beauty. Each is masterful.

It is now time to consider the third member of this Lieder triumvirate, *Dichterliebe*.

11

Dichterliebe (Heine), Opus 48

Most performers rely on either the dependable decades-old Peters Max Fried-länder *Dichterliebe* edition or the newer International Music Company's Sergius Kagen edition that includes nonrhyming translations useful for inclusion in program notes. An excellent supplementary source for both study and performance is *Schumann: "Dichterliebe,"* edited by Arthur Komar. Komar supplies an authoritative score that includes settings of poems that Schumann later eliminated from the cycle, with historical information, musical analysis, and a sampling of critical commentary. Rufus Hallmark's *The Genesis of Schumann's "Dichterliebe"* considers the sources and the evolution of the cycle and offers detailed analyses that provide insight to performers.

Heine's *Buch der Lieder* (Book of Songs), published in 1827, comprises five parts, one of which, *Lyrisches Intermezzo*, first appeared in1823. (For the complete *Lyrisches Intermezzo*, see *Heine*, 1975, pp. 131–203). Jeffrey Sammons, in his *Heinrich Heine*, suggests that many evaluations of Heine as poet are based on misapprehension, owing to the fact that the poet's verse was frequently set to music by composers who altered his intent (p. 65):

> Beginning around 1840, Heine's poems became prime texts for the German art song. It is said that no other poet excepting the Psalmist has been set to music

as often as Heine; settings of poems from the Book of Songs alone number close to three thousand. Unquestionably this is a significant feature of Heine's standing in the world and not out of keeping with his own intentions; he himself generally denominated his poems Lieder and he showed an interest in having them set to music. But it is possible that the art song has obscured part of the view into his poetry. On the whole, the musical Lied re-lyricises and re-Romanticises his verse, for by its nature it elides the spoken and conversational component of Heine's tone. It tends to reimpose sincerity of feeling upon poems in which the truth and reliability of feeling are the very problem; thus it softens the hard edge, smooths out the cross-grained skeptical tension that troubled much of Heine's original public, which often wanted to abstract from him a poetry of sincere, soulful experience while deploring those inextricable gestures by which the poetry calls itself into question.

Sammons's remarks are particularly perceptive with regard to Robert Schumann's treatment of Heine's texts in *Dichterliebe*.

Schumann was not the first major composer to turn to *Buch der Lieder*. In August of 1827, a year before his death, Schubert set six Heine poems (from *Die Heimkehr*) that, together with seven Rellstab settings and the Seidel *Taubenpost*, were issued six months after Schubert's death as *Schwanengesang* (the title supplied by the publisher, Hasling). The lover of Lieder finds historical rightness in circumstances that led Franz Schubert at the close of his life to a poetic source that thirteen years later would so inspire Robert Schumann. Subsequently, the 1827 version of *Buch der Lieder* became a wellspring for a number of composers, including Mendelssohn, Franz, Brahms, and Strauss. With the exception of Schubert, no settings of Heine by any composer were more successful than those from the hand of the creator of *Dichterliebe*.

In a description of the silent mad knight, in the *Prolog* to *Lyrisches Intermezzo*, Heine (Grappin, p. 131) moves his plot forward with

> Doch hat er kein Wörtlein gesprochen,
> Kam aber die Mitternachtstunde heran,
> Ein seltsames Singen und Klingen begann—

Professor S. S. Prawer, in his chapter "The Poet of the Buch der Lieder" in *The Penguin Book of Lieder* (p. 1), points to Heine's melodious use of language, and the poet's "Singen und Klingen" approach to word selection. Whatever Heine's intention in choosing *Book of Songs* as a title (did he do so in anticipation that all of its poems would be put to music?), composers took him literally. Schumann's 1840 settings are from a revised edition of *Lyrisches Intermezzo* that for the first time included the opening poem of *Dichterliebe*, *Im wunderschönen Monat Mai*. Several months in advance of *Dichterliebe*, the composer had set *Die Lotosblume*, also from the *Lyrisches Intermezzo*. Is it probable that Schumann's return to the *Lyrisches Intermezzo* collection was sparked by his earlier satisfaction with *Die Lotosblume*?

Heine's poetry has often been characterized as heavy with nostalgia and bitterness, which are commonly thought to be the result of disappointment at re-
jection by his cousin Amalie. Sammons (p. 43) dismisses this assumption:

> The story of the great unrequited love of Heine for his cousin[s] is almost en-
> tirely a creation of literary historians, working on the same principle by which
> touching stories were constructed for barely visible courtly love poets of the
> Middle Ages. His lack of cooperation in the effort made it the more piquant. If
> ever a poet was more silent about the primordial love experience of his life than
> Heine, it would be hard to think who he was.

Heine himself maintained that the poetry of *Dichterliebe* had no autobiographical implications.

There remains a question as to whether Schumann failed to fully recognize
the degree of Heine's pervasive cynicism or simply chose to subdue it. Perhaps
Schumann's anxiety regarding the outcome of court procedures (which finally
terminated in permitting his marriage to Clara) and his uncertainty that Clara
would really become his wife drew him to the mixture of love and pain so evident in the Heine poems. Yet Schumann's hope for ultimate marital triumph
may be an additional reason for his downgrading Heine's bitterness. Another
possible factor may have been Schumann's concern with how his betrothed
might respond to settings of poetry overlaid with bitterness and nostalgia. Clearly,
Clara Wieck is the object of Schumann's expressions of love in his *Dichterliebe*
settings.

In a creative burst that paralleled Schubert's own flood of song and recalls
the still-to-come eruptive creativity of Hugo Wolf, Schumann began composing
Dichterliebe (including four settings later dropped from the cycle) on May 24,
1840, and finished a week later. It should be recalled that this energy was in
keeping with the achievement of composing nearly 150 songs in a single year of
lyrical explosion.

Komar (p. 4) details the *Dichterliebe* alterations, including title selection
and the change of dedication from Felix Mendelssohn to Wilhelmine Schröder-
Devrient. For two reasons the dedication revision is of interest to performers.

First, Schumann greatly admired the singing of Schröder-Devrient, an internationally famous opera singer of dramatic vocal character who numbered
among her roles Donna Anna, Euryanthe, Norma, Desdemona (Rossini), Agatha,
and the *Fidelio* Leonora. (Schumann [p. 294] writes that he is "still elated by
Schröder-Devrient's lofty performance of Fidelio.") The soprano later added Wagner's Senta and Venus to her repertoire. Thus sopranos and mezzo-sopranos
should not be excluded from singing a cycle that was dedicated to a professional
female vocalist.

Second, the dedication to Schröder-Devrient suggests that *Dichterliebe* is
not the property of the vocal miniaturist, whether male or female. John Warrack
(p. 744) quotes a telling 1854 description of Schröder-Devrient by one of her
contemporaries, H. Chorely: "Her voice was a strong soprano . . . with an inher-

No Autobiographical content

ent expressiveness of tone which made it more attractive on the stage than many a more faultless organ. . . . Her execution was bad and heavy."

Schumann (pp. 233–34) had this to say (March 18, 1841) about a Schröder-Devrient performance (not of *Dichterliebe*) in which she was accompanied by Felix Mendelssohn:

> If we speak last of the climax of the evening, there is a good reason for it. In one word: Madame Schröder-Devrient sang. What there is human in a person and an artist of course succumbs to time and its influences: the voice, for instance, and the beauty of appearance. [Schröder-Devrient was thirty-seven at the time!] But what there is beyond—the soul, the poetry—remains fresh throughout all ages in the favorites of Heaven, and thus this artist and poetess will ever enchant us as long as her heart and throat contain one single tone.

Further, Schumann stated that Schröder-Devrient was the only singer who could survive Liszt as an accompanist. Clearly, not a voice of small proportions! Schumann called her singing of *Ich grolle nicht* "nobly projected." The composer's great admiration for this operatic soprano and his dedication of *Dichterliebe* to her make it clear that dramatic vocal abilities as well as beauty of vocal timbre were of importance to him. In *Dichterliebe*, the vocal demands grow as the cycle proceeds, and they must be met by appropriate increases of sound intensity. Among the aphorisms by Schumann (p. 31), published in connection with the *Album für die Jugend*, op. 68, one reads: "If you possess a sonorous voice, however, do not lose a moment's time but cultivate it immediately, and look upon it as a most precious gift bestowed by heaven." Schumann, the prolific Lied composer, advised (p. 35): "Never miss an opportunity of hearing a good opera," and at another moment (p. 34), perhaps tongue in cheek: "Much is to be learned from singers male and female. But do not believe all they tell you."

Most major composers of the period, including Schubert, Loewe, Mendelssohn, and Liszt (and later Strauss), played publicly for noted professional singers of the day. Schumann's awareness of the potential of the skilled vocal instrument often made him far exceed the range limits and the sustaining abilities of the nonprofessional vocalist. This is demonstrable in Lieder such as *Warte, warte, wilder Schiffmann*, *Der Hidalgo*, *Stille Tränen*, *Aufträge*, *Geständnis*, *Der Contrabandiste*, the Mignon Lieder, *Wanderlied*, the late ballads, and numerous songs within the well-known cycles themselves. His vocal compositions, including those of more intimate genre, were generally not written as salon pieces.

In *Dichterliebe*, Schumann does not violate poetic scanning of the Heine texts as much as he does with most verse. Perhaps the innate "Singen und Klingen" nature of the Heine poems is responsible for what appears to be Schumann's greater respect (in this cycle, at least) for the poetry of Heine. In *Dichterliebe*, text repetitions occur only in *Ich grolle nicht*. Contrariwise, the setting of a poem such as *Er ist's* (to Mörike's verses) offers a prime example of

Schumann's free treatment of poetic sources in a fashion that would have greatly upset Goethe, Zelter, and Professor Stein. (Later in the century, with regard to the question of how musicians set poetry, Tennyson would query: "Why do these musicians always make me repeat myself?")

As Komar points out (pp. 3–12), in *Dichterliebe* Schumann's respect for the poetic structure restricts him largely to syllabic settings. Lyric declamation is evident in most of these songs; it is the task of the singer to retain the overall lyricism of the Schumann Lieder while "declaiming" them. Lyric declamation in Schumann should not, it must be emphasized, take on the nature of recitativo or of *Sprechstimme*. The songs are not simply to be declaimed, but to be lyrically sung.

It may be that the cyclical character of the thematic material gives *Dichterliebe* greater unity than op. 39, *Liederkreis*. Yet *Ich grolle nicht, Aus alten Märchen, Die alten, bösen Lieder*, and to some extent *Ein Jüngling liebt ein Mädchen* depart from the lyric-declamatory style of *Dichterliebe*. They are insertions that break up uniformity of style and atmospheric color. *Liederkreis*, op. 39, is equally unified, despite its almost total lack of obvious cyclical recall and its less compelling tonality relationships. The significant difference is that *Dichterliebe*, although closely constructed, at times suddenly thrusts us into new directions, whereas *Liederkreis* plays with less starkly defined lights and shadows.

For many performers and listeners, *Dichterliebe* has the more immediate appeal, but *Liederkreis* has the greater enduring quality. A higher degree of unity is attributed to *Dichterliebe* and *Frauenliebe und -leben* than to *Liederkreis* only if more weight is placed on structure and form than on vocal and pianistic colors and moods as elements of unification. The nature of the poetry contributes directly to the dissimilarity of these three compositional triumphs (*Dichterliebe, Liederkreis,* and *Frauenliebe und -leben*), but it is creative genius that explains their individuality.

In his consideration of the structure of *Dichterliebe*, Hallmark deals extensively with the textual choices and alterations that Schumann made, as well as with the cycle's musical construction. Komar offers musical analysis of the individual songs as they relate within the cycle. He, as others have, points out that the vocal motifs rely heavily on C♯, B, and A. Every singer has been struck by the cycle's habitual hovering around a melodic axis—often a four-note nucleus of D–C♯–B–A.

The opening vocal line of *Im wunderschönen Monat Mai*, #1, based on the pianoforte's initial statement (bars 1–6), sets forth the melodic unit that is maintained throughout much of the cycle. Sams (pp. 22–26) posits that Clara themes (C–L–A–R–A equals C–B–A–G♯–A), in a number of variations, pervade the symphonic works, the Lieder (particularly *Dichterliebe*), and the pianoforte compositions (Ex. 11.1).

Linear connections between D-C♯ and B-C♯ occur in the four-bar keyboard introduction of *Im wunderschönen Monat Mai*. One might assume from these bars that the song is grounded in F♯ minor, but no tonic harmony emerges during the course of the entire song. Key ambiguity provides a sense of longing,

Example 11.1.   *Im wunderschönen Monat Mai*, bars 1–6.

unrequited love, and suffering, propelling the cycle through poetic and musical questioning. Suspensions and appoggiaturas occur (as Komar reminds us) with high frequency, centered around the intervallic nucleus previously described. Komar's analysis (p. 70) of *Im wunderschönen Monat Mai*, which he calls germinal to the rest of the cycle, succinctly concludes:

> Thus, Song 1 stresses linear displacements of the Note B, leaving the direction of its final displacement undetermined. . . . To sum up, Song 1 is in the key of A but makes a point of hanging onto B. This suggests the remaining course of the cycle; to hang onto B and eventually resolve it to either A or C♯.

Komar (p. 77) finds the cycle to be constructed on integrated harmonic and modal schemes. His observations in that regard follow:

> The overall form of Dichterliebe can be viewed as an outgrowth of the initial tonal events of the cycle. As tonic of song 1, A is the principal note at the beginning of the cycle, yet B and C♯ impinge on the primacy of A at the beginning, middle and end of that song. In fact, the $C\sharp_7$ chord raises doubt about the key of the first song, and it is only the clarity of A major in Song 2, along with numerous similarities between Songs 1 and 2, which relieves that doubt. As the only pair of adjacent songs in the same key, Songs 1 and 2 make a strong case for hypothesizing A major as the key of the cycle. The incomplete linear motion A–B of Song 1 . . . is completed with the resolution of B to C♯ at the outset of Song 2. Songs 1–5 represent a still larger unit in which A also moves to B, as in the incomplete linear motion of Song 1. The key of B minor gives way to vari-

ous other keys after Song 5, but B returns as tonic (in the major mode) in Song 14, followed by C# minor at the end of the cycle. I propose an overall view according to which the arpeggiated interval A-C# is filled in by the passing-note B, with an interruption in the motion from B to C# between Songs 5 and 14.

The intervallic nucleus of A–B–C# produces melodic lines with restricted excursions. What does this mean with regard to emotive potential for the performers of the cycle? Schumann's close intervals that equate with intimacy can only be realized through the smoothest connection of vocal sound, not by the pointing up of each individual word or note. The most expressive interpretation comes from the vocal legato, which is mirrored in the keyboard.

To be explicit, the pianist begins *Im wunderschönen Monat Mai,* #1, with fingers close to the keys, avoiding marked articulation of individual notes while maintaining exact rhythmic steadiness in the first half of the initial bar and allowing only the subtlest of improvisatory rubato in the phrase that sings out B-G#-F#-E#. This interpretative suggestion is supported by Gerald Moore's advice (p. 3) that "at no time should we be made aware that he is playing on a percussive instrument; the fingers touch the keys, the tone floats."

A word of caution is in order regarding late-nineteenth-century ritardandos as a mode of introducing vocal entrances in Schumann. In the opening measures of *Im wunderschönen Monat Mai,* there should be no Romantic torturing of the pianistic harmonic web, yet some slight rhythmic accommodation for the rising arpeggiated figure is called for. One of the premises of this work is that singers and pianists tend to ignore the progression of stylistic changes that occur during the nineteenth century. For example, Schubert should not be sung like Wolf, Beethoven not like Brahms, and Schumann not like Schubert, Brahms, Wolf, or Strauss. Schumann has his own unique Romantic flavor.

Edvard Grieg (pp. 447–48), in pointing out the extent to which the pianoforte plays a conspicuous role in the compositional style of the Schumann Lieder, states: "Up to a certain point, he who cannot play Schumann cannot sing him either." There have been a few performers who attempted to combine vocal and pianistic skills in public, generally with limited success. Grieg's statement, of course, was not to recommend that the singer publicly accompany himself or herself but to make performers aware of the need for integration of vocalism and pianism. With regard to vocal and pianistic collaboration in the Schumann Lieder, one might rearrange Grieg's statement to read: regardless of keyboard technical facility, the pianist who does not thoroughly understand the texts and who cannot (at some level) *sing* the Lieder should not perform them.

An argument has been made previously for the desirability of legato singing applied to the close-intervalled melody of the opening Lied of *Dichterliebe.* The poet's play with the sonorities of nasal continuants (**Im wunderschönen Monat Mai**) can be advantageously used by the singer to ensure continuous flow of smooth legato sound.

The same is true of the nasals that complete climactic endings of each line of poetry: "spra**ngen**," "aufgega**ngen**," "sa**ngen**," "gesta**nden**," and "Verla**ngen**." (This certainly is "Si**ngen** und Kli**ngen**"!) The singer should aim to maintain

Example 11.2.   *Aus meinen Tränen spriessen*, bars 1–8.

these voiced consonants (nasal continuants) *on the same dynamic level* as neighboring vowels. All too often, because of a loss of acoustic energy and vibrancy during nasal-consonant intrusions, one hears a sagging line at exactly those moments when harmonic movement demands sustained, or even increased, energy from the voice.

There is no reason to diminuendo the phrase climax at "aufgegangen" or the final vocal phrase on "Verlangen." Indeed, the composer has indicated a crescendo both times. Though *f* is not required, some increase in intensity is desirable. To introduce a decrescendo or subito piano (as is sometimes thought to be an artistic maneuver here) is to belie the phrase structure and to induce a mannered effect contrary to the musical and poetic language.

Lied #2, *Aus meinen Tränen spriessen,* closely follows the language intonation typical of Schumann's lyric declamation, built on the by-now-familiar melodic nucleus C#–D–B–A (Ex. 11.2).

Because of the melodic structure, the singer may be faced with a dilemma: declamation or lyricism? Much of the genius of Robert Schumann lies in his ability to fuse the elements of language and music. A singer's stylistic appropriateness in this, as in many Schumann Lieder, is dependent on his or her ability to implement the composer's conscious synthesis. It is a mistake to take on a quasi-recitative style; all too often in the performance of Schumann Lieder (and in this Lied in particular) the percussive inflections of spoken language are transferred to the singing voice. This negates the intention of the close-intervalled vocal line, which should move forward in tandem with the keyboard harmonies. There is then no conflict between declamation and lyricism.

The pianoforte offers not only a countermelody in the left hand but also additional melodic development. The vocal line anticipates the harmonic event at "spriessen"; the singer must not dawdle en route with disjunctive syllabification. Interweavings of small motifs between voice and piano contribute substantially to the integration of the two instruments, beautifully illustrated at bars 3 and 4, bars 7 and 8, and bars 11 and 12 and in the final pensive statements of voice and pianoforte.

The brief Lied is constructed on four phrases in a modified AABA form. A common temptation is for the singer to fill these few measures with such emotional weight that both vocalism and communication are hampered. While it is true that the first two phrases deal with flowing tears, blooming flowers, sighs, and a chorus of nightingales (generated typically in melodic single-note fashion), they are diatonically direct. Longing, not weeping, should be the interpretive mood. (One cannot cry and sing at the same time.)

The phrase that begins with "Und wenn du mich lieb hast, Kindchen," assisted by the chromatic play in the middle keyboard octave (in both left-hand and right-hand descending voices), not only expresses the poetic sentiment but questions tonality as well. Shall we be deceived by the final B in the vocal line, or shall we accept the concluding A major of the pianoforte? Komar (p. 70) comments that "song 2 is among the briefest of songs, but its apparent simplicity belies the perplexities of its structure." His analysis (p. 73) of *Aus meinen Tränen spriessen* concludes:

> Finally, the end of the song leaves B unresolved in the voice part, just as Song 1 leaves B unresolved in the piano part. So while Song 2 supplies a resolution (C♯) for the unresolved B of Song 1, it also leaves B very much in evidence at the end of the song. The function of Song 2 in the cycle is generally to strengthen the harmonic support for B while clarifying the key of Song 1. A major is not in doubt as tonic of Song 2, and the associations between the two songs—we should not overlook the fact that in neither song does a C♯₇ chord ever resolve to an F♯ minor triad—forges them virtually into a single entity.

Allen Forte (in Komar's *Schumann: "Dichterliebe"* [pp. 23–24]) selects *Aus meinen Tränen spriessen* to discuss Schenkerian analysis.

In turning to #3, *Die Rose, die Lilie, die Taube*, it should be remarked that using this Lied simply for the display of a singer's skill in breath support is one of the least tasteful tricks encountered on the recital stage. Blustering through it in a single breath is inexcusable. The indicated ritardando at bars 11 and 12 ("ist Rose und Lilie und Taube und Sonne") should be observed but not exaggerated. Schumann, as usual, does not indicate *a tempo* following the ritardando. However, at bar 13 ("ich liebe alleine, die Kleine, die Feine, die Reine, die Eine"), the performers need to return to tempo in preparation for the second ritardando at bar 16 ("Eine!"). Once again, following the final "Eine!" there is not an a tempo marking. But in order to retain the *munter* (lively, gay, blithe, merry, vigorous) atmosphere of this miniature, a return to the original tempo for the final six bars is essential. The diatonic forthrightness of #3 counters the introspection of songs #2 and #4. Within the cycle, *Die Rose, die Lilie, die Taube* expresses the exuberance of love but should not become an exhibition of bombastic diction or airflow and subglottic-pressure controls.

Brief and *munter* as it is, *Die Rose, die Lilie, die Taube* is neither a Gilbert and Sullivan patter song nor a Rossini buffo arietta but a delightful momentary insertion of bright splashes of color on a larger mural that is often composed of more subdued shades. Crisp diction, exuberant delivery, and excitement are called for from the singer, with dry articulation from the pianist, who will need to sing out the left-hand countermelody. Excerption of *Die Rose, die Lilie, die Taube* for performance outside the cycle violates the canon of good taste.

Lieder #3 and #4 have been briefly analyzed by Schenker and by Ernst Oster and Felix Salzer, using Schenkerian principles. (Analyses by Schenker, Forte, Oster, and Salzer are included in Komar's excellent compendium [pp. 95–110].)

The same integration of poetry, musical construction, voice and keyboard found in #2 is present in #4, *Wenn ich in deine Augen seh'* (bars 1–5). Lyric declamation is built on speech inflection. No better example of the effectiveness of Schumann's mastery of this idiom, which is of his own creation (there are tentative indications of it in late Schubert), can be found than in this brief song. A version of the ubiquitous melodic nucleus, first appearing in a B–D–B–G–C–A sequence, persists throughout. A struggle for primacy among these pitches creates melodic organization, surfacing even in the pianoforte postlude (Ex. 11.3).

Just as the singer must move to the first syllable of the word "**Augen**," so also must the pianist, adhering to the written crescendo-decrescendo nuance on the final beat of bar 2. Marked only in the pianoforte score, the same dynamic level belongs to the vocal line, so that the keyboard, in imitation of the voice, is heightening textual implications.

Eusebius/Florestan elements teem within this brief Lied, The single-note contour of the opening phrase and the more expansive melody of bars 5, 6, and 7 assume a level of emotional surging, moving to the forte dynamic. Legato— not detached syllabification—brings conviction to this exquisite example of lyric declamation. The *ossia* in bar 7, with its doubling of keyboard voicing, is a performance essential. The halting of melodic and harmonic movement at the word "sprichst" (bar 13) momentarily suspends declamatory lyricism, but the pianoforte, even while retarding, propels the singer forward to "ich liebe dich!"; there follows Heine's typical expression of the painful aspects of love. The poet's purposeful understatement of the climactic moment is wonderfully caught by Schumann. His handling somewhat tempers critical comment that composer Schumann fails to take into account poet Heine's tendency to find a worm in the center of every Romantic apple.

The postlude is much more than a keyboard reflection on what the singer has just asserted; additional symbolism that stems from the Clara theme is woven into the melody and the inner voices of the pianoforte. Robert Schumann interjects himself into the poetic process, with a D–C–B–G symbolic nu-

Example 11.3. *Wenn ich in deine Augen seh'*, bars 1–5.

cleus in tight distribution within each bar. Schumann not only brings about textual recall through musical motifing, thereby expanding the sentiments expressed by Heine, but also inserts Clara herself and his own feelings about her into the poetry and the music.

The melodic nucleus of *Ich will meine Seele tauchen*, #5, bears close relationship to the opening lines of songs #1, #2, and #4 (as did the deleted Lied *Dein Angesicht, so lieb und schön*), but now Schumann relies for quiet excitation upon his arpeggiated keyboard pattern (bars 1–5). Pianists should not fail to make the two outer voices distinct as they move in contrary motion. The combination of gently upward-curving vocal line and pianistic excitation yields a high level of synthesis among poetic and musical elements. Florestan is singing (Ex. 11.4).

Exact attention should be given by the singer to the differentiation between quarter-note *gruppetti* and the triplet figure of bar 15, in keeping with rhythmic exactitude among the sixteenth notes of the vocal and pianistic motifs. The quiet agitation of this sensuous text, with its intimate implications, must be portrayed through smooth *p* dynamic, while retaining vital vocalism. The postlude is among the most distraught and driving to be found in the cycle. As was mentioned previously, the polarity between the two outer voices, such an integral part in the development of a familiar thematic nucleus (particularly in the postlude), turns pianist into poet as well.

Performers and listeners enter another world with *Im Rhein, im heiligen Strome*, #6. The grandeur of the Rhine that flows through German physical and literary landscapes is majestically portrayed through slow, ponderous dotted rhythms for voice and piano and a strong anchoring of the long-note octaves in the bass. One kinesthetically experiences the strong current of the river as it relentlessly moves along, especially in the pianoforte interlude between bars 27 and 30. (It is of interest to see in what varied ways Liszt successfully set this poem.) Time is allowed for the singer to deal firmly with voiced consonants and nonvoiced consonants that help define harmonic goals. The performers may now indulge in higher dynamic levels than heretofore in the cycle. It is of utmost importance to give full, unhurried value to the eighth-note portion of the dotted-quarter/eighth-note rhythmic motif that permeates the composition. The Rhine glides majestically.

Beginning at bar 35, intimacy reaches its peak with "die Augen, die Lippen, die Lippen, die Wänglein," by which poet and composer describe the physical attributes of the beloved. The consonants of each noun must be savored and underscored with the warmest vocal color in the singer's palette. There is in this Lied a coupling of harmonic angularity and sturdy melodic sweep that never loses tenderness despite its strength. An extended postlude demands noble, decisive, and unhurried pianism.

The position of *Im Rhein, im heiligen Strome* in the cycle gives performers

Example 11.4. *Ich will meine Seele tauchen*, bars 1–5.

and listeners relief from previous harmonic and melodic webbing, and it prepares for departures yet to come. This change in musical textures reaches its fullest in the subsequent *Ich grolle nicht*.

Ich grolle nicht, #7, has found favor among singers of all categories and artistic persuasions. Yet it probably is one of the most violated songs in the Lied literature. Operatic voices who find themselves compelled to include some token Lieder on a recital program lurch through it. (It has even been kidnapped from the cycle to join a catchall "operatic" group of Lieder, performed together with such other hostages as Schubert's *Die Allmacht* and *Der Atlas* and Strauss's *Zueignung*.) It is, indeed, a vigorous song; it requires a display of vocalism capable of matching the bitter intensity of the poetry. However, treating *Ich grolle nicht* as an occasion for vocal verismo is unacceptable. No ritardandos other than those marked should be introduced. Octaves of the left hand and the pianistic accentuated first and third beats of each bar, with reiterated insistent chording, must be heavy. But the singer is not required to rupture the spleen beginning at bar 1. The composer's intention is not to offer a dash toward a climactic high note. The climax (although they may not have been the composer's original intention, the *ossia* notes should be taken) is not exciting if the entire Lied has been bellowed and punched out at a hurried tempo. The inherent emotion is not one of rage and destruction but one of bitter recall, regret, and pain.

Because of time restrictions in academic degree recitals, a truncated performance of *Dichterliebe*, consisting of the first seven songs, sometimes is necessary. This is not a satisfactory route for the established artist. However, songs #1 through #7 do bear tonality and idiomatic relationships that afford them cohesion as a group.

A different but related question arises regarding the wisdom of reintroducing into the cycle, as a means of sprucing up old and familiar literature, the four songs that Schumann omitted. (These are to be found in other opus numbers in the Friedländer edition and as #4a, #4b, #12a, and #12b in the Komar and Hallmark *Dichterliebe* analyses.) The omitted Lieder may bear some musical relationship to the final canon, but it seems musicologically presumptuous to put them back in, even in academic recital circumstances, inasmuch as Schumann took them out.

In *Und wüssten's die Blumen, die kleinen*, #8, the rapid configuration of thirty-second notes provides a complete about-face from the ponderous unbroken chordal progressions of *Ich grolle nicht*. They also supply a unifying rhythmic principle. Without doubt, this is "finger music." Perhaps the poetic imagery of small flowers ("die Blumen, die kleinen") dictated the composer's choice of rapid clusters of "small" notes for both hands, or it may be that he found the lover's suffering, so movingly present in the text, best expressed through pianoforte flutterings. More tellingly, at work here is a principle that originated in the eighteenth-century *Melodram* of Zumsteeg, where descriptive figures underlay texts, a heritage passed on by Schubert. Superimposed over this figure, outlining the melody itself, is a phrase characteristically shaped by descending small intervals, the whole providing a sense of intimate excitation. The pianist's technical task is considerably more involved than is the singer's.

The postlude material introduces new ideas, moving to triplets that comment on Heine's embittered last line of verse, "zerrissen mir das Herz." This is another occasion on which it cannot be said that Schumann misses the irony of Heine's concluding line. Indeed, the composer seems to magnify it through his energetic postlude; there has seldom been such an expression of bitterness from Schumann. The doubling and dotting of the forceful octave figure underlying the triplet agitation should be strong, with the sforzandos and the crescendos fully realized, rushing headlong to the concluding note. Whereas it might be advisable to use una corda and discreet pedaling through most of this Lied, the postlude requires percussive right-hand articulation matched by competing hammered left-hand octaves.

The Lied that follows, *Das ist ein Flöten und Geigen*, #9, is a remarkably refreshing insertion into the cycle. This folklike melody is so structured with its dotted rhythms, its sudden leaps following more closely intervalled melodic movement, and its directness that were one to sing the isolated melody there would still be an awareness that not all is well. However, the actual "song," with its imitation of the flute, the violin, the trumpet, and the drum, is in the keyboard. The downbeat of each bar, often acting as a pedal-point anchor, portrays the percussive drum, which, rather than contributing to the gaiety, offers an ominous impulse to the strange dance. The second and third beats of each bar must be executed loudly and clearly, with rhythmic exactitude; the sixteenth-note configuration requires a character of wildness that seems to deny the pleasures of the ongoing dance. Here is no festive wedding whirl but a musical realization of Heine's bitterness as the rejected lover observes the celebration. Despite the folk character of the vocal line, singer and pianist must not treat this Lied as either festive or folklike. Subdued rage is present in both poetry and music (Ex. 11.5). (Peter [Heine's *Der arme Peter*] is another rebuffed lover who watches a wedding dance.)

The voice drops to low intensity and pitch levels as the singer intones "die Herzallerliebste mein," describing perfidy. The pianist must do the same, then swoop passionately onward with the arpeggiated figure between the strophes. The nineteen-measure postlude is not only pianoforte music at its best but a summation of the pain previously expressed poetically. Perhaps it equals or even surpasses the bitterness present in the postlude of #8. An enraged Florestan here takes charge. This keyboard commentary reiterates without words what the poetry has previously said. The last four bars, diminishing to *pp* level, with their chromatic inner voice and bass-line descent, constitute painful suppression of anger. Musically and emotionally, the position of this Lied within the cycle serves a function that takes it far beyond its individual merit. To excerpt this song for inclusion in a potpourri group of selected Schumann Lieder or in a general Lieder group from several composers is to be party to desecration.

Hör' ich das Liedchen klingen, #10, returns to the kind of writing that most endears *Dichterliebe* and its composer to traditional critics and performers alike. The pianoforte first intriguingly announces, in an offbeat dotted eighth note from which an arpeggiated figure slowly drips (bars 1–6), what the voice

Example 11.5. *Das ist ein Flöten und Geigen*, bars 1–10.

will sing. These delays of melodic outlining produce tenderness and nostalgia. Perhaps the touching pianoforte writing has more to tell us about the real meaning behind the words than does the vocal line itself (Ex. 11.6). In the melodic structure, B♭ substitutes for the recurrent B of the previous Lieder in the cycle, and the nucleus of neighboring notes gravitates around it. B♭ at times alters to B♮; the near pitches C and D♭ play back and forth. Phrase movement should be directed to these pivotal melodic events with momentum but without rushing. The closeness of the intervals, the minor mode, and the language-inflection rhythms delivered at slow (*langsam*) tempo strike a compelling mood of contained emotion. An expressive embellishment on "auf" in "dort löst sich *auf* in Tränen" momentarily breaks out of this restraint. On the embellishment itself, the singer must articulate the thirty-second/eighth-note figure by slightly increasing vocal intensity within an aura of subdued emotion.

The postlude is again a dominance contest among notes lodged in the tight melodic conglomerate. (Is it possible to detect a bit of the "flute" theme of #9?) Pianistic recall of the opening material now becomes contemplative, discoursing over mounting and descending alternating bass lines and harmonic permutations. Komar (p. 85) points out the effective prolongations of the I$^6_4$ and the I$^5_3$ chords. Sams (p. 117), adept at discovering thematic relationships between disparate compositions, finds that bars 24–25 have parallels in the *Abegg* variations, in *Papillons*, in *Carnaval*, and elsewhere.

Ein Jüngling liebt ein Mädchen, #11, at first seems foreign to the structure of the cycle. A closer analytical look reveals that while providing a startling shift of mood *Ein Jüngling liebt ein Mädchen* manages to remain within the framework of the total *Dichterliebe* tableau. Sams (p. 118) finds "the song is all dancing high spirits," the composer affecting an amused frame of mind that serves to mask a later bitter expression of jealous despair. The octave downward leap at "ist eine alte Geschichte," with its immediate return to the upper octave, expresses scorn and irony. In addition to introducing a folk element that is strikingly dissimilar to the Lieder on either side of it, *Ein Jüngling liebt ein Mädchen* makes use of the by-now-clear compositional concept of a concentrated pitch nucleus. Indeed, the postlude seems almost a banal argument between the pitches Bb and C, now the fifth and sixth scale degrees of the Eb major tonality. Directness in a forthright narrative manner is called for.

/12   *Am leuchtenden Sommermorgen*, #12, brings back the world of romantic dreaming and longing that demands beautiful lyric vocalism and improvisatory pianism. This improvisatory style is "composed in," and the pianist must avoid taking too much license with it. The initial Gb serves as the bass of a German 6th chord in Bb major, from which the opening arpeggiated descriptive keyboard figure is germinated, thereby creating a model of poetic and musical contemplation. Komar (p. 86) finds the same chord to be spelled enharmonically as the V_7 of Cb major (that is, B♮) in bar 8. The previously mentioned compact melodic kernel (now Bb–Cb–Db–C♮) insistently lingers on (Ex. 11.7).

The final vocal phrase evolves melodically until its conclusion on the note C, over which the piano begins to improvise with changing harmonies in a manner reminiscent of *Hör ich das Liedchen klingen*. This pianoforte reverie illustrates Schumann at his Romantic best. Without in any way creating an intrusion, Schumann calls on the equal partner of this performance duo—the pianist—to sing out the irregular resolutions of the augmented-sixth chords in a memorable metamorphosis of "the song" (Komar, p. 87). This is best done by giving fullest concentration to the sonorities and introspective colors of which

Example 11.6.   *Hör' ich das Liedchen klingen*, bars 1–6.

Example 11.7. *Am leuchtenden Sommermorgen*, bars 1–5.

the keyboard is capable, avoiding percussive sound. (It is not necessary to drive home the harmonic language.) As every lover of *Dichterliebe* is aware, Schumann will return to this material for the cycle's remarkable conclusion. In this Lied, a thing of enduring beauty, the synthesis of word and music, voice and keyboard, is complete.

The composer must have intended that the beginning of *Ich hab' im Traum geweinet*, #13, should recall *Aus meinen Tränen spriessen*, #2. The initial one-pitch intoning on B♭ moves only as far as C♭. Like the interjectory keyboard chordal staccatos between the intoned phrases, it shows an indebtedness to the late-Schubertian declamatory style. Schumann's design bears no direct melodic or rhythmic relationship to the late Schubert Lieder, yet it reveals itself as a not-too-distant cousin. These common techniques include interjectory phrases, the *Bläserchor* (brass choir) or *Männerchor* (male chorus) harmonies of the keyboard lower-middle octave so beloved by Schubert, and the use of multiple moments of silence. In *Ich hab' im Traum geweinet*, the *Luftpause* so dear to Schubert is put to equally effective use by Schumann. These rests in the concluding bars must be given full value. Silence here is more meaningful than sound. The balanced chiaroscuro timbre of the singing voice determines the effectiveness of this Lied.

(What a lesson this cycle provides in the skillful employment of small patterns of motivic material to create unity and compactness without a hint of boredom or lack of melodic invention!)

How can vocal coloration be used by the re-creative artist to convey the poetic and musical synthesis characteristic of Schumann? It is tempting for a singer to try to manufacture special colors of the voice in the hope of conveying profundity of feeling. This is to overlook the fact that the voice itself is expressive as an instrument. A violin does not attempt to make itself into a trumpet, nor a flute into a clarinet, in order to execute coloration. Likewise, the voice need not disguise itself or masquerade. The communicative parameters of the voice are timbre, dynamic variation, phrase shaping, and textual portrayal.

The most expressive thing the singer can do in this Lied is vocalize a mezzo piano that is efficiently balanced in harmonic partials (the historic chiaroscuro timbre mentioned previously) while giving each phrase its unique shape and direction. Vocal mooing and cooing are out of place. It should be remembered that one cannot be overcome with emotion and sing at the same time. Art is not reality; it is the elevation, the ennoblement, of reality.

Allnächtlich im Traume, #14, plays with a by-now-familiar compact pitch nucleus: B and C♯ repeatedly occur in the pianoforte voices as well as in the vocal melody, and they compete until the song's conclusion. The short, spurting comments given to the singing voice must be bound together (although the rests are to be thoroughly observed) so that phrases are shaped in groups of four and eight bars; otherwise there is peril of their becoming disjunct and nonsensical. Duration aspects of the speaking voice are judiciously imitated in these short segments, leading to a recitative-like conclusion of the opening phrase ("und laut aufweinend stürz' ich mich zu deinen süssen Füssen"). *Allnächtlich im Traume* makes a gradual transition from the introspection of the two previous Lieder to the straightforwardness of *Aus alten Märchen,* #15.

If divorced from its vocal line, *Aus alten Märchen* could survive as an instrumental piece. Yet vocally the song is technically demanding. Once again the constant drumming on the pitch B by both pianoforte and voice is unmistakable. In its swinging pianism and vocal directness it reminds us somewhat of another Schumann Lied, *Mit Myrten und Rosen.* At "und laute Quellen brechen aus wildem Marmorstein, und seltsam in den Bächen strahlt fort der Widerschein, Ach!" *Aus alten Märchen* builds to one of the three chief vocal climaxes of the cycle. An earlier one is the dramatic "und sah die Schlang', die dir am Herzen frisst" of *Ich grolle nicht* (particularly in the *ossia*), the second is this passage, and the third will be found in #16 at "als wie der starke Christoph, im Dom zu [K]öln am Rhein."

This singular climax in *Aus alten Märchen* occurs following a passage in limited lower range; the vocal line then ascends into upper range, under and over which the pianoforte figuratively pounds pain into the listener. Modest vocal instruments get lost when singing this Lied. Strength and full sound from both performers are requisite. The triumphant outburst of "Ach!" and its reiteration on the pitch B are spine-chilling. In winding down this emotional burst, Eusebius reins in Florestan's volatility in bars 96–103, yet Florestan's voice is still to be heard in the final nine *pp* measures.

It is not marked as such, but a segue should occur at the final fermata chord of #15, the performers embarking immediately on the concluding Lied, *Die alten, bösen Lieder,* #16. The latter begins as a forceful, direct expression, the melody based on diatonic harmonies. As the vocal line rises to the climax, the drama requires powerful vocalism. Upward and downward melodic motion is constructed on I, IV, V harmonies, with resulting intervals of fourths, fifths, and octaves or of seventh-intervallic variants. This squareness counters the introspective nature of much of the cycle.

Performers and listeners understand the composer's insertion of what at first seems disparate material for this last song of the cycle. Schumann's intention gradually becomes apparent. The four occurrences of C♯ (including the grace note) of the *sf* embellished chord reaffirm the victory of C♯ at that point in no uncertain terms, as do several subsequent phrase endings. The pianoforte confirms the importance of B, B♯ (C), C♯, and D as members of the pitch nucleus, regardless of where the reiterated eighth notes take us in scale ascent. Finally, the weightiness of the quarter-note chords, slowed down by half-note enriched harmonies, then reverting back to seventh-chord quarter-note progressions (under almost same-note vocalism), leads to a final adagio. But the battle among C♯, D♮, B♯, C♯, and A is not yet over. Has A major perhaps become the established key? No, the problems of unrequited love are not so easily resolved.

Schumann moves onward, recalling in improvisatory manner thematic material of *Am leuchtenden Sommermorgen.* He originally notated this postlude in C♯ major, then changed to the enharmonic tonality of D♭ major, which of course makes no perceptual difference (except for ease of reading). So the key of C♯ and the C♯ member of the melodic nucleus claim final victory in the cycle after all!

Schumann has sometimes been assessed as having written postludes that become "songs without words," but here the words have written the postlude. Schumann is as much poet as musician. With its thematic recall, this postlude is perhaps unmatched in beauty by any other in the Lied literature. How should it be played? Perhaps no more appropriate assessment of the pianist's task is possible than that by Moore (pp. 21–22), who probably has publicly played it more times than any other person:

> But the inspired peroration to *Dichterliebe* is not imbued with tear-choked retrospection; it breathes a different air, we float from darkness into light. No longer a reflection of self-pity, it is a new structure; in truth there are moments of nostalgia, but they are gentle and without smart, with a fragile beauty.

12

Opus 45 and Opus 57

Opus 45

Musicologic criticism customarily attributes good nineteenth-century ballad writing to Carl Loewe while lamenting that Schumann did not possess sufficient dramatic capability to compose equally successful ballads. The Loewe ballads are an excellent genre deserving of more performance than they get, but many Schumann ballads compare favorably with or even surpass those by Loewe. Some of these are found in op. 45: *Der Schatzgräber,* #1, *Frühlingsfahrt,* #2, and *Abends am Strand,* #3. They represent first-class ballad writing, but because they are far removed from the *Dichterliebe* idiom, they are falsely accused by traditionalists of displaying lack of inspiration.

Composed in November 1840, to an Eichendorff text, *Der Schatzgräber* recalls the Schubertian technique of inventing mechanical keyboard figures to serve as unifying musical means. An energetic ascending chromatic motif introduced in the first four bars of *Der Schatzgräber* contrasts with another motif that consists of chordal progressions. The two motifs—motion/arrested motion—support the distinct narrative character of the ballad. Some singers may feel warned off by the low G on the syllable "hub" (bar 8) and again at "herab" (bar 41). Considering his written advice about a composer's need to be familiar with vocal ranges, one wonders exactly what kind of singer Schumann had in mind here. A dramatic mezzo-soprano, a dramatic baritone with strong low register, or a bass-baritone may prove best.

Schumann catches the intensity of the lonely digger. The G minor motif opens with a *sf* introduced by a heavy grace note in the left hand. Moore (p. 171) remarks that "the impact of the first note in the pianoforte is earth-shattering." The three mighty pianistic swings with the pickax must be deliberate and unhurried. In its chromatic propulsion, the passage becomes one of the most effective descriptive moments in the Schumann Lieder. The vocal narration logically follows this telling preparation. For the singer, "und wirst doch mein, mein, mein!" (bars 26–28) comes as a cry of triumph at the releasing of the precious treasure. It is the pianist, then, who must paint the scene of frenzy induced by the greedy search (Ex. 12.1).

The keyboard, in its *f* chords, has the task of hammering out the sound of crashing rocks as they fall on the foolish digger. Can anyone doubt that Schumann anticipated a voice of generous proportions for the performance of this Lied? At the words "Hohnlachen wild erschallte" Schumann has found in stac-

Example 12.1.   *Der Schatzgräber*, bars 20–28.

catoed, harmonically enriched triplets a remarkably able musical representation of sarcastic laughter. Here is first-class dramatic writing. It requires from both singer and pianist ample sound and the ability to depict, through musical means, Eichendorff's strange, gripping verse.

Another Eichendorff poem, *Frühlingsfahrt*, set in October 1840, begins as a straightforward ballad with angular melodic contour and buoyant dotted rhythms. During the poetic and musical portrayal of the domestically directed first lad, who finds a sweetheart with whom to settle down in a comfortable life, both pianist and singer should express exuberance through energetic playing and singing.

At the introduction of the second lad, who is lured by the siren call of the sea, lightheartedness disappears in favor of measured reiterated eighth notes in the right hand superimposed over a version of the lustier motif of the opening section. Schumann matches Eichendorff's account of the perils of the sea and a weary old sailor's disillusionment. The twenty bars of harmonic progression, beginning with the text "die tausend Stimmen im Grund," are highly inventive. The singer must diminish tonal brilliance, and the pianist needs to bring solemnity to this section.

In the interest of unity, at the final section Schumann reverts to the brisk opening motif that described the two lads' expectant embarkations on life's journey, even though the text pictures the now-old salt as pensive and tearful. Schumann's reaction is to indicate a ritardando at "die Tränen im Auge mir schwellen" and a *langsamer* at the pious reflection "ach Gott, führ' uns liebreich zu dir," which concludes the vocal line. Careful handling of tempo changes is essential; otherwise, text and music seem somewhat at odds with each other. The final four keyboard bars are liturgical in nature; they offer relatively small compensation for the dour, pietistic concluding sentiment of the poem.

Abends am Strand, #3, written in November 1840 to a Heine poem, is appropriately included in this ballad opus. Again, a pianistic motif catches the inner emotion of the poetry. Not only is it a fortunate descriptive figure, but it is also an engaging musical idea that shows the range of Schumann's talent even when he is faced with a curious tale. The insistent eighth-note *gruppetti* move relentlessly forward, first as a single voice, then in octaves, followed by a bass/tenor keyboard duet in tenths (bars 1–16). A musical foil to the close-intervalled contour of the vocal line is created, eliciting an atmosphere of calmness that characterizes the deep sea itself. A sudden tonality shift transports us to another geography and another scene (the Ganges with its lotus blooms), and comes as a shock. Almost immediately we are whisked to yet another locale (Lapland), whose inhabitants here suffer immeasurably from the uncomplimentary caricature given them by both the poet ("schmutzige Leute, plattköpfig, breitmäulig, klein" [dirty people, flat-headed, wide-mouthed, small]) and the composer (Schumann's sustained note on the word "schrein"). The singer must give a full-bodied sound devoid of beauty on this "howl." (Can this Lied still be performed, despite its obvious note of ethnic prejudice?) The song is an oddity but nonetheless an imaginative composition.

Example 12.2.   *Belsatzar*, bars 1–5.

Opus 57

Belsatzar (*Belsazar*), a great ballad, is among Schumann's earliest Lieder (aside from youthful attempts), having been written in February 1840 and later published as op. 57. Based on the biblical scene of Belshazzar's feast, the poem itself is ranked among Heine's greatest. His representation of Belshazzar's violent demise is fresh and imaginative. Heine's creativity leaps out from every line. Schumann's setting of this poem propels him at once into the category of outstanding ballad composer. One stands in awe at the way Robert Schumann in his earliest efforts in the genre so completely mastered the ballad tradition.

The eerie seventh-chord arpeggiation of the opening keyboard measures (bars 1–5) is full of mystery and agitation. The pianist has the task of conceiving this figure in an improvisatory way that evokes midnight and impending doom. It is a mistake for the singer to begin with simple storytelling, as though he or she were unsuspecting of what lies ahead. Schumann already is showing us in the keyboard that something is amiss. There must be a secretive, confidential quality of sound at *p* dynamic level that sketches the sinister night atmosphere of ancient Babylon and announces the strange and fascinating tale that is about to unfold. The first thirteen bars are mood-evocative in a different mode from that found in *Aus den hebräischen Gesängen* or in *Zwielicht*, yet the same technical method of enriched harmonic arpeggiation prevails (Ex. 12.2).

All the more effective then, beginning at bar 14, is the distinct change in thematic figuration to present the bustle of feasting and drinking and the racket of the shouting and singing vassals. Broken octaves in sixteenth notes in the right hand, leaping above the square harmonies in the left, adeptly catch the pandemonium of the royal banquet. The singer casts aside the intimate tone of the first fourteen bars to portray wild, exuberant, abandoned drunkenness. While cleanly articulating each note of the right hand with its open-octave harmonies, the pianist accents the harmonic foundation given to the left hand.

Back-and-forth playing across the Ab–B♮–C–Bb melodic nugget (undergirded by the swaying harmonic figure) catches the drunken boldness growing apace in Belshazzar (bars 23–32). The king's drunkenness will lead him to fatal blaspheming. (Those who discover Clara-related signs and symbols in melodic nuclei that play around these pitches will be given pause here!)

As the vassals urge the king onward, a brief pianistic episode is suddenly introduced in bars 32–35 by detached accented solid chords, effecting a tumultuous scene. In bar 36, the reemergence of the opening chromatic improvisatory arpeggiation, with a compelling *sf* struck in the left hand, reminds us that we were, at the very beginning of the Lied, forewarned of impending tragedy.

The account of the king's sacrilegious grasping of the golden temple goblet filled with wine, which he drains in one gulp, begins melodically with a narrow-intervallic pattern that moves up the scale by semitones over an insistent pianistic ostinato. Above this left-hand figure, the right hand is restricted to small-intervallic *gruppetti*. The effect is one of mounting tension in anticipation of the climactic lines that lie ahead. At the king's loudly calling out with foaming lips, the doubling in the bass clef and the broken octaves in the right hand press forward to the frightening first climax: the king cries, "Ich bin der König von Babylon." At this moment, there is a freezing of motion at the *sf* applied diminished seventh chord on "ich" that leads to a cadence in G minor. The subsequent harmonic commentary, with its chromatic rumble of astonishment and fear (in contrast to the halting of all movement the moment before), crashes in on the sensibilities with tremendous intensity. The audacity of the self-centered, godless king erupts (bars 55–61) like a volcano (Ex. 12.3). Next comes the result of such blasphemy. The laughter vanishes; the mysterious hand writes in letters of fire on the white wall. The voice descends into lower register, and the pianoforte traces the eerie event by means of dissonant seconds in the right hand, over upward interjectory semitones.

The drama would appear to be over; a recitative marked "to be lightly and clearly recited" transpires at slower tempo. The vassals sit in stunned astonishment; the wisemen cannot decipher the fiery inscription. Purposely understated by Heine, the violent conclusion is also handled by Schumann without fanfare. The final poetic climax, "Belsazar ward aber in selbiger Nacht von seinen Knechten umgebracht," is delivered almost dispassionately. No postlude is appended. Nothing but deafening silence concludes the abrupt "was slain." All ends in a whisper. Schumann's penetration of the drama is as close to perfection as one could wish.

Sams (p. 35) offers a different assessment:

In the heat of this first song-writing inspiration it all boils over and goes to waste. The fine poem . . . is perhaps the best in all Schumann's Heine settings; not so the song. The necessary objective treatment was not in Schumann's na-

Example 12.3.   *Belsatzar*, bars 55–61.

ture. His music expresses, instead of the drama, the changing moods of an imagined onlooker.

Regarding Schumann's climactic treatment of the word "ich" in the passage "ich bin der König von Babylon," Sams (p. 36) finds that the sense of the words is ignored, "e.g., the over-emphatic *'ich* bin der König,' as if the Babylonian succession were in dispute." Quite to the contrary, the king is *exalting*, not identifying, himself. By this pronouncement Schumann catches the egocentricity of the wildly drunken king in his defiance of God, which is, of course, the point of the ballad. The Lied is not the tentative searching of a composer working in a new medium; it is an accomplished narration in the manner of the classic balladeer.

Contrasts in dynamic levels and between speech-inflection and melodic segments, together with an improvisatory keyboard idiom, make *Belsatzar* a major contribution to the ballad literature. The singer and pianist are offered full opportunity for the realization of the dramatic potentials of their instruments.

13

Opus 53

Opus 53 comprises five Lieder. There is little logic for linking the first two songs with the three brief songs that make up the *Der arme Peter* cycle.

The first song of op. 53, *Blondels Lied*, is a setting of J. G. Seidl's poetic version of how Richard the Lionhearted's place of imprisonment was discovered by his minstrel Blondel. Schumann creates a medieval flavor without attempting historical authenticity; there is an archaic, chorale-like quality about *Blondels Lied*. (A number of Baroque chorales have their melodic sources in the *Minnelieder* and *Meisterlieder* literatures.) The strophic structure of *Blondels Lied* depends on an echoing dialogue between the king and his minstrel. (Schumann omits Seidl's third strophe.) Proper delineation of the protagonists and penetration of the inherent drama bring charm to this neglected Lied. *Blondels Lied* calls for straightforward pianism and vocalism, delivered with dignity and reserve. However, it seems orphaned in op. 53; it might prove more interesting when placed among a group of ballads.

Blondels Lied is a point of departure for the consideration of a performance-practice matter. The interpolated grace notes instruct the pianist to strike parts of the chord slightly in advance of the rest. It is significant that when Schumann wants an anticipatory note he writes it. The vicious habit (mentioned in chapter 2) of striking one hand, or portions of a chord, in advance on chordal changes inhibits harmonic fluidity. It is tasteless exaggeration of a late-Romantic pianistic style. The "ker-*plunk!*" of left hand/right hand (nonsynchronization of the notes of the chord, or of notes in both hands) serves Schumann adversely. This "ta-*dum!*" affectation introduces more sentimentality than is inherent in a literature that already tends to strike the modern listener as verging on excessive sentiment. Such pianistic practice goes together with the vocal straight-toning "hearts and flowers" school of naive Romantic music making. When Schumann wishes independence of the two hands in the striking of chords—which he sparingly requests—he writes out the embellishments. Infrequent but typical bars, in which one hand anticipates harmonic movement, can be found in, among others, *Du bist wie eine Blume*, *Lied der Braut I*, *Stille Tränen*, *Melancholie*, *Hauptmanns Weib*, *Ins Freie*, *Kommen und Scheiden*, *Jung Volkers Lied*, *Ich wandelte unter den Bäumen*, *Schöne Wiege meiner Leiden*, and *Der Schatzgräber*. In a few songs, such as *Blondels Lied*, *Warnung*, and *O wie lieblich ist das Mädchen*, anticipatory notes at chordal changes are written out for both hands.

The second Lied of op. 53 is a setting of Wilhelmine Lorenz's *Loreley*, about which Sams (p. 85) says: "Only some . . . domestic or family connection could explain how the greatest living song-writer came to set such pitiful trash." (The poetess was Schumann's sister-in-law.) Although it is not competition for Eichendorff's *Waldesgespräch*, the verse is not trash; it is a modest setting of a frequent theme in German Folk Romanticism. The song itself is seldom highly rated, partly because of its somewhat academic, etudelike keyboard attributes and partly because of its brevity. Vocally and pianistically it is at least as meritorious as a dozen other Schumann Lieder held in higher regard. It could be useful in a group of Schumann miniatures. The keyboard must be kept *zart* and *leicht* (tender and light), with flowing arpeggiation. The affable melody has an ease that invites a bel canto line. One regrets that it all is over so soon.

Compared to the major Heine cycles considered thus far and to the larger opus collections, the small, compact *Der arme Peter*, op. 53, #3, consisting of three songs, appears vocally and pianistically slight. It is, nonetheless, intense. By the nature of the poetry, a folk idiom is required. But the result goes far beyond simple folk-song parameters. The embellished right-hand and left-hand drones of the opening chords call to the wedding dance. There is both celebration and gravity. A melodic kernel, in this instance deceptively easy and gracious, hovers around the familiar A, B, C, and D. (This is one version of the pitch combinations some critics see as a hidden sign of Schumann's obsessive love for Clara. What could possibly be the connection here? Probably such coding, here and in many other instances, was not intended.)

The slow waltz introduces Hans and Grete, bridegroom and bride, dressed in rustic wedding finery. Even when nothing amiss is yet evident, the nuptial gaiety is subdued. The octaves in the right hand must be played with nonchalance and should share in equal voicing with the left-hand figuration. Noticeably, the keyboard motif alters at mention of the bridal pair, and the melodic line abandons its static contour, taking on a new and distinctive upward turn. *Der arme Peter I* becomes a *Ländler* (slow country waltz). At bar 26 the pianoforte resumes its insistence that the conjugal dance will continue while Peter's pain is ignored.

An eerie, wraithlike Peter appears with the phrase "Der Peter spricht leise vor sich her." Only with Peter's "Ach! wenn ich nicht gar zu vernünftig wär', ich täte mir was zu Leide" do we realize we have been deceived by the simple folk-song frame within which this small tragedy is encapsulated.

The E minor chord of Lied II that segues from Lied I sounds a death knell. The eighth notes of the vocal line, hovering at first around a familiar pattern, soon give way to a more extended range at "will's mich von hinnen drängen." The melodic direction at *etwas ruhiger* ("es treibt mich nach der Liebsten Näh'") descends again as it paints the effects of despair; the low range of the voice is reached, beginning with "Ich steig' hinauf des Berges Höh', dort ist man doch alleine." The voice then rises again over expanded harmonies and reaches a *f* dynamic level with "und wenn ich still dort oben steh'." The subsequent phrase, "dann steh' ich still und weine," full of pathos, is remarkably sculpted out of the sustained chord that undergirds it. A pattern reminiscent of the dance motif that concluded Lied I intensifies Peter's pain. The pianoforte reminds us that, despite Peter's emotions, the wedding dance still goes on.

The chordal progressions of Lied III have a funereal mien; the octave dou-blings must be lugubrious and weighty yet remain at *p* dynamic. Until the last tragic sung phrase, the melody stays within limited confines. A dirge completes the Lied.

Schumann catches the folk narration with a precise combination of sim-plicity and profundity. *Der arme Peter* is sometimes mistakenly taken for a mi-nuscule exercise in intimate interpretation rather than as a live human experi-ence of considerable immensity, deceptively set to small scale. There is as much drama crowded into these brief pages as can be found in many an operatic *scena*. The singer initially assumes the character of narrator. Vocal intensity stays within dynamic levels appropriate to dimensions of the cycle. Then the performer must enter into the personal tragedy of Peter and contrast Peter's an-guished outburst with the contentment of Hans and Grete.

14

Some Other Early Lieder: Opuses 27, 30, 31, and 49

No particular significance attaches to the date of composition for most of the songs written by Schumann in 1840 and 1841. But because of the nature and extent of critical comment regarding the merit of early versus late Lieder, it is well to keep in mind which ones were written in 1840 and which were of later composition. Publication dates and sequential opus numbers may be misleading as to when the songs were written. Now that the major cycles have been considered, it is appropriate to turn to other early Lieder.

Opus 27

The songs assembled in op. 27 are sometimes not regarded as of sufficiently consistent quality to enhance the reputation of Schumann as a major Lied composer. *Sag' an, o lieber Vogel mein*, #1, to a poem by Friedrich Hebbel, probably was composed in 1840. This song is pleasant and innocuous, even commonplace, and it could have come from any number of skilled hands. Phrases should be shaped dynamically in accordance with poetic questioning and answering, yet artlessness remains paramount.

Dem roten Röslein gleicht mein Lieb, #2, to a Burns source, may generate more musical interest than does *Sag' an, o lieber Vogel mein*, but there is little here to spark great enthusiasm. Aware of the limitations of this Lied, Sams (p. 78) nevertheless finds that the tune "nods and droops very winningly." The lilting re-current dancing sixteenth-note figure, in both pianoforte and voice, must be well accented.

Of much greater moment is the setting of Chamisso's *Was soll ich sagen?*, #3. A slow tempo is called for by its descending keyboard octaves, shifting harmonies, and several intriguing tightly constructed interludes. Overall unity is enhanced by compact melodic kernels. However, even the most committed Schumann afi-cionado may find it difficult to laud the banality of the final four bars.

Jasminenstrauch, #4, to a Rückert poem, is a worthy Lied. It is built on an arpeggiated figure originating in the left hand, joined to pianistic filigree in the right hand, over which a melody (the C♯–[and later C]–B–A nucleus again) sal-lies forth in bright A major. The song should be sung with fresh expression. It must be played with gently surging well-articulated *gruppetti* in the right hand. The verses of *Jasminenstrauch* do not easily adapt themselves to musical set-ting, because they succinctly mirror the quickly changing fortunes of love as symbolized by Nature's seasonal turns. Schumann often was able to transform Nature's volatility into human sentiment (as in the Eichendorff Lieder). In this brief excursion, his interest lay in describing the transformation of the green jas-mine bush by an overnight snowfall. The compact sextolets of the right hand depict gently falling snowflakes, which are then momentarily halted by a di-minished seventh chord fluttering downward in the keyboard as the crucial question "Was geshah mir in der Nacht?" moves upward in the vocal line (bars 12–13). *Jasminenstrauch* remains the most appealing song of op. 27. Stephen Walsh (p. 28) also offers *Jasminenstrauch* high praise:

> "Jasminenstrauch," inexplicably left out of *Myrten*, is another example of Schumann's genius for catching the essence of a poetic idea and crystallizing it in a few seconds of unforgettable music. In this case the music is purely de-scriptive, but the style—folk-tune, aerial semiquaver accompaniment, and elu-sive chromatic harmonies—contains everything Schumann later required for the deeper insights of *Dichterliebe*.

Although Walsh rightly identifies several Schumann compositional earmarks found in this Lied, it is not clear that *Jasminenstrauch* contains everything that ennabled the composer to achieve the unique *Dichterliebe*, a cycle largely dis-tinguished by its lyric-declamatory style.

Nur ein lächelnder Blick, #5, to a poem by Georg Wilhelm Zimmermann, is something of an anomaly. It feels out of step with the poetry, and its final liturgi-cal cadence seems questionably appended. One feels this Lied could have been written by a number of creators of tuneful melodies and grateful pianism. Yet Fischer-Dieskau, while suspecting (as does Sams, p. 164) that the composer was making use of material originally intended for solo pianoforte, comments (p. 105):

> Schumann found a felicitous solution to a problem that must have seemed dif-ficult at the time: to set to music a text employing both hexameter and pen-

tameter. We are here witnessing a new esthetic of song writing; the delicate emotions of the text are convincingly expressed. The music readily shows that the vocal line, rising chromatically, is not self-sufficient. Without the underlying harmonies it is meaningless; it can be understood only as forming part of the sequentially rising seventh-chords that extend and enhance the emotional meaning.

Further, Fischer-Dieskau finds similarities in the shaping of melodic lines, in harmonic choices, in phrasing, and in underlying rhythms between *Nur ein lächelnder Blick* and the first movement of Beethoven's Sonata op. 101. Sams (p. 164) believes Schumann here was under the influence of Mendelssohn and that, in turn, the last page of Brahms's *Auf dem See*, op. 106, #2, owes much to several bars of *Nur ein lächelnder Blick*. The saccharine text induced a musical setting that exudes sweetness, giving *Nur ein lächelnder Blick* a pleasant old-fashioned flavor. Because of its easy vocalism and its swinging pianism, the song proves especially useful in the studio. Should it be included within a group of outstanding Schumann Lieder? Probably.

Opus 30

Opus 30, *Drei Gedichte*, dating from the 1840 Lieder Year, seldom pleases academic Lied evaluators, who fret over its improper poetic scanning and absence of lyric declamation. A closer look is in order. Emanuel Geibel's *Der Knabe mit dem Wunderhorn*, #1 (the title comes from the *Des Knaben Wunderhorn* folk-poetry collection edited by Ludwig Achim von Arnim and Clemens von Brentano), speaks in direct and expressive spirit, with its *lebhaft, rasch* tempo. Yet the vocal requirements include an extensive range and vital sound far exceeding the folk-tune frame. This is a bravura Lied, with ballad-like components. The singer (of either gender) must give a convincing masculine expression. Vivid portrayal of the bounding horse should come from both voice and keyboard. An opening horn-call motif is reiterated. There are many examples in the Schumann Lieder—in this instance, a prancing steed and a sounding horn—to illustrate Schumann's use of literal imitative musical figures; it is perplexing to read repeated critical commentary about the composer's avoidance of descriptive writing. In accordance with the forthrightness of the text, Florestan is in full command; there is no introspection, no Eusebian psychological probing.

At the risk of stating the obvious, it can be mentioned that the phrases of *Der Knabe mit dem Wunderhorn* and much of *Der Page*, #2, demonstrate Schumann's fixation on a recurring melodic conglomerate that hovers around the pitch B. The opening vocal lines of these first two of the three Geibel songs begin with similar notes and similar intervallic leaps. The $\frac{6}{8}$ rhythms and their angularity also bind the two Lieder as a unit. In *Der Page*, the singer's assignment is to proceed in narrative fashion, like a balladeer; the pianist's role is largely secondary. An exuberant spirit must permeate both songs.

Another far departure from Schumann's lyric declamation is *Der Hidalgo*, #3, a song that requires as much vocal prowess as many operatic arias. Exactly because the *Drei Gedichte* of Geibel go beyond the narrow confines imposed by adherence to a *musica/parola* synthesis doctrine (on many occasions Schumann's aim, but not here), these songs (particularly #1 and #3) are excellent for technically secure singers and pianists. In support of the argument that Schumann had skillful performers in mind, we recall that he frequently attended concerts presented by the chief professional singers of his day. He did not write his songs in an aesthetic Lieder vacuum. For a significant part of Schumann's song output, an intimate salon genre was not intended. (The parlor Lied had already begun to disappear during Schubert's lifetime. Schubert himself happily accompanied the noted opera singer Vogl.) Public recital appearances of leading professional singers of the day regularly took place. Some of the Schumann Lieder preserve an intimate chamber quality about them, but frequently they were conceived for concert-hall listening, not just for living-room performance.

When Schumann turns to Spanish themes, he finds the right mode in appropriate bolero rhythm and instrumental strumming. *Der Hidalgo* is full of humor, splash, and, above all, bravura. Sams (p. 158) refers to it as "this most brilliantly original love song." The operatic tenor need search no further for a dashing vehicle that offers vocal challenge and affords fruitful possibilities for the display of professional timbre and technical control. Ascending vocal lines explode with energy, fully supported by instrumental scoring in the keyboard (bars 75–90). It is hard to find any Lied that brings more joy to audiences and performers (Ex. 14.1).

Opus 31

Opus 31 is a group of songs from 1840 sometimes judged to be below the level of other Lieder from the "Clara Year." *Die Löwenbraut*, #1, begins with an arresting octave keyboard motif that describes the dignified pacing of the caged lion. It is followed by a quasi recitative as the young woman enters the cage. Interest continues to be held by a ballad-like excursion, but a problem arises at the *etwas langsamer*. One has the feeling the composer relies on an underlying unobtrusive accompaniment to get on with storytelling, accomplished for several pages at slow pace. It has been suggested that the less-than-stellar quality of the Chamisso poetry excuses Schumann from taking more care. However, such a gory plot can properly be treated only as a subject for high drama, something Schumann avoids until he reaches the moment of leonine rage at "er im Zorn den Ausgang wehrt." His continuing solution consists of heavy chromatic chords that the pianist should deliver with abandon.

Unfortunately, the vocal writing, limited to lower-middle range, is no match for what occurs in the keyboard. A distinct vocal climax is lacking, as though understatement were necessary to the narrative style. A singer will need to help the composer by underscoring the heightened dramatic moments, and the pianist will have to exercise restraint in those sections where

Example 14.1.   *Der Hidalgo*, bars 75–90.

the vocal tessitura is low and the keyboard is aggressive. Large voices are most successful with these songs. A solid baritone voice of good size and facility or a sturdy tenor voice might best promote this interesting but somewhat flawed Lied. Given the wonderful reservoir of Schumann Lieder available to performers, is this Lied worth programming? Yes. But *Die Löwenbraut* may be best included in a group of ballads.

Schumann's setting of the second Chamisso poem, *Die Kartenlegerin* (based on Béranger's *Les Cartes, ou l'Horoscope*), is much more successful. Its parlando-like vocalism (Fischer-Dieskau [p. 93] calls it "subtle nuances of declamation") is here particularly suited to the timbre of the mezzo-soprano voice. The keyboard motif in the opening measures depicts the flicking of cards. It occurs four times, with intriguing variations, as at bars 116–27 (Ex. 14.2).

Moore (pp. 141–42) finds *Die Kartenlegerin* "one of our composer's happiest compositions . . . almost every bar provides a descriptive commentary on the girl's emotions." Sams (p. 141) considers it "a wholly novel contribution to songwriting." A direct ballad style must be employed. Yet a skillful singer will not entirely sacrifice vocalism for parlando narration. The pianist must play the thirty-second-note motif of the flicking cards with snappy articulation.

The last song of this Chamisso set, *Die Rote Hanne*, #3, although notated in treble clef, is designated "für eine Bassstimme," with optional choral commentary. There is, from time to time, a quality about all three of these Lieder reminiscent of the eighteenth-century *Melodram* (recitation of a text over descriptive music), attesting to the continuing influence of that dramatico/musico form on the mid-nineteenth-century Lied. The Chamisso verses (all based on Béranger's *Jeanne la Rousse, ou la Femme du Braconnier*) seem not to have inspired Schumann to his highest level.

Schumann's answer to plots of this sort is to take the quasi-recitativo route, resulting in somewhat pedestrian vocal settings. It is evident that Schumann is unequal to Schubert in managing long sectional narrative scenes. This may also be the reason that Schumann has been considered a less successful ballad composer than Loewe. Nor is Schumann always able to match Wolf's ability to make outstanding musical drama from small poetic forms. Most of Schumann's outstanding ballads are set to tight, nonrambling poetic structures.

Once more, the favorite lower-middle keyboard octave brings solemn sonority. Schumann skillfully sketches the characters of the novice and the man who loves her and loses her. Repetitions of the passacaglia pattern in the inner voices, for the purpose of motion, seem nearly endless. Over this figure the voice must maintain an unalterable legato. Because of its *chor ad libitum*, *Die rote Hanne* might prove of value to the choral conductor in search of a performance occasion for a strong male solo voice in the ensemble.

Since the inherent musical value of these Lieder is not at Schumann's most

Example 14.2.   *Die Kartenlegerin*, bars 116–127.

compelling level, singer and pianist must make a strong character portrayal for each of the protagonists of the three Chamisso poems.

Opus 49

Die beiden Grenadiere, #1, op. 49, is deservedly one of the most beloved of all ballads. Heine's narrative is first-rate dramatic material, and Schumann's reaction is equal to it. The opening march is strong and compelling. Its distinctive rhythms, including the dotted-quarter/sixteenth groups, the four sixteenth-note *gruppetti*, and the descending quarter notes in octaves, produce a masculine, military air with a Florestan boldness seldom so consistently maintained during an entire Lied. The bars of half notes that move the recitative-like passages forward bring additional rhythmic interest without losing the squareness of the march. Touches of genial imagination are everywhere apparent.

Eight bars of triplet movement in the middle section provide a sense of desperate urgency. This is further heightened by the offbeat right-hand eighth notes over a legato bass-clef ostinato figure. The revolutionary *Marseillaise* breaks out as a natural evolution of the foregoing materials. Its integration into the previous rhythmic and melodic keyboard motifs is stunning. As he does frequently in the ballads, the composer closes with a brief chordal commentary, eschewing his tendency in more intimate literature to develop an introspective pianistic transformation of themes encountered earlier.

Die beiden Grenadiere is so sturdily constructed and emotively written that even a weak performance can hardly diminish its impact. Characterization of the two soldiers must be clearly differentiated. Blind adoration of the emperor can be expressed through vocal grandeur. References to wife and child must contain manly pathos; the threatened resurrection from the grave needs to sound insanely victorious. The pianoforte should resound forcefully and unhurriedly on each rhythmic pattern.

This engaging ballad has a wide range of emotions, and it requires a commensurate range of dynamic and timbre intensities from both instruments. It is ideally suited to mature male voices, but young tenors and baritones fall in love with it. Its very directness is often of pedagogical value in assisting a young male singer to find the proper balance between energization and vocal freedom.

Die feindlichen Brüder, #2 of op. 49, cannot be awarded the same kudos as *Die beiden Grenadiere* but is still a worthwhile ballad. It is unfortunate that the two Lieder are not programmed together more often. Sams finds Heine less successful here than in his treatment of other myths and he judges Schumann's setting to be stilted (p. 91). On the contrary, there is about *Die feindlichen Brüder* a forthrightness and a verve that make it ideal for the young voice of good proportions. It is a splendid "teaching" exercise. Aside from the subdued sarcasm that remains challenging, a vigorous singer will be able to manage the grateful lines successfully. The song serves well in a group that includes *Belsatzar* and the Andersen ballads from op. 40.

Die Nonne, #3, op. 49, to a poem by Abraham Fröhlich, was composed in

November of 1840. Schumann achieves a fitting ambience for the nun in the convent garden through an eight-bar hymnlike motif in D♭ major that is picked up by the singing voice for a subsequent eight bars. This theme could well be adapted to organ.

Suddenly one jumps from the legato solemnity of D♭ major to a bright E major through a bridge of four bars in march-like staccato that decisively departs from the convent-chapel organ harmonies. This radical change compares the happiness of the bride at the wedding festivities with the unhappiness of the other young woman in the convent garden. From nearby comes a wedding party, a topic much in Schumann's thoughts during the "Clara Year," and he writes a wedding march for the occasion. Poetry concerning marriage and the sorrow of those denied the marital state always intrigued Schumann. There is a relationship between *Die Nonne* and *Stirb, Lieb und Freud!*, #2 of op. 35, although the latter is the more successful of the two.

In *Die Nonne*, performers must make much of the difference between nun and bride by using darker coloration for the nun and brighter timbre for the bride. This can be done by the singer without altering basic vocal production, simply by lowering or raising upper harmonic partials (overtones) and adhering to the dynamic-intensity indications. The contrast of legato and staccato and the shift in keyboard octaves give the pianist similar color possibilities.

15

Opus 127 and Opus 142

As mentioned earlier, it is a mistake to assume that high opus numbers indicate late composition dates. Some songs written in 1840 bear late opus numbers. Among these are four Lieder originally intended for inclusion in *Dichterliebe*: *Dein Angesicht* and *Es leuchtet meine Liebe*, now located in op. 127, and *Lehn' deine Wang' an meine Wang'* and *Mein Wagen rollet langsam*, now located in op. 142.

With the exception of *Mein altes Ross* (1850), the *Fünf Lieder und Gesänge*, op. 127, were written in 1840 but published in 1854. Opus 127 includes *Sängers Trost* (1840), *Dein Angesicht, so lieb und schön* (1840), *Es leuchtet meine Liebe* (1840), *Mein altes Ross* (1850), and *Schlusslied des Narren* (1840). Published in 1858, *Vier Gesänge*, op. 142, includes *Trost im Gesang* (1840), *Lehn' deine Wang' an meine Wang'* (1840), *Mädchen-Schwermut* (1840), and *Mein Wagen rollet langsam* (1840).

Opus 127

Sängers Trost, op. 127, #1, in contrast to most of *Dichterliebe* and many other 1840 Lieder, allows the singer to display vocalism in its purest form. A singer steeped in nineteenth-century Lieder and not familiar with the authorship of

Sängers Trost might logically attribute it to Mendelssohn (as is also true of several other conventional Lieder from Schumann's hand). The melody is gracious and eminently singable. The pianoforte score has an etudelike character yet remains incomplete without the melody that unfolds above it. This is a sumptuous, sensual setting of Kerner's poem. Unlike a number of Schumann songs that raise questions as to which vocal category is intended, *Sängers Trost* lies favorably in upper-middle range for soprano or tenor voices, maintaining a comfortable *tessitura*.

The vocal climax (the lower *ossia* notes are not desirable) at "Stern und Mondenlicht" (bars 28–29) is further heightened by the underlying modulatory harmonies in the keyboard, which must be pointed up in support of the voice. From the pianoforte there ought to be steadiness in the arpeggiated ostinato that supports the vocal line, yet through dynamic variation the pianist should accomplish an improvisatory effect, as though the singer were accompanying him- or herself on the lute.

This is a wistful moonlit serenade. Schumann's vocally favorable melody evokes the lonely protagonist—forgotten by every living soul—whose songs will be remembered only by Nature. *Singing* is the composer's answer to the poet's melancholy and introspection. Because the compositional style is unlike that of the better-known Schumann Lieder of 1840, one suspects that if historical evidence as to the date of composition of *Sängers Trost* were uncertain, some critic would be certain to complain that it shows a lack of invention, caused by advancing mental illness. A parodistic analysis of some Schumann criticism could cite the reliance on a single Czernyesque rhythmic motif, traditional high lying vocal lines that do not offer synthesis of word and music, and unsuitable language accentuation.

Sängers Trost has little of the flavor of the much-loved cycles of 1840 but nonetheless has great merit. Disparity in style is probably the reason the composer chose not to publish *Sängers Trost* with songs of the then-prevailing Schumann compositional mode. Its bel canto line wings gracefully. The climactic vocalism of bars 28–29 is underpinned by a significant tonality change to D♭ major. The tessitura is vocally demanding. Beauty of vocal sound, richness of the warm lower-middle keyboard octave, elegant phrase shaping that follows melodic contour, and an increase in rising emotion are performance requirements. A gentle Lied, lovely to sing and play, *Sängers Trost* unfortunately is neglected.

In *Dein Angesicht, so lieb und schön,* op. 127, #2, the right-hand sixteenth notes over sustained bass-clef harmonies must be played sonorously, assisted by judicious use of the sostenuto pedal. Congenial motion in the pianoforte supplies an underlying phrase pointing for the vocal line as it moves upward from the single-tone opening to "so lieb und schön" and as it descends to the region of the favorite melodic nucleus (D–C–B♭–A) that germinates so much of *Dichterliebe,* from which *Dein Angesicht, so lieb und schön* was removed (Ex. 15.1). Rolled three-voiced dominant seventh-chord harmony in bar 4, while underscoring the change of phrase direction, reminds us that when Schumann wants a partially rolled chord, he *writes* it (also the case in bar 8).

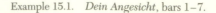

Example 15.1.   *Dein Angesicht*, bars 1–7.

That rolled right-hand chord should be executed with an almost imperceptible tenuto. The same pianistic emphasizing of harmonic change is indicated through a more widely distributed harmonic roll at "Erlöschen" (bar 14), following the ritardando of bar 13. The seventh-chord harmonies at the beginning of bar 8, with recurrences through bar 17, lead to evocative moments. Schumann's use of alto and tenor keyboard voices in sixteenth-note *gruppetti*, for momentary modulatory tonal excursion, catches the pathos and sentiment of Heine's verse. The ascending vocal line and the increasing keyboard sonorities produce an agonizing expression that justifies any tendency on the part of the composer toward Romantic excess. *Dein Angesicht, so lieb und schön* is a clear-cut example of mid-nineteenth-century emotive Romantic song literature.

The return to original melodic material at bar 18 and the subsequent harmonic and melodic adjustments for the conclusion bring cohesion: textual and musical synthesis. It is exactly this form of synthesis (not primarily based on lyric declamation but on equality of voice, keyboard, poetry, and musical construction) that is overlooked in many critical analyses of Schumann's song-writing. While understanding Schumann's decision to omit *Dein Angesicht, so lieb und schön* from the Heine cycle, one regrets that this Lied is thereby denied the frequent performance opportunities it richly deserves.

The singer must bind one syllable to the next and dynamically shape each phrase according to its rising and falling contours. The ritardandos ought to be fully realized. Schumann does not indicate when *a tempo* should be resumed, but the harmonic language (bar 12) makes that obvious. At "und nur die Lippen, die sind rot," the singer must prepare for Heine's typical tragic interpolation ("bald aber küsst sie bleich der Tod") through intensification of the legato, especially on "Tod." The tragic phrase itself should be unrushed, so that the underlying harmonic deviation that leads to "der Tod" can be properly savored. Modulations fit exactly the changes of poetic mood. The postlude, in its harmonic development, is skillful commentary on the concluding poetic sentiment "doch so bleich, so schmerzenreich." These final six bars should be played warmly and deliberately.

It is difficult to imagine a more appropriate musical reaction to Heine's prose than that represented in *Dein Angesicht, so lieb und schön*. Sams (p. 125) assesses the final page otherwise: "The last page, down to the unctuous final chords, wears an uncomfortable air of formal mourning apparel." Most performers will not agree with that assessment.

Es leuchtet meine Liebe, #3 of op. 127, creates a world of fantasy wherein Florestan loses all inhibition. This is the sort of Schumann Lied that remains incomprehensible to listeners who have an affinity with only the diminutive Eusebius blossom and are offended by the rampantly growing Florestan bush. What an interesting anomaly would have been created had Schumann incorporated *Es leuchtet meine Liebe* into *Dichterliebe*! If it had followed *Am leuchtenden Sommermorgen*, #12 of *Dichterliebe*, as was the original plan, its impact would have been overpowering; its presence would have changed the nature of the entire cycle, perhaps jangling the ear even more than would have the inclusion of *Mein Wagen rollet langsam*, which was to have followed it.

Joan Chissell (p. 185) finds, as does Sams (p. 126), that material from *Es leuchtet meine Liebe* will reappear in 1842 in the scherzo movement of the Schumann Quartet in A minor, op. 41, #1. Fischer-Dieskau (p. 86) agrees that *Es leuchtet meine Liebe* bears "many similarities to the string quartet in A minor." He considers the song "an exciting and ingenious reflection on Schumann's experience of deprivations" and believes it to be autobiographical, with Wieck the giant, Clara the virgin, and Robert the bleeding knight.

The pianistic energy exhibited in the opening bars of *Es leuchtet meine Liebe* never ceases. This animation is matched by the exciting long vocal lines with relatively high tessitura. Both singer and pianist must deliver sufficient sound to adequately meet the poem's enigmatic but sinister depiction. If ever a pianist needed to pound chromatic octaves, it is in this Lied, beginning at bar 20. (It could, particularly from bar 30 onward, serve as an excellent technical study in chromatic octave doubling.) The seventh-chord harmonies particularly require strong keyboard pummeling. The conclusion is not merely a Lied postlude; it is a frenzied pianistic etude. Regarding the postlude, Moore (p. 231) comments:

> It remains, however, for the pianist to draw the curtain which he does in a succession of wailing chromatic octave passages—noxious winds blowing over the prostrate knight. Horror is made apparent in the surging rise and whimpering fall; the *crescendo* and *diminuendo* cannot be overdone, nor can the terror of it be held in check. From [bar] 30 an *accelerando* begins and its momentum [is] maintained until the penultimate bar of the postlude.

Moore assesses *Es leuchtet meine Liebe* as a capital song for a fine singer and fine pianist. Sams (p. 126) is far less pleased: "The accompaniment goes crashing off in triumph while the voice dies in despair. But just as in other Heine songs, the music seems too innocent and innocuous to make its intended effect."

Es leuchtet meine Liebe is pianistically (even orchestrally) conceived; there is a certain bitterness and an inexorable, tornado-like thundering in the keyboard. The harmonic language, with its diminished sevenths, adds to the driving full-chorded keyboard sonority. Such drama must be matched by vocalization that competes with the orchestral sound level of the pianoforte. The challenging vocal line is not bound by the same aesthetic that produced most of the popular songs of 1840.

The singer must deliver sturdy vocalism to match the high degree of pianistic energy, not by being excessively loud but by producing a suitably full sound. An operatic voice could find this song a happy solution to Lieder programming, in preference to pulling out *Ich grolle nicht* one more time. It is not amiss, despite its early composition date, to program *Es leuchtet meine Liebe* with late dramatic Schumann Lieder.

Partly because it is not typical of Schumann's lyricism, *Es leuchtet meine Liebe* is unduly neglected. Extensive association with the song increases admiration for a composer who so successfully amalgamates pyrotechnical keyboard and vocal skills with the strong emotional content of the text. *Es leuchtet meine Liebe* is an excellent medium for singers and pianists who can combine the potential colors of both instruments. As an independent Lied it has much challenge for both performers. This is big, exciting Schumann, indicative of what was to come in his Lieder composed a decade later.

Just as Schumann's aim in 1849–52 was mostly to elevate poetry to a dramatic musical genre rather than to achieve lyric declamation and synthesis, so it was in 1840 with *Es leuchtet meine Liebe*. This makes questionable the oft-repeated notion that the reason the late songs do not sound like those of 1840 is that Schumann had lost his ability to achieve lyric declamation. As is evident here, in his earlier as well as in his later productive periods Schumann called on a variety of techniques for Lieder construction.

Mein altes Ross, a poem by Count Moritz of Strachwitz, who died at age twenty-five in 1847, was well suited to the kind of energetic, masculine-oriented expression Schumann turned to in later years. The song, #4, was composed in 1850. Schumann uses two basic means for portraying the male rider: an angular chordal motif and a dotted-eighth/sixteenth motif, the latter signifying the old horse's hooves as he charges ahead. Considering *Mein altes Ross* and many other Lieder of the late period that reveal artistic athleticism, one questions the oft-repeated critical judgment that weariness, weakness, and decline are characteristic. In the instance of *Mein altes Ross*, even Sams (p. 250) modifies the negative criticism he usually directs to Lieder of this period:

> Thoughts of that lost youth [Strachwitz's], and of Schumann's own, converge in a stronger current of music than any other of the 1850 songs. The opening strains are Schubertian in their guilelessness and their response to the words.

The first page is all resignation. Then as recollection becomes livelier a rider's memory dominates the song. . . . The harmony halts on a dominant; and now the hoofbeats change imperceptibly into a knell tolling for a young love and a young life.

While sharing Sams's approval of *Mein altes Ross,* this writer has difficulty identifying a stronger current in it than in any other song of 1850. One might even choose to question whether its two central motifs form an ideal compositional whole. The song is, however, a superb performance medium for a male voice of virile resonance and sizable proportions. The pianist who enjoys collaborating with singers on instrumentally conceived Lieder should find happiness here.

A translation of verses 1, 3, and 5 of the clown's song that closes Shakespeare's "Twelfth Night" is the text for *Schlusslied des Narren,* #5, which was composed in February 1840. Its brevity and its being tucked away in op. 127 tend to invite neglect of this delightful Lied. The song is of more than passing interest as an example of the diversity to be found in the early Lieder, and as a prediction of the bold explorer Schumann would become. Sams (p. 33) raises an interesting question: "Can it be just coincidence that the opening figure and recurring melody echo Mendelssohn's *Midsummer Night's Dream Overture,* also about a Shakespeare clown, while the two composers had met the evening before this song was written?" Sams's detection seems well on target.

What do we do with these two pages? With what other Lieder can the song be associated? *Schlusslied des Narren* makes a splendid concluding song for a set of Schumann miniatures, where it will not be lost because of its brevity and will lend a touch of lightheartedness. Further, although the suggestion may be a bit pat, what more delightful way to conclude a group of intimate Lieder than with the German translation of Shakespeare's original "But that's all one, our play is done; and we'll strive to please you every day"?

Opus 142

Trost im Gesang, op. 142, #1, was composed in 1840. Like the text of *Sängers Trost,* that of *Trost im Gesang* comes from the pen of Kerner. Clara Schumann considered the Lied "magnificent." Sams (pp. 177–78) draws a different conclusion: "The poem's pedestrian metaphor deserves a similar setting. In the result the music is unconvincing; it conveys not so much a real comfort, as a resolve to march up and down and sing to show that it is not afraid. But fine interpretation can make it most moving."

An objective evaluation may lie somewhere between the assessments of Clara Schumann and Eric Sams. The construction is intentionally conventional, but *Trost im Gesang* should be sung and played without bravura. The marking is *durchaus leise, doch nicht langsam.* This song does not deserve a place among the greatest Schumann Lieder, but it is not pedestrian just because it marches along in very un-Eusebian fashion. The almost martial character seems to take its initiative from "Er schreitet mutig weiter die menschenleere Bahn" and, later, from "Doch geh ich mutig weiter die menschenleere Bahn." The song should be felt rhythmically in a moderate 2 rather than in 4 and must be sung lightly, despite the marching impulse.

Fischer-Dieskau (p. 108) suggests that the Kerner songs form a performance unity. Although *Trost im Gesang* might not be entirely at home in the published Kerner group of twelve songs, it does not seem out of place among the late opus numbers. One finds certain similarities between *Trost im Gesang* and some late Lieder in conservative style; it could easily have come from 1850.

In bars 1–4, an alert in the pianoforte is sounded through a dotted rhythmic pattern built on octaves followed by somber scale passages also doubled at the octave. The voice enters with a chorale-like melody. A straightforward quality catches the meaning of the verse admirably. A plodding character to the octave motif is relieved by the insertion of the static chords (resurfacing in bar 34) that first appeared in bars 9–11. Careful attention to the indicated wide range of dynamics helps bring off the song.

Lehn' deine Wang' an meine Wang', #2 of op. 142, comes from a remarkably creative week in May 1840. It and its companion Heine Lied, *Dein Angesicht, so lieb und schön*, were subsequently omitted from *Dichterliebe*. The triplet keyboard figure was probably introduced to offer relief from other pianistic configurations within the original cycle sequence. The Lied's brevity (to be performed *schnell, leidenschaftlich*) and its concluding bars suggest that it was meant to fit with something yet to follow. For those reasons, *Lehn' deine Wang' an meine Wang'* stands with difficulty on its own two feet, despite its exuberant charm. Had it been included in *Dichterliebe*, its vocal mounting to high Ab could have strenuously competed with and diminished the effect of other climaxes in the cycle. *Lehn' deine Wang' an meine Wang'* and the other omitted Lieder would have disturbed the compactness that characterizes *Dichterliebe*. (*Lehn' deine Wang' an meine Wang'* was to follow the purged *Dein Angesicht, so lieb und schön*, the two Lieder then to be inserted between *Wenn ich in deine Augen seh'* and *Ich will meine Seele tauchen*. *Lehn' deine Wang' an meine Wang'* would thus have introduced a climactic vocal event at the wrong moment, disrupting the overall unity of *Dichterliebe*.)

The emphatic "und an mein Herz drück fest dein Herz, dann schlagen zusammen die Flammen" (beginning at bar 9) must be sumptuously sung and crisply played. During the sustained high Ab, full attention should be given to the ritardando. Immediately after this passionate expression, Florestan withdraws and Eusebius enters, perhaps to accommodate death in the bliss of love. A wide range of dynamics as well as of emotions takes place within such a brief period of time that we are left feeling that the song would be more effective as part of a larger whole, as originally conceived. The same melodic compactness that prevails in many *Dichterliebe* Lieder is apparent in *Lehn' deine Wang' an meine Wang'*. Performers should take seriously the "passionately" marking and not slow down to make a long song out of a brief one. Schumann indicates that the song begins at a *f* dynamic level, which develops into a prolonged crescendo. The Lied is to be sung and played with impatience and a rush to conclusion. An inherent danger is for the singer to bring sweet sentimentality to its performance; *Lehn' deine Wang' an meine Wang'* must be vigorously sung. Any thought of reincorporating it into *Dichterliebe* should be abandoned.

Op. 142, #3, *Mädchen-Schwermut,* is set to verse by an unknown poet, who may have been Clara's friend Lily Bernhard. Despite the disparate poetic sources, the publisher later inserted *Mädchen-Schwermut* in op. 142 between *Lehn' deine Wang' an meine Wang'* and *Mein Wagen rollet langsam.* The only plausible connecting link among the songs is that *Mädchen-Schwermut* comes from 1840.

Mädchen-Schwermut is at least the equal of several 1840 Lieder published during Schumann's lifetime, but it is not among his greatest. The keyboard begins in plaintive three-part harmony, the two lower pianistic voices stepping downward in sorrowful semitones. The harmonic compactness and the limited melodic excursion are clearly meant to ask: "Little drops, are you tears on the flower cup?" This use of close intervals as a motivic principle also frequently indicates smallness in the Lieder of Hugo Wolf and is an example of one of several influences of Schumann on Wolf. The sudden appearance of a widely swinging arpeggiated keyboard figure comes as something of a shock, even though it does prepare for the emotional and musical climax on "Sternlein in dem Himmelszelt!" An abrupt return to the "klein" motif causes disjunction. Do the pianoforte's final four bars (including the ascending scale) seem somewhat ill at ease?

Mein Wagen rollet langsam, op. 142, #4, was also meant to find a home in *Dichterliebe,* together with *Es leuchtet meine Liebe,* between *Am leuchtenden Sommermorgen* and *Ich hab' im Traum geweinet,* as mentioned previously. On one hand, we should be happy that Schumann and his publisher made the decision to eliminate all of them from the cycle. On the other hand, the charge of bordering on sentimentality sometimes leveled at *Dichterliebe* might have been mitigated had Schumann included them. The omitted Lieder also pose questions regarding their relationship to the cycle's tonality structure. Was Schumann's decision to exclude them related to that schema? (See Komar on the *Dichterliebe* key relationships, pp. 63–94.)

Mein Wagen rollet langsam carries an odd notation from the composer: "after the meaning of the poem." This remark has been seen as a conscious admission by Schumann that he was not completely certain of Heine's intention and that he was requesting the singer and the pianist to bring their own imaginative interpretations to the setting. Sams (p. 127) goes so far as to suggest that Schumann "proceeds to repeat the poem arbitrarily, misquote it senselessly, and, to judge from the curiously innocent music, misunderstand it completely. At the same time he feels and expresses a part of the poem's essential content with consummate insight and mastery."

Whatever the intrinsic meaning of the text, journeying slowly through pleasant green woodlands and blossom-filled sunlit valleys is juxtaposed with disquieting introspective thoughts of the beloved. The lurching motion of the carriage is established at once. As the rider sits and dreams, Schumann introduces staccato chords (bars 17–23) in the pianoforte to lend support to the short interjectory phrases in imitation of speech that break up the vocal line. At the entrance of

the three sinister figures, the voice grows more agitated, with brief spurting ut-
terances. As the three mysterious forms hop, mock, and whirl, the pianoforte
and the voice (bars 35–46) take on an even more marked recitative-like aspect.
Schumann relies first on vocal lyricism and legato, then on melodic interjections
and lower-register keyboard staccatos. The three shadowy figures who invade
the carriage must be starkly characterized by a decisive change from the vocal
timbre with which the Lied began. The close-intervalled interpolated phrases
should be delivered at *pp* dynamic, perhaps with an admixture of breathiness
and with diminished vocal resonance. The pianist will need to replace the earlier flowing legato with dry, short, percussive *pp* chords. Moore (p. x) makes interesting comparisons between Schumann's setting of the poem and that of
Richard Strauss in *Waldesfahrt*, op. 69, #4, which uses the same text:

> [*Mein Wagen rollet langsam*] has a languid and graceful movement, soothing to
> the somnolent passenger, who becomes absorbed in tender thoughts of his in-
> amorata; without warning, three ghosts appear at the carriage window, float in,
> mocking, gibbering and grimacing. Do they frighten the day-dreamer or dis-
> turb his train of thought? Not in the slightest degree. Richard Strauss sets the
> same verses . . . and the spectres he elicits, hopping, floating, skipping for three
> pages of pianistic pyrotechnics, do most decidedly startle their victim and inci-
> dentally scare the living daylights out of the pianist.

In Schumann's setting, the two thematic elements devoted to quietude and tur-
bulence are metamorphosed into a lengthy epilogue. The pleasant movement
of the carriage passing through a serene landscape and the sudden disturbing
figures (representing evil thoughts?) are caught in the confluence of rhythmic
motifs.

There is an enigmatic aura about *Mein Wagen rollet langsam* that makes
one seriously question the comment that Schumann misunderstood it completely. The music is *not* "curiously innocent" (Sams, p. 127): it is alluringly subtle. Performers must play up the contrast between "all is well" and "but something is wrong" that makes both the poem and the musical setting so intriguing.

Mein Wagen rollet langsam is a topflight Lied that is unfortunately neglected, partly because of Schumann's decision to omit it from *Dichterliebe* and
partly because of its having been placed in a late opus number. As has been
seen, the chief complaint against it is that it is so pianistically oriented that it
does not remain within the confines of the classic Lied. Must Lied composers
always embrace the Goethean dictum that music is but a frame to poetry?
Schumann's attitude in this regard was manifestly not Goethean, nor were his
aesthetic principles based on a single compositional mode. The contrasting figurations in *Mein Wagen rollet langsam* are in keeping with its poetic source.

If one insists on the narrow view that Schumann was committed to avoiding
the use of mechanical figures for musical representation then one cannot justify
the pianism of *Mein Wagen rollet langsam*. Once that barrier is surmounted, this
Lied can be appreciated for what it is: musical representation of events described in a poetic narrative.

Schumann, one of the most sophisticated of the great Lied composers, was familiar with traditional assumptions as to what constituted a proper Lied, and at times he knowingly rejected those concepts. As has been stressed repeatedly, it was Schumann's specific intention to expand the boundaries of the Lied, as evidenced in this case.

Yet the genesis of *Mein Wagen rollet langsam* lies in a compositional model inherited from Franz Schubert: a mechanical keyboard figure that embodies the emotional content of the text. (The spinning wheel [*Gretchen am Spinnrade*] and the mechanism of the mill and the flow of the water [*Die schöne Müllerin*] are classic examples.) In this instance, the wheels of the carriage are set into motion through a tumbling-and-turning figure that falls through several half-hinted tonalities over a pedal point. (Brahms would later make use of these devices in his Lieder.) As well as describing the turning carriage wheels, the figure catches the romantic dreaming about the beloved. It should not be regretted that Schumann features the pianoforte here, nor can we unqualifiedly endorse Hallmark's comment (p. 98) in his 1979 study of *Dichterliebe* that "'Mein Wagen rollet langsam' is a piano piece with voice added." There is no reason that the composer, after reading the poetry, should *not* initially have sketched the pianistic motif over which to develop the vocal narrative. Mood evocation through pianistic means is plainly the composer's intention. Schumann, early in his career (and later as well), moves into territory extensively cultivated by Schubert.

Why should there be concern over the length of the postlude? It combines pianistic configurations with vocal interjections representative of speech, in a remarkable recalling of what has gone before. The lengthy keyboard commentary should be fully realized as a solo performance. This Lied does not belong in *Dichterliebe* but does have a place in the active repertoire of serious singers and pianoforte collaborators. Such a joy to play is this Lied that pianists welcome the work its preparation entails.

16

Opus 51

Opus 51, published in 1850, includes *Sehnsucht, Volksliedchen, Ich wandre nicht, Auf dem Rhein,* and *Liebeslied.* The first three songs were composed in 1840. It is not possible to definitively date the composition of *Auf dem Rhein,* but *Liebeslied* first appeared in 1850.

What a remarkably new kind of song was *Sehnsucht,* #1! In the following extract, Alfred Einstein (p. 187) had in mind Lieder exemplified by the final song of *Dichterliebe,* but his assessment is equally pertinent to songs such as *Sehnsucht,* in which Schumann introduces an expanded pianoforte idiom:

> It was highly important for Schumann the song composer that he already had in his background twenty-three piano works—a world of instrumental poetry and pianistic, virtuoso perfection and originality. From the beginning on, the piano, the "accompaniment," had to play a different role in his songs than it had done in Schubert's. In Schubert, an equilibrium prevails; in every gentle fluctuation of the balance, the word always leads, the piano subordinates itself. In Schumann, from the very beginning, the piano plays a new role: it is more refined in sonority, more cunning in technique, although it seems to be simple; to it falls the task of emphasizing "the finer traits of the poem," of creating transitions in the song-cycles, of rounding out a group of songs, of supplying a commentary in the prelude and particularly the postlude, of giving final impression to the sur-

plus feeling—in short, as Schumann himself has expressed it, of contributing to a more highly artistic and more profound kind of song.

Einstein's comments are always perspicacious. In his remark about the subordination of the pianoforte in Schubert, he may momentarily have excluded from consideration some of the pianistically conceived Schubert Lieder such as *Auf dem Wasser zu singen*, *Gruppe aus dem Tartarus*, and the two *Suleika* Lieder, to mention but a few familiar examples.

In the setting of Geibel's *Sehnsucht*, following an initial keyboard flourish in offbeat thirty-second notes in $\frac{12}{16}$ meter, the vocal melodies are literally lifted upward by means of the keyboard's agitated triplets in rich reiterated chordal patterns. The cumulative phrases given the singer demand rapid, silent breath renewals that must be executed without impeding the driving forward motion of the song. The motif of the postlude is a relative of material heard in the prelude. High pianistic skill and vocal prowess are demanded by this fascinating composition.

Tune detectives enjoy pointing out that the melody of the first phrase of *Volksliedchen*, #2, to poetry by Rückert, resembles many other opening phrases in Schumann Lieder. Suggested melodic relationships of *Volksliedchen* to *Schöne Wiege meiner Leiden* and *Widmung* (Sams, p. 82) are only superficial. Gaiety and unmitigated pleasure are accomplished by small, intimate strokes of pleasant construction. Simplicity of the staccatoed bass-clef melody, the introduction at bar 3 of a legato duet between right and left hands that brings contrast to the staccato figure, and the harmonic movement that points to the delightful figure of bars 8 and 9 (followed by a three-bar interlude) add up to pure joyfulness. Word inflection is a model of musical setting. Felicity reaches a high point, both melodically and vocally, at the concluding bars of the strophe, elevating this folklike Lied far beyond that genre and turning it into an example of grateful vocalism and pianism without loss of inherent simplicity.

Carl Christern's *Ich wandre nicht*, #3, set by Schumann in 1841, was published separately in 1843, again in 1844, then included in the 1850 op. 51. This is a charming song, its neglect difficult to understand. While retaining strophic directness, it has an engaging sense of happiness brought about through a descending keyboard chromatic figure in octaves and by an upward-swinging vocal line. Here Eusebius is completely shunned and Florestan given free rein. *Heiter* is the marking, and joyously played and sung it should be. The pianist needs to make distinct the alternation of the legato of the two opening bars and the semi-staccatos of the subsequent offbeat measures. The chromatic figure—now descending, now ascending—will be particularly effective if the performers carefully follow the crescendo-decrescendo markings. The lengthy note F for the voice is further sustained by a ritardando. Especially striking is the long crescendo on that note (bars 18–19), subsequently evolving into a decrescendo at high A with the word "die" ("die Heimat ist so schön!"). Mezza voce on the final two vocal bars is advised. These dynamic changes add zest and interest. The third strophe is varied. Its dynamic forward motion must never be lost. *Ich wandre nicht* should be sung and played exuberantly.

Auf dem Rhein, #4, is set to a poem by Immermann. Both Sams (p. 188) and Fischer-Dieskau (p. 187) suggest that the Lied portends Schumann's attempted suicide in the Rhine. Speculation regarding a pathological attraction to the Rhine on Schumann's part, based on his selection of this poem, would seem to be negated by the mood of his several other Rhine settings. Schumann's approach to the brief text is somber in mood, and its harmonic language is hymnlike. Low octaves suggest the water's depth. Both performers should achieve tenebrous sound commensurate with the poetry and the musical setting.

Liebeslied, #5, comes as something of a surprise. The text by Goethe is enigmatic, the words apparently representing a private code between lovers. Schumann is faulted by Sams (p. 231) for selecting these verses: "The words are of course gibberish, and hopelessly unsuitable as a song text; but they well illustrate Schumann's attitude to song-writing, and his obsessive love of mystification." *Liebeslied* is *not* illustrative of Schumann's general attitude toward the selection of poetic sources (nor is the poetry "gibberish"). Although the date 1850 is generally suggested, Sams (who with some frequency questions the date of composition for the late songs that he finds meritorious) suggests that the song probably was composed in 1840 as a kind of secret message between Clara and Robert—"a private communication in code."

Liebeslied is constructed with traditional vocal lyricism and idiomatic pianism in mind. Perhaps the uncertain meaning of the Goethe text—an expression of abstract love?—permitted Schumann greater concentration on musical rather than textual matters. In any event, *Liebeslied*, as is true of many late Lieder, can be sung and played with beauty of tone as its sole reason for being.

17

Opus 64

For those critics who hold that only the songs of the 1840 "Clara Year" are top-drawer Schumann, the Lieder of 1847 must be an anomaly. Sams (p. 189) finds that when Schumann resumes songwriting in 1847 his style has become more "objective." Fischer-Dieskau (p. 137) also identifies an objective character in *Die Soldatenbraut*, op. 64, #1, which he sees "revealed in its folk-like flavor." Hallmark (1996, p. 108) suggests that "what Fischer-Dieskau and others identify as greater objectivity in Schumann's later works" may be an economy of emotion, a quality of understatement. Donald Ivey, to the contrary, finds Schumann becoming "intensely subjective" (p. 198).

Die Soldatenbraut is a worthy song. The directness that distinguishes *Die Soldatenbraut* is equally present in *Wanderlied* and *Die beiden Grenadiere*. Like them, *Die Soldatenbraut* is basically diatonic in its harmonic structure, and its forthrightness is completely in keeping with Mörike's engaging poem. The marchlike beginning is, in spirit, understandably, not unlike the opening of *Die beiden Grenadiere*, inasmuch as both deal with military themes, although here treated in milder fashion. Mörike paints a sympathetic portrait of an unsophisticated young girl whose naive view of military life and of her lover's capabilities captivates us. Schumann finds the right tone for combining humor and sympathy.

The pianist must lightheartedly touch the short opening rhythmic figure that so aptly echoes the poet's underlying playfulness as he unfolds the young woman's vision of her soldier lover and her longing for him. (The term *Soldatenbraut* does not imply actual marriage but an amorous relationship.) In the opening vocal bars, the singer should not hesitate to emphasize the nearly audacious complaint of the soldier's sweetheart through exaggerated diction and syllabic articulation. As the girl's emotional intensity grows ("Für den König da liess' er sein Blut"), a more sustained vocal line becomes necessary. Pointing up semi-detached articulation and sostenuto will bring variety. Schumann heightens the simplicity of the young woman as she speaks of her lover, and at the same time the composer expresses the depth of feeling she experiences. Particularly in the A section, the folk elements of the poem and the musical setting itself demand a narrative style. In section B (*etwas langsamer*), an increase in the sostenuto of the vocal line requires the purest legato. The subsequently alternating octave sixteenth-note keyboard figure must have about it pertness and cheekiness.

Schumann's repetition of the first strophe rounds out this delightful vignette in traditional ABA form. The return to the A section can be expressed by more forceful treatment than was afforded the original statement, but a better effect is achieved by the opposite mode—treating its reappearance wistfully. This is justified by the nature of the four-bar ending in which Schumann has the young woman almost whisper her repeated "für mich aber ebenso gut!" When encountering the alternating octave sixteenth-note figure eight bars before the end the pianist must play without the previous sauciness, producing plaintive, sighing commentary instead. This Lied, indebted to both folksong and ballad, is first-rate Schumann. Most narrative Lieder are appropriate to both genders, but *Die Soldatenbraut* works best for the female vocalist.

In the same op. 64 is Schumann's setting of Mörike's *Das verlassene Mägdlein* (titled *Das verlassne Mägdelein* in the Peters edition), #2, which is generally overshadowed by Wolf's haunting treatment of the same poem in March 1888. Wolf, who was inclined not to compose Lieder to poetry he believed already effectively set, had this to say about his own version:

> On Saturday I wrote, without having intended to, a setting of *Das verlassene Mägdlein*, already set to heavenly music by Schumann. If I set it again, it was almost against my will. But perhaps just because I was suddenly caught up in the magic of this poem, the result was outstandingly good, and I think that my song can stand comparison with Schumann's. (Eric Sams, *The Songs of Hugo Wolf*, p. 44.)

Wolf's *Das verlassene Mägdlein* is far more frequently performed than is Schumann's. Unquestionably, the Wolf Lied has great appeal. However, the Schumann setting, in its own way, is equally remarkable.

The emotional detachment of Schumann's music mirrors the hopelessness and despair of the abandoned girl. He uses the inner voices of the keyboard (the melody is nearly always doubled by voice and the pianoforte soprano line) to bring out pain and weariness through chromatic harmonies that, although reminiscent of Bach chorales, extend far beyond them. The

Example 17.1. *Das verlassene Mägdlein*, bars 1–8.

choice of this chorale-like harmonic structure, so often in an earlier century associated with introspection and sorrow, evokes exactly the right setting for Mörike's moving poetry (Ex. 17.1).

The singer should use a somewhat detimbred vocal color without forsaking her legato. No emotion other than despair intrudes. (Wolf's maiden, in her emotional surge, is almost accusatory at "Plötzlich da kommt es mir, treuloser Knabe"; Schumann's maiden [bar 19] experiences total hopelessness, placing no blame.) It is left to the pianoforte to express the abandoned girl's inner turmoil through the weight of the descending chromatic bass and through the tortured harmonies that lie above it. Each passing tone of the keyboard reveals the extent of the interior pain that is monochromatically understated by the singing voice. Op. 64, #2, challenges the artistry of both performers.

There is no need to search for new objectivity in the Lieder of 1847 but rather to acknowledge that the powers of Robert Schumann in effectively setting diverse poetic materials remain undiminished. Nor should undue importance be given to any increase in outside influences (for example, a growing indebtedness to Bach, already evident in some of the earlier Lieder) as explanation for Schumann's unique treatment of this Mörike poem. The explanation is simpler: Robert Schumann subtly penetrated the poet's meaning and translated it into intimate pianistic and vocal terms.

Tragödie, #3, was written in 1841, when Schumann was still much drawn to the poetry of Heine. While the poetry of *Dichterliebe* sings for Schumann, the poetry of *Tragödie* does not. This may account for the curious manner in which

Schumann treats its three disparate sections. The most enthusiastic Schumann admirer may have difficulty determining the composer's intention in this grouping of three brief poems.

Part 1, "Entflieh mit mir," #1, with its *rasch und mit Feuer* marking, its high dynamic levels, its angular melodic line, and its mounting tessitura at climactic moments, calls for a dramatic singer. The Lied requires vigorous singing and blustering pianism.

The pianoforte becomes almost submissively pensive in part 2, "Es fiel ein Reif." This section of *Tragödie* exhibits folklike charm but cannot be considered inspired writing. Singer and pianist should deliver it without pretension. It might well be included in a group of folk-oriented Lieder, in which environment it might find a happier musical home than in its original place, but that would violate the poet's intention and Schumann's as well.

As for part 3, "Auf ihrem Grab da steht eine Linde," Schumann's purpose in setting the poem as a duet for tenor and soprano is not clear. First of all, the tessitura is high-lying for the tenor, while that of the soprano is low. Unless a *leggiero* tenor is given the task, it is doubtful that dynamic balance between the two voices could readily be achieved with a soprano of any *Fach*. Second, part 3 does not accord with the diverse vocal demands of part 1 and part 2. Third, there is the problem of how to program *Tragödie* in a recital situation. The duet seems less than compatible with Lieder from other opus numbers that include two or more solo voices. Imitative keyboard figures that move from right to left hand are of musical interest, but all in all, this is not a highly distinctive composition.

18

Opus 77

Opus 77 contains songs written in the years 1840 and 1850. *Der frohe Wanders-mann*, #1, comes from the Spring of 1840. It was originally intended as the first song of the Eichendorff *Liederkreis*, op. 39, but was wisely removed by Schumann from the 1850 edition. It is hard to understand how Schumann could have initially considered *Der frohe Wandersmann* appropriate to *Liederkreis*. The setting matches Eichendorff's boisterous expression but comes close to the banal. It goes beyond the confines of a folk song and should be sung and played in exuberant fashion.

Mein Garten, #2, is a charming little song (to an August Hoffmann von Fallersleben poem) that some critics find derivative of other sources, including Schumann himself. Both Sams (p. 245) and Fischer-Dieskau (p. 179) mention an affinity with or similarity to Chopin's G minor Nocturne, op. 37, #1, which was published in June 1840. Sams concludes that "this is a piano piece from 1840 or earlier, perhaps part of some Chopin variations, refurbished to make a song in a barren period." In addition, because the "Ob die heimisch ist hie-nieden" phrase makes use of a series of notes found at "Nimm Sie hin denn diese Lieder" from Beethoven's *An die ferne Geliebte*, both Fischer-Dieskau and Sams consider it a deliberate quotation. Walsh (p. 91) expresses the following reservations about *Mein Garten* :

149

The sententious point of the verse is in the composer's mind from the start, hence the self-conscious solemnity of the music, its surprising failure to paint the scene, and the otherwise inexplicable move to F major (from A minor) at the saddest part of the poem—"only the flower of happiness will you *not* find in my garden."

The practical performer will discover that the means for expressing gentleness, linear vocalism, elegant phrase termination, and directness of emotion are inherently present in *Mein Garten*. It is, in fact, a sweet Schumann Lied at about the same level of merit as many another sweet Schumann song.

Geisternähe, #3, was written in 1850. Schumann's pianistic motif may be intended to portray both the yearning that blows about the lover's brow like a gentle, sad Spring breeze and the sound of a harp. A melody that is rewarding for the singer, though not particularly adventuresome, unfolds above the keyboard. Fischer-Dieskau (p. 197), seeing only slight identification of the composer with the text (a poem by Friedrich Halm), believes such detachment reflects the composer's growing withdrawal that will eventually lead to silence and escape. Walsh (p. 90) also makes an unfavorable appraisal:

> In "Geisternähe". . . the chromaticism has become superfluous, serving neither a functional purpose nor—except in the sense that it disguises a fundamental dullness in the harmony—a decorative one. . . "Geisternähe" shows only the danger of a Mendelssohnian drawing-room style without the benefit of Mendelssohn's supreme craftsmanship.

Moore, in his *Miscellany of Songs* section (p. 189), thinks highly enough of *Geisternähe* (Near in Spirit) to include it among the Schumann Lieder he selects for special attention. Moore speaks about the sense of yearning in the singer's first phrase and the keen impact made by the unanticipated F♮ of bars 3 and 4. He concludes by saying: "The postlude repeats the charming introductory figure and contentedly subsides."

A case could be made for the composer's having found the overall meaning of the poem through an intentional vagueness and by keyboard motifs that alter with poetic imagery. *Geisternähe* provides singer and pianist with a performance channel that requires finesse and skill from both of them. It should be sung and played introspectively, despite its somewhat virtuosic demands.

It is doubtful that the removal from reality one perceives in the setting has anything to do with the 1849–50 mental condition of Robert Schumann. Rather, it is a becoming musical response to the strange circumstances surrounding the poet Halm, who chose to make a wedding gift of verse to a woman he had loved who was about to marry another man. Schumann reacted in 1850 with the same interest in the notion of unrequited love he had displayed a decade before when Clara seemed forever beyond his reach. This lyrical Lied does not indicate growing withdrawal leading to silence and escape, nor does it exhibit superfluous chromaticism. Singers and pianists may program this engaging song with confidence.

The Peters edition carries the note that the text of *Stiller Vorwurf*, #4, is by an unknown poet. This "unknown poet" was Oskar Ludwig Wolff, who had once been a suitor of Clara. That may be why he goes unmentioned by Schumann and might further explain why the left-hand opening bars of *Stiller Vorwurf* hover around the pitch nucleus C–B–A–G–A (C–L–A–R–A), frequently used in the songs of 1840. For that reason, and because the poetry could well have spoken personally to Schumann by recalling his time of separation from Clara, it is presumed (Sams, p. 247) that the original form of the song dates from 1840, although it was first published in 1851. Fischer-Dieskau (p. 180) evaluates the setting as evidencing "very careful declamation, and the abrupt changes in harmony point to techniques which would be further developed by Hugo Wolf."

Stiller Vorwurf is a gentle song, full of emotional depth. The poetry may appear maudlin when viewed from a twentieth-century perspective, but is it more so than numerous poems chosen from nineteenth-century Romantic sources by Schumann and his contemporaries? The poet's pain is echoed, with remarkable plaintiveness, in unanticipated enriched harmonic language.

Singer and pianist are offered a Eusebian Lied that should be delivered with quiet passion. The pianist will, of course, carefully observe the scattered *fp* markings, pointing up changing harmonic structures, dynamics, and rhythmic accents. Although the vocal lines are subdivided into bars of two, the singer, while observing notated rests, must unite these brief phrases into larger units, thereby mirroring the tightly constructed harmonic movement.

In *Aufträge*, #5, to a poem by Christian L'Egru, composed in 1849, performers encounter one of the most charming compositions to come from the hand of Robert Schumann or any other Lied composer. It could not have been written without knowledge of a number of the *spumanti* Lieder of Franz Schubert. The pianoforte motif is remarkable, with exactly the right mechanical figure put to emotive purpose, as so often with Schubert; the effervescence of the vocal line is captivating and contagious. Singer and pianist have an opportunity to exhibit technical skill and artistic temperament (Ex. 18.1).

The excitement of the unrelenting, scintillating pianism and the inexorable rapidity of the text, which demands clear articulation of the syllabic setting, stimulate a rush of adrenaline that both performers should enjoy. The keyboard configuration must remain crystal-like in its clarity, but the use of the sostenuto pedal as indicated by the composer is essential. Pedaling should be accomplished through brief in-and-out touches, discreetly altered at each chordal change. Dry harpsichord effects are to be avoided. Right-hand arpeggiated figures in thirty-second notes demand the pianist's skillful attention, and the *fp* notations in the left hand indicate that the whole texture requires harmonic grounding by giving special voicing to the left hand. Granted that in *Aufträge* territorial rights belong to the pianist, the singer's exuberance and vocal charm will make equal partners of the two performers. The dynamic markings in the vocal line must be carefully observed, as should the alternation of staccato and legato passages.

There is danger that a singer appropriately interested in good diction and

Example 18.1.   *Aufträge*, bars 1–3.

clear enunciation may indulge in detached syllables. The sweeping nature of the melody demands a forward line best achieved through articulated legato singing. The singer ought, by all means, to take the *ossia* high A in the fifth bar before the end; only a purist would object to a brief tenuto on that note, in anticipation of the subsequent ritardando and vocal conclusion. This remarkable Lied has elicited a wide range of critical comment. Walsh says (pp. 89–90): "Anyone listening to 'Aufträge' is likely to recall Schubert's 'Liebesbotschaft' with regret, as no doubt Schumann was doing when he wrote the song."

Sams (p. 232), remaining constant to his general assessment of the Schumann Lieder of this period, has this to say: "But sooner or later it [its charm] will pall just a little. What seems to be a spring of ebullient invention is after all hardly more than a threefold repetition of music which though full of its own special grace is, like the verse, rather too hectic and florid for what it has to say." An opposite viewpoint is expressed by Fischer-Dieskau (p. 172): "An attractive song, it displays virtuosic élan, yet its simple form of three repeated sections keeps it from sounding hectic and exaggerated. This is another love song in lighter vein, with precise declamation and a playful piano part. Such an effective song needs to be better known." Ivey (p. 199) somewhat surprisingly remarks: "(*Aufträge*) features a vocal style that bears an uncanny resemblance to fully developed Debussy, but without the latter's suavity."

Moore's enthusiasm for *Aufträge* (pp. 189–91) spills over and deserves extended quotation:

In the whole field of song there are few with more exuberance than this. . . . Every note sparks and bubbles but its joyousness depends on lightness of touch, for though the burden of the song is largely born[e] by the accompaniment, the singer must be able to deliver her message blithely and without effort.

. . . It provides the only specimen in my experience, where the singer, finding the pianist endeavoring to cope with so many notes, does not urge him to play faster. On the contrary, here the player is continually charged not to sweep along so quickly. With refreshing independence the pianist ignores the singer's bidding. It is a novel situation which is so enjoyable for him that he is irresistibly spurred on to feats of unheard-of velocity.

Moore (p. 191) is adamant that only a soprano should undertake *Aufträge*. He expresses a particularly strong feeling against its adoption by the countertenor. The text, however, indicates that a tenor (and why not a skillful male falsettist, i.e., the countertenor?) with the capability of much flexibility might also find this Lied rewarding. Transposition is unacceptable, because the sparkling pianistic timbre needs to stay in the range in which the composer conceived it.

19

Liederalbum für die Jugend, Opus 79

Having had considerable success with his 1848 *Album für die Jugend* for piano-forte, written in part as a birthday gift for daughter Marie, Schumann turned to the poetry of Hoffmann von Fallersleben for a similar song album for the young. To von Fallersleben's verses were added poems by Geibel, Ludwig Uhland, Hermann Kletke, Andersen, Goethe, Schiller, Mörike, and Rückert. Individual songs from this opus might at first blush support the contention that Schumann's powers as a song composer were waning. However, Schumann had not only an artistic intention in assembling this collection but also an instructional one. To his publisher he wrote: "They [the songs] themselves will best explain what I had in mind. I have composed songs for young people, selected only from the best writers, progressing from the easy to the more difficult. Mignon provides the conclusion, giving insights into a more complex soul."

It would be a rare child who could perform all the songs of op. 79. Further, if the composer's intention was that the songs be *sung* by children, one would have to assume that the children of 1848 were better musicians and vocally more prodigious, with sturdier larynges and greater pulmonary capacities than their modern counterparts. Some of the Lieder, such as the earlier numbers of the opus, may be plausible literature for young vocalists, but it is doubtful that others such as *Er ist's* and *Kennst du das Land*, which later became #1 of op.

98a, could ever have been thought ideal for young voices. Because of the disparate characters of the songs, it is difficult to recommend that a singer program all of op. 79, except as a musicological exercise. What is the assessment of this collection? Fischer-Dieskau (p. 155) awards the composer high marks:

> Schumann succeeded admirably; he found the tone of what then was popular, thus ensuring the songs' appeal to young singers. None of the pieces became a true folk-song—but Schumann's intention was to lead subtly to a higher level of artistry. . . . The songs reflect Schumann's, the teacher's, interpretation of what attracted young people to music. . . . In this sense these miniature pieces, though easy to play, can be considered small works of art.

Hallmark (1996, p. 104) assesses op. 79 favorably:

> Many of these songs possess great beauty and charm. Despite a certain cultivated naiveté, nearly every song contains artfully nuanced elements that make for satisfying performance. . . . Such simplicity, frequently cited as a waning of creative power, was more likely a conscious artistic choice. One may question Schumann's judgment, but one should not fault him for failing to accomplish what he did not set out to do, or upbraid him for artistic growth and change.

Some of the songs are better than others. Several editions disperse the songs of op. 79 among other opus numbers. The sequence of the Lieder as found in the first edition and repeated in *The New Grove Dictionary of Music and Musicians*, vol. 16, pp. 860–61, is followed here. Fallersleben is the poet for the first six songs.

Der Abendstern, #1, is a brief song that plays with key relationships through a cycle of falling intervals. With *Schmetterling*, #2, Schumann illustrates for his young musicians the principle of webbing together a pianistic motif and an echoing vocal response. Sams (p. 199) finds "here is mastery and sensitivity too, lavished on a trifle." *Frühlingsbotschaft*, #3, offers a joyful setting without relying on pitches imitative of cuckoo calls. Children should find it fun to sing. Both Sams (p. 199) and Fischer-Dieskau (p. 156) consider this miniature to have a military character; the poet was the author of *Deutschland über Alles*, of which fact Schumann and his critics would have been aware. *Frühlingsgruss*, #4, has a triplet figure resembling the one found in the preceding song and seems a close relative to it. Sams (p. 200) finds merit in it: "a jolly song about eating and drinking, suitable for a child's song-book; and he makes it, in its way, a very fine one." *Vom Schlaraffenland*, #5, with its gleeful text, is suitable for a trained treble voice. Its gaiety is appealing.

Sonntag, #6, has an atmosphere of innocence and serenity best achieved through constant legato. Moore (p. 191) restricts the song to a female singer because he believes the deeper pitch of a man's voice destroys the illusion. Pianist and singer aim for noncomplexity of expression but must not be misled into treating *Sonntag* as a folk song. The performance requirements of *Sonntag* go beyond expectations for a child's voice.

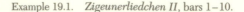

Example 19.1.   *Zigeunerliedchen II*, bars 1–10.

Geibel's translations for *Zigeunerliedchen I* and *II*, #7, from an anonymous Spanish source, spark Schumann to compose two estimable songs for vocal and pianistic characterization. The gypsy lad's plight—his rebellion against a society to which he does not belong—is caught in the opening vocal motif of *Zigeunerliedchen I*, "Unter die Soldaten," as it develops over the alternating eighth notes of the left and right hands in the pianoforte part. The pianist then sets forth a reminiscent figure in a four-bar commentary that occurs three times. This heightens the intensity of a brief but stark portrayal, making for a tightly knit vignette.

Zigeunerliedchen II, "Jeden Morgen, in der Frühe," is justifiably a favorite Schumann Lied. The composer catches the pain and tears of the young gypsy girl stolen away from her homeland. Schumann, with simple means, vividly mirrors the depth of her longing. Triplet figures previously seen in the songs of this opus provide an important rhythmic pillar. The pianist needs to exaggerate the rolling of the chords so as to emphasize anguish. The harmonic progressions cascade downward, like the flow of tears described in the text (bars 1–10). This is poignant poetry, poignantly set. The expressed ardor extends far beyond mere storytelling. Despite the modest construction of the song, the cumulative long phrases require a singer with substantial breath-management technique. Performers should portray each of the gypsy children as though directly and personally involved. These two songs belong together (Ex. 19.1).

Yet another striking image occurs in a setting of Uhland's *Des Knaben Berglied*, #8. The dotted rhythms and the familiar triplet figure are the means by which the mountain boy expresses buoyancy of spirit. Notwithstanding its ranginess and its vocal demands, there is directness about this strophically set Lied. It should be vigorously played and sung with full voice and with supporting pianistic dynamics. If public performance is intended, as opposed to a study for developing musical interests, a young tenor voice would appear apropos for delivering the song's aggressive exuberance.

(*Mailied*, #9, a duet *ad libitum*, is briefly considered in chapter 26.)

From *Des Knaben Wunderhorn* comes *Käuzlein*, #10. Schumann catches the pathos of the little owl. The awe-inspiring character penetration so frequently managed in the miniature songs of this opus is realized here through the descending close intervals of the first few vocal bars. *Käuzlein* is a sweet and charming song that could be included in a group of other Volkslieder or among a group of songs selected from op. 79 itself. It requires intimate word painting from the singing voice and playful sincerity, without coyness, from the keyboard. It is *not* a comic expression. There must remain deep understanding of and sympathy for the little owl's sadness.

Fallersleben's *Hinaus ins Freie!*, #11, is given a forthright, vigorous arpeggiated melody based on the triad. It needs to be sung with generous tone while maintaining its inherent relationship to the folk idiom. *Hinaus ins Freie!* fits well in a group composed of several better known Lieder from this opus. Since it is without sophistication, it should be sung and played that way.

Der Sandmann, #12, to Kletke's poetry, illustrates perfectly Schumann's ability to write a song that is successful both as an inducement for the young to enjoy music and as a miraculous miniature that appeals to all ages. *Der Sandmann* is an endearing song constructed over an appropriate keyboard mechanical figure (calculated rhythmic monotony [bars 1–9]) of the kind so successfully used by both Schubert and Loewe (Ex. 19.2). The pianist must touch the

Example 19.2.   *Der Sandmann*, bars 1–9.

Example 19.3.   *Marienwürmchen*, bars 1–10.

keyboard in such a way as to elicit playful detail; for the singer, the mythologi-
cal Sandman becomes as much a reality as he is for the sleepy little children.
Any attempt at cleverness destroys the wonderful entry into the child's imaginative world created by Schumann. This is not just a lullaby; it is an ingenious
event.

Des Knaben Wunderhorn supplies the charming *Marienwürmchen*, #13.
Each of the three strophes seems perfectly fitted to Schumann's folk-song invention. As with *Käuzlein* and *Der Sandmann*, *Marienwürmchen* must be delivered not by an adult performing childishly but by an adult singing with childlike
belief. Parodistically mimicking infantile vocal mannerisms spoils the impact of
this gem. *Marienwürmchen* must be earnestly depicted through gracious vocalism. Who can imagine a more successful miniature? (Ex. 19.3).

Die Waise, #14, with Fallersleben as its source, deserves a better critique
than has been afforded it. The dignity and seriousness of this brief Lied manage
to shun the maudlin. Its engaging folk melodies should be sung and played with
controlled emotion.

(*Das Glück*, #15, a duet for two sopranos to a poem by Hebbel, is considered briefly in chapter 26.)

A devotional nativity song, *Weihnachtlied* (*Weihnachtslied*), #16, to an un-
identified Andersen translation, begins conventionally with hymnlike part writing for the keyboard and a sturdy melody for the voice. Forthwith, intervallic
leaps push the phrase toward the concluding "Hallelujahs" that outweigh what
has gone before. Schumann may have hoped the song would fit liturgical occasions for children, because he concludes each of the strophes with two-part
choral bars. These final bars seem incongruously like a festive choral finale at-
tached to a hymn, terminating with an octave drumroll. Perhaps the composer

felt this would be especially appealing to the young musician. There is, indeed, considerable charm here. Schumann appears to have intended the song to contrast with other musical idioms in the *Liederalbum für die Jugend*.

Goethe was the source for #17, *Die wandelnde Glocke*, as he was for some of the finest Schumann Lieder still to be conceived. Goethe's delightfully imaginative tale appealed to the ever-present child in Schumann. He approached *Die wandelnde Glocke* with the kind of conviction for fantasy that he evinced in setting *Der Sandmann*, but through dissimilar musical means. The opening mock seriousness of the deep-toned tolling bell, with its inner-voice *f-p* play between the pitches D and E♭, establishes the ideal balance between reality and fantasy. We hear the bell, which vies with the child as chief protagonist, even while the recalcitrance of the child is narrated. (The marking from Schumann is *im erzählenden Ton*.) The child is warned by his mother about being absent from church, he shoots off into the fields anyway, and the bell pursues him. He dashes back into church, thereby escaping the bell; never again does he fail to answer an invitation to go to church when the bell calls.

Schumann has chosen a melodic contour and a chordal progression that remain adjustable to all segments of the developing story. As it unfolds, the urgency of the boy's race against the advancing bell, now booming away with dissonant *sf* strokes announced through left-hand octave triplets, is introduced at "das arme Kind im Schrecken, es läuft, es rennt, als wie im Traum." At this point, the singer must bring an additional sense of urgency to the vocal timbre, and the pianist should make much of the octave tripleting. The incessant tolling of the bell that opened the song completes the framing of this beautiful little ballad by reappearing forcefully in the concluding bars. Once again Schumann's creative powers discover a musical language that grasps the spirit of the poetry. It is simply not true that he bends the poetry (despite minor text modifications at times) to suit his personal wishes; he creatively interprets his poetic source.

Two other assessments of this ballad are of interest. Says Fischer-Dieskau (p. 158):

> Quite convincing . . . is the dry, pedantic beginning of *Die wandelnde Glocke*. . . . The intentional rhythmic monotony is interrupted by accents and jarring chords when the bell comes, hobbling along. Even though the great Goethe is involved Schumann deviates from the text three times, for the sake of his melodic line. The song is just right for a child's comprehension; it is in no way inferior to Loewe's famous setting.

Sams (p. 207) has this to say:

> The poem is full of affectionate indulgence. But Schumann is at first rather square and schoolmasterly about it, as if it really were a cautionary tale. The tolling in the piano prelude and occasionally in the first three verses is all too predictable. Then his imagination like the child's is seized by the idea of the pursuing bell. The sudden clangour in the piano at the moment when it suddenly appears just behind "doch welch ein Schrecken hinterher," and the fol-

lowing of grotesque wobbling-movement (at "die Glocke kommt gewackelt") are given equivalents so compelling that the song comes to life; and becomes, within the limits imposed by its miniature framework, a spirited and effective ballad.

Schumann unites a strong dramatic situation to a small structural design. Too often neglected, *Die wandelnde Glocke* adds humor and musical substance to a group of Schumann miniatures. Singer and pianist must firmly believe in the unfolding fantasy; they must not laugh at it but experience it. Schumann has produced a song that appeals to the child of any age.

(*Frühlingslied*, #18, is a duet ad libitum. See chapter 26.)

Calling on Fallersleben's *Frühlings Ankunft*, #19, the composer invents a reflective inner-voice keyboard figure that reminds one of some of his close-intervalled improvisatory middle-keyboard motifs from the previous decade. A melody sensitive to the inherent meaning of the text weaves through the song. The poem speaks of the stirrings of Spring ("seed and bud struggle towards the light, and many a flower blossoms in silence up towards heaven"); there is in Schumann's setting more of hope than of action, as is evident with the concluding affirmation: "O heart, let that be a sign to you; be happy and brave!" Voice and piano must find apt lyricism that grows in emotional intensity (not in decibels) for the concluding admonition.

(*Die Schwalben*, #20, is a duet for two sopranos set to a *Des Knaben Wunderhorn* text. See chapter 26.)

Kinderwacht, #21, by an anonymous poet, is unpretentious. There is a sweetness about it; it is one of the few songs in the entire opus that could actually be sung by a child. That makes it all the more difficult for an adult to pull it off successfully in performance. Perhaps it is best to reserve *Kinderwacht* for the precocious child who sings.

Schumann, turning to Schiller's *Wilhelm Tell*, evokes the Swiss Alps in *Des Sennen Abschied*, #22, through a continuous bagpipe bass drone, which some critics point out is more easily imitated on the keyboard than would have been the anticipated Alphorn theme. Above all, Schumann produces a folk dance, rhythmically set in two-bar units. The vocal melody is based in part on an authentic herdsman's tune. The constant drone and rhythmic ostinatos, together with turns and grace notes, serve up a Swiss/Tyrolean Volkslied. The melody is full of leaps of fourths and fifths, which are dictated in part by the harmonic stability of pedal-point droning. This produces foursquare melodic, harmonic, and rhythmic elements to which singer and pianist must rigorously adhere. Again Schumann finds a pertinent musical idiom for the text. Forthright, energetic, yet tender in its expression of seasonal farewell, *Des Sennen Abschied* is a congenial performance agent. But it cannot stake out a claim for being included among topflight Schumann Lieder. Moore (p. 193) includes *Des Sennen Abschied* among the relatively few songs he selects for special discussion, commenting: "It is very much in the nature of a country dance with the dancers more on their heels than on their toes. The singer should bear in mind that a rustic, simple and untutored, is giving voice to a bagpipe accompaniment."

Example 19.4.   *Er ist's*, bars 1–8.

What a joy it is to turn to *Er ist's*, #23! Schumann here is at his most in-sightful with regard to textual involvement; his creativity (April 1849) was never at higher peak. The opening bars in the keyboard prepare perfectly for the vocal entrance that emerges from the brief prelude (Ex. 19.4). Schu-mann's setting contains all the joy and gentleness of Spring. There is no blus-tering, no whipped-up agitation. Spring comes with soft breezes and dream-ing violets; all is as beguiling as the stroke of the harp (bars 18–21). *Er ist's* is the ultimate Spring song. Pianist and singer are not asked to indulge in fits of unabashed energy. Subdued exuberance, anticipation, and, above all, appre-ciation for the coming of Spring are characteristic of *Er ist's*. Walsh (p. 82) does not agree: "Its [*Er ist's*] already insubstantial charm is seriously diluted by the amorphous treatment of the poem, which leaves out words and repeats the last two lines, in whole or part, no less than eleven [*sic*] times to accom-modate a reprise and coda." The accusation that Schumann, whose immersion in the reservoir of German poetry and whose own literary accomplishments exceed that of any other Lied composer of the nineteenth century, misunder-stood his poetic sources is not tenable. Schumann not only was aware of the literary heritage out of which he himself came but also intentionally made use of it in new and intriguing ways to expand the concept of the Lied, as in this particular instance.

Sams (p. 209) devotes a brief paragraph to the Schumann *Er ist's* :

> Music-lovers may consider this song a witless travesty of a beautiful poem. However, the music is undeniably charming and effective. Schumann's treat-ment of the verse suggests that the stolid kindergarten solemnity of the earlier spring songs has grown into the dancing pulse of a girl's first lovesong.

There is no desire here to take away the deserved reputation of Wolf's version of this lovely Mörike poem, but its excellence is no reason for denying a favorable assessment of the Schumann Lied. Fischer-Dieskau (p. 158) finds that Wolf, in his setting of the poem, is "far more convincing" than Schumann. Moore (pp. 194–96) prefers the Wolf but finds "much to appreciate" in Schumann's handling.

Schumann's *Er ist's* catches more convincingly the wonderment of Spring's arrival than does the marvelously frenetic Wolf setting. Schumann paints Nature's awakening in the opening syncopated bars and *then* builds to a dramatic climax with a "Ja, du bist's" series. It is true that repeating a text segment ten times is extraordinary, but such repetition admirably manages to accumulate joyous reactions to the coming of Spring. More than that, it expresses the hopes of a longing, loving heart.

The Wolf postlude is enthralling keyboard bombast. It has little or nothing to do with Spring and everything to do with virtuosic pianism. Wolf's postlude is exciting, great to play (for facile fingers), makes the adrenaline run, and induces immediate and thunderous applause. But it outdistances the poet's intent. Moore (p. 196) fittingly asks: "Why does Wolf promote the 'süsse Düfte' to a whirlwind in his postlude?" Indeed, why should critics who value a Lied for not exceeding its poetic frame often still extol Wolf for this bit of excess? The conclusion can only be that even the most scholarly critic is not immune to the visceral excitement skillful virtuosity can induce in a listener.

Moore is right to suggest that the meaning of Schumann's *Er ist's* is found in one musical phrase (bars 14–16), about which he writes (pp. 195–96):

> This is the core from which my love for the song springs. First of all it is beautiful, with voice and piano moving independently but intimately involved. Much more than that, however, is the hesitation, the maiden meditation asking, "Can violets really be waiting there? Is it possible?" The uncertainty, so eloquently expressed by the questioning line of the voice and the unresolved harmony, [is] the personification of innocence. It cries out for restraint and space, and for this reason is marked *etwas zurückhaltend* (somewhat held back). The singer allows time for its significance to be absorbed.

Er ist's should not be transposed. Schumann has found the range where keyboard color can best paint the hues of spring; equally, the chosen vocal tessitura is ideally suited to warm expression. The singer must not allow the voice to bloom fully until the climactic high A. A soprano is clearly the preferred vocal type, but *leggiero* and lyric tenors may be excused for insisting on singing this vocally rewarding, musically and emotionally fulfilling masterpiece.

(*Spinnelied*, #24, a trio ad libitum. is not considered here.)

Des Buben Schützenlied, #25, was selected, as was *Des Sennen Abschied*, by Schumann from Schiller's *Wilhelm Tell*, the chosen text being spoken by Tell's son. The demands of *Des Buben Schützenlied* far exceed the capabilities of a child's vocal instrument. Several commentators believe this song and the marches of op. 76 (the "barricade marches") were Schumann's limited reaction to the

Example 19.5.   *Schneeglöckchen*, bars 1–6.

revolutionary events that took place in Dresden on May 3, 1849. Sams (p. 210) suggests that the motifs in this song are "stock-in-trade; e.g. joyous manliness . . . in the outdoor key of B♭ major." He also believes that Schumann's heart was not really in it. It is difficult to disagree about the stock-in-trade aspects, yet the square "manliness" of the musical structure seems required by the poetry. Fischer-Dieskau (p. 159) remarks: "The boy's song, however, does not suggest that Schumann was unusually inspired, for the musical lines do not bring anything new. The melodic declamation is in stubborn conflict with the text's basic rhythm." Performers need not concern themselves with great subtlety of expression. The best advice may be to enthusiastically sing and play this Lied with uncomplicated vocalism and pianism.

Schneeglöckchen, #26, is a jewel. (The poem is by Rückert; a second *Schneeglöckchen*, by an anonymous hand, is found in op. 96.) Schumann's gift for synthesizing word and music, voice and pianoforte, is illustrated perfectly in this magnificent little song. Its initial hesitation to go beyond the gentleness of snowflakes soon is graciously modified by upward mobility, only then to fall downward with equal grace. This development is realized over a rhythmic ostinato that catches the feel of soft fallen snow while expressing the wonderment and quiet joy a lover of Nature experiences on discovering a delicate flower blooming in the snow. Little harbinger of Spring, the snowdrop touches Rückert's poetic muse and arouses Schumann's musical imagination; the combined result is exquisite (Ex. 19.5).

Schneeglöckchen must not be hurried. (*Nicht schnell* is the tempo indication.) A perfect small world has been created on two pages. The dynamic level ought not to exceed *p* in either instrument, except for the indicated *fp* notes in the keyboard that are necessary to accentuate harmonic movement. The vocal melody should be sung nearly portamento at such phrases as "hängt nun geronnen heut als Glöckchen," and the singer and pianist must allow a little time for the sixteenth-note *gruppetti* of those phrases.

Sams (p. 210) considers *Schneeglöckchen* "the apotheosis of salon art." Further, "the appealing verse charmed Schumann into a melody worthy of the 1840 songs, while the accompaniment is vivid and sonorous with Rückert's imagery." Fischer-Dieskau finds that *Schneeglöckchen* "sounds easy and natural as though it came from his [Schumann's] most successful period of song writing." (In both of these critiques lies the mainstream assumption that artistic deterioration was the norm for Schumann during this April 1849 period.)

Schumann returns to Goethe for *Lied Lynceus des Türmers*, #27, which now is the concluding song of this instructional opus for the young. The sturdiness of the song was doubtless intended to appeal to boys and youths, who were among the audience Schumann wished to reach with his *Liederalbum für die Jugend*. (*Mignon*, the original conclusion of this opus, was meant to accomplish the same purpose for young female musicians.) Thus, it should not come as a surprise that Schumann attempts a certain masculine bravado. *Lied Lynceus des Türmers* may not be one of the greatest songs of the opus, but it has attractive energy.

(*Mignon* [*Kennst du das Land*]), #28, was removed from the opus to lodge more suitably in op. 98a. It will be considered with the other *Wilhelm Meister Lieder*.)

Soldatenlied was published in 1845 in another collection of songs for children, to which Mendelssohn and others contributed. For that reason, *Soldatenlied* does not bear an opus number. When taken out of context as a song meant to be accessible to childish ears, it does not enhance the reputation of Robert Schumann as a Lied composer.

From op. 79 a remarkably fine group of Schumann Lieder may be selected. The following order (to be listed as "from *Liederalbum für die Jugend*") is suggested:

Sonntag

Zigeunerliedchen I

Zigeunerliedchen II

Käuzlein

Der Sandmann

Marienwürmchen

Frühlings Ankunft

Schneeglöckchen

Er ist's

This group would be particularly appropriate for a young lyric soprano and almost equally so for a youthful lyric tenor, in which case *Die wandelnde Glocke* might be appropriately substituted for *Zigeunerliedchen II*.

The dilemma in which critics find themselves when confronted by the great songs of the late period of Schumann's creativity is exemplified by op. 79. Such a quandary results only when an attempt is made to neatly codify Schumann's efforts within rigid predetermined rules. Critics aware of the composer's personal history tend to search for evidences of deterioration in his songwriting following the feverish creativity of the "Clara Year." A typical negative assessment comes from Astra Desmond (p. 44):

> The chronicler's job begins to be a sad one, for though there was a recrudescence of song-writing in 1849 the strain of the intervening years was beginning to show. The wonderful spontaneity of genius [1840–41] had gone. Though Schumann could still write beautiful songs they become rarer. Where other composers have gone from strength to strength Schumann shows a deterioration until he ceased writing altogether.

That conventional assumption will be further questioned in what follows.

20

Opus 83 and Opus 87

That most of the Lieder of 1850 no longer sound like those of 1840 is indisputable. There is considerable controversy as to what this change may mean. Traditional criticism, passed from one pen to another, long maintained that Schumann's mental and physical condition was responsible for changes in his compositional mode. For that reason, in-depth consideration of the inherent value of the late Lieder has been neglected. For example, for performing musicians intrigued by *Resignation*, #1 of op. 83, the following pejorative evaluation (Sams, p. 232) is upsetting: "Here is the new and disturbing voice of the 1850 Schumann; the bland vagueness of its harmonic language is only too fitting a match for the sickly drivel of the verse."

On the contrary, Schumann's change in compositional technique was intentional. He purposely altered his style of the previous decade. The "vague harmonic language" in actuality shows a forward-looking approach to the setting of poetry, from a composer exploring new vistas for the Lied. *Resignation* is not an easy song to comprehend without examining its free structure. Its adventuresome melodic contour is wedded to passages almost of the *recitativo accompagnato* sort. The first six bars are a fascinating combination of harmonic and melodic complexity, taking on an almost *arioso* comportment that in some ways anticipates the mature Wagnerian declamatory technique. These are followed by eight bars of sustained melodic motion that ascends and falls, often by

166

semitones, producing a sense of musical kinship with the poetic quest: "To love, to love with my whole soul, with my whole heart, that I never can conceal; completely must I love you; how is this possible? how can I know it?" The poetry by Schumann's friend Julius Buddeus is not of the highest literary level, yet the text has an intensity of emotion that twentieth-century critics find distressing; unpolished emotion it may be, but "sickly drivel" it is not. Rather, it is a highly personal assertion of unrequited love. Schumann identified with the poem completely.

The keyboard becomes almost orchestral, requiring warm sonority from the pianist. (Orchestral conception will also pertain with many Brahms and Wolf Lieder and later with those of Strauss and Marx.) Schumann might well have moved even further into this genre, had health and life been extended. There are interjections that take on a recitative character. Although not entirely new to Schumann, the manner by which he alternates a "tortured" melodic line with such passages indicates an additional departure.

Fischer-Dieskau (p. 172) offers a positive evaluation of the direction Schumann is now taking: "Many of Schumann's late works no longer bear the marks of thinking in pianistic terms. . . . This compositional approach leads to a richer harmonic language, subtly reflecting every nuance. Being a free fantasy, the song offers special challenges to the interpreter." With the kind of insight expected from a scholarly performer of major international stature, Fischer-Dieskau (pp. 172–73) provides a perspicacious critique of *Resignation* and additional comment on Schumann's developing compositional style:

> There is no longer any trace of the traditional strophic song. In this miniature Schumann created what Wagner had envisioned for the musical theater: a mixture of speech-like song and of melody derived from words. . . . Such freely-flowing melody runs counter to the conventions of the time, leading one to wonder what Schumann, had he lived, might have created to take a place next to Wagner's "Art Work of the Future" of the second half of the century. . . . There is no real recitative, no elaborate arioso, no "cantata song" in Schubert's manner; rather we meet an entirely new medium of a vocal fantasy.

Voice, pianoforte, text, and music are integrated into a performance unity.

Having, in *Resignation*, expanded the vocal line beyond that found in many Lieder of 1840, Schumann turns to more traditional melodic invention with the Rückert poem *Die Blume der Ergebung*, #2 of op. 83. There is a Mendelssohnian winging of the vocal melody, with almost a *bel canto* flavor. If one considers only the well-known cycles, a case might be made for saying that Schumann never wrote songs such as this in 1840. However, the total output of the 1840 literature refutes that assumption.

Die Blume der Ergebung is rewarding for both singer and pianist: pure vocal lyricism for the singer, and romantic improvisatory arpeggiation, with solid sonority in the anchoring bass line, for the pianist. The composer makes use of his arpeggiated harmonic filler of other years.

Der Einsiedler, #3, a setting of an Eichendorff poem, may not qualify as one of the greatest Schumann Lieder, but it has as much appeal as at least a dozen Lieder from an earlier period. Hymnlike, despite unexpected harmonic progressions, *Der Einsiedler* should be sung and played with straightforward dignity.

Opus 87

Schiller's outstanding poem *Der Handschuh* comprises op. 87. It bears an 1851 publication date. Critics have difficulty knowing what to make of it. Sams, who is generally critical of the late Lieder, makes this assessment (pp. 235–36) of a late Lied that he basically admires:

> This long poem is admirably matched by Schumann; indeed it is hard to think of a better setting of a Schiller ballad in the whole literature of the Lied. . . . Most of the music is typical of 1840. . . . Only the last page, with its quirky harmony, suggests a later date. *Finally the music as a whole seems too lively and inventive to have been within the grasp of the Schumann of 1850.* This may well be an early work, revised, not necessarily to its advantage, in 1850. (Italics mine.)

This kind of critical speculation, which occurs frequently, attests to an unwillingness to rate the late Lieder highly. Fischer-Dieskau (p. 174) does not come down as positively as does Sams: "There is little here that approaches the intensity of Schumann's best ballads save for the descriptions of the 'frightful cats' which compare favorably with the corresponding section of the *Löwenbraut.*"

Der Handschuh is a ballad equal to many composed by Loewe. The song seems disjunct because of numerous scene changes, which is also true of some Loewe ballads. The pianist is reduced to "accompanying" and must provide the proper *Melodram* as background for the ballad narration. What vocal type should perform *Der Handschuh*? The song is not comfortable for a lyric-tenor voice, since much of the narration takes place in low register; because of its upper-range extension, a lyric baritone may find the ballad too dramatic. Perhaps a very rangy dramatic baritone or a dramatic soprano would find it a good source. More probably, a dramatic tenor or a mezzo-soprano would have the best luck with *Der Handschuh*. Whatever the vocal category, the singer will need to dramatize the poetry in true balladeer style.

An accurate evaluation of Schumann's contribution to the Lied during his late period comes from Fischer-Dieskau (p. 216), who, more completely than any other artist, has immersed himself in the study and performance of the entire Lied literature:

> It has appeared to many, and not only to those who observe from the periphery, that during his last decade Schumann failed to find the musical equivalents for the ideas he espoused. However, he had in point of fact reached a new

starting point; a new stage of musical expression which, due to his illness, was never fully explored and developed. . . . Schumann, experimenting with speech-related song, came close to the declamatory style of the giant of Bayreuth—but this was not intentional, but rather the result of Schumann's rigorous pursuit of a new and simple vision of music. . . . His outstanding songs soon made their way, affecting the genre far into the future. Their influence on later song writing may have been greater than that of Schubert. Richard Strauss, Hans Pfitzner, Othmar Schoeck are indebted to Schumann above all, whether they were prepared to admit it or not. . . . *Only familiarity with his entire oeuvre can lead to appreciation of a different Schumann speaking from each one of his songs.* (Italics mine.)

The discussion of the effects of Schumann's mental condition on his Lieder output should now be taken more fully into account. Schumann was troubled by fears of insanity as early as 1828 (at age eighteen). There were reports in 1831 of Schumann's "illness," the nature of which was a point of embarrassment and dismay to some of his friends. It has been suggested that there was concern among them that Robert was syphilitic; there is a suspicion that syphilis may have been the reason for Wieck's opposition to Clara's marriage to Robert. Sams (pp. 276–80) gives an account of medical and psychological studies that have been directed to an examination of the causes of Schumann's health problems.

It has been proposed that as early as 1831 Schumann suffered deteriorating results from the administration of mercury, a cure for syphilis. Peter Ostwald (p. 93) comments on the theory that the mercury treatment used to combat syphilis caused damage to Schumann's right hand:

Two neurologists, Drs. R. A. Henson and H. Urich, who have reviewed various theories of causation of this hand "injury," claim that neurological symptoms of syphilis "would hardly be manifest at the age of twenty or twenty-one." (Actually, Schumann's problems with his hand began when he was only nineteen.) As for the conjecture that mercury poisoning was a pathogenic factor, Henson and Urich point out that "mercurial neuropathy was so rare during anti-syphilitic treatment as to raise doubts on the causal relationship."

Others find medical and psychological evidence that points toward schizophrenia (Eusebius/Florestan), even in the early creative years. A study by E. Slater and A. Mayer contains a chart designated "Mapping Madness and Genius" reprinted in the *New York Times* in October 1993. As established by researchers, Schumann was in severe depression as early as 1833, was moderately manic throughout the year 1840, experienced severe depression throughout 1844, but then became moderately manic throughout 1849. Five years later came his attempted suicide; his death at the Endenich Asylum was in 1856. Ostwald, himself a psychiatrist, concludes (p. 303):

The most comprehensive diagnosis for Schumann's psychiatric illness would be a *major affective disorder.* He suffered from severe, recurring depressive episodes. The symptoms consisted of feelings of extreme sadness and irritability. Often he was sleepless, agitated, and hopeless. Guilt and self-accusatory ideas accompanied many of these depressive episodes, occasionally leading to self-destructive behavior. Thoughts about death, and a wish to die, were prominent.

Ostwald (p. 305) goes on to discuss Schumann's personality disorder:

He had what seems to have been a severely divided self, with conflicts centering around dependency versus independence, attachment versus separation, and femininity versus masculinity. . . . Schumann made an effort to meliorate his disorder through his creativity. Florestan and Eusebius were temporary, poetic solutions.

Says Ostwald: "There is no evidence that Schumann became demented, except possibly at the very end of his hospitalization" (p. 305). As would later be true of Hugo Wolf, there were periods of depression and times of exuberant behavior, in Schumann's case less dramatic because of being spread out over the creative years 1833 to 1852.

The hypothesis that divergences from the Schumann compositional style of 1840 were the cumulative result of advancing illness and of progressive mental deterioration is a romantic viewpoint not based on reliable information. Schumann did not become unstable around 1849; he always had been unstable. It was a continuous factor in his life and his work.

The kind of negative criticism cited with frequency in this work has hindered the performance of some of the most imaginative Schumann Lieder. As Fischer-Dieskau (p. 217) points out, only about forty of the solo songs from Schumann's hand are known by many singers and the public, most of them from the two best-known cycles, the other songs comprising a handful of *ausgewählte Lieder*. Songs from Schumann's last decade must be approached with a mind swept clean of limited critical insight and academic prejudice. Many outstanding Lieder are to be found in the opus numbers yet to be considered.

21

Opus 89 (von der Neun) and Opus 90 (Lenau)

Opus 89

In May 1850 Robert Schumann turned to six poems by Wilfried von der Neun, whose real name was Friedrich Wilhelm Traugott Schöpf. (The pseudonym refers to the nine Muses.) Schumann met with the poet to discuss plans for setting the texts. There is nothing in these Lieder to suggest, as has been alleged, that Schumann's mental faculties had deteriorated so that he no longer was able to distinguish between good and bad poetry. He was looking for a genre of poem through which to realize his changing attitudes toward Lied composition. Sams (p. 236), in line with prevailing criticism, believes otherwise: "By May 1850 Schumann's mind and music are in perceptible decline. Both return to a weak and sickly subjectivism. He believes the turgid claptrap of 'Wielfried [*sic*] von der Neun' to be 'very musical poetry'; his own music for them is mainly stereotype from earlier and better songs." By contrast, Fischer-Dieskau (p. 174) finds that "settings of poems by Wilfried von der Neun are distinctive, not merely reversions to an earlier style."

Presume for a moment that the Lieder of op. 89, dating from the year 1850, have just been unearthed and that they are considered to be by an unknown hand. The excitement of discovering such an addition to the Lied treasury would be enormous. As mentioned previously, this kind of composition points to the orchestrally accompanied Lieder of the second half of the century and to other Lieder for voice and piano that, although not originally scored for voice and orchestra by their composers, were essentially orchestrally conceived by them.

Whatever its intrinsic poetic virtue, *Es stürmet am Abendhimmel*, op. 89, #1, became in Schumann's hands a remarkable Lied that requires skillful singing and playing. The pianist must aim for an orchestral sound. The singer is given ascending lines that require greater sustaining power than do most of the well-known early Schumann Lieder. In *Es stürmet am Abendhimmel*, the melodic structure has technical demands of phrasing and dynamic contrast that destine it for high-level vocalism. There may be a good reason, in that these songs from May 1850 were dedicated to an artist considered by her contemporaries to be the greatest soprano of her time: Jenny Lind. Lind had visited the Schumanns the previous year and spent several hours sight-reading a number of Schumann Lieder. Fischer-Dieskau (p. 176) gives a detailed account of Lind's visit and of the joy Clara and Robert experienced at hearing beautiful vocalism applied to his songs. Clara could not resist making a comment that may throw light on the Lind performance that so pleased Robert: "If we could persuade her to sing nothing but good music and to get rid of all that rubbish by . . . Meyerbeer, Bellini, Donizetti, etc.; she is too good for that." One suspects that Lind did not substantially change her vocal production when singing Schumann Lieder, but that Clara preferred Schumann to Meyerbeer. These songs are intended for the accomplished vocal artist capable of a bel canto line. Regarding *Es stürmet am Abendhimmel*, Fischer-Dieskau (p. 175) finds other significant factors:

> In this kind of "speech-song" we detect the first influences of Wagner. Dramatic expression here takes precedence over any intrinsic musical values or thematic work. In spite of some evident banality and intense dramatic expression Schumann manages to refrain from posturing. The broad sweeping lines of the dark ending are convincing, as they are in *Herbstlied*. Brahms did not hesitate to make use of such effects in his Platen songs.

Heimliches Verschwinden, #2, calls on Schumann's arpeggiated trademark keyboard figure, here appearing in triplet patterns. This rhythmic scheme and the keyboard sonority support a sustained melody. The phrases are long, and the vocal line wends its way in a somewhat circuitous fashion, requiring a technically skilled singer. This is yet another example of the advance the Schumann Lied is making in 1850. As the nineteenth century draws to a close and the twentieth century dawns, the flowing style exhibited in *Heimliches Verschwinden* will be much imitated by other composers. The indication *nicht zu schnell* should be carefully observed (m. = 88–92 seems appropriate).

The same can be said of *Herbstlied*, #3, as indicated in the preceding extract from Fischer-Dieskau. The noble keyboard bass quasi-ostinato brings unity to the extensive composition as it progresses through several keys. *Herbst-*

lied must be sumptuously played at a low dynamic level. Over it a sixteenth-note *gruppetto* harmonic filler moves the expansive vocal melody forward. Nostalgia alternates with hope. There is a soulfulness about this Lied that presages the Lieder of Johannes Brahms. Singer and pianist encounter an expanded form of the traditional mood-evocative song (*Stimmungslied*), rich in interpretative opportunities for both instruments.

Abschied vom Walde, #4, is a superior Lied. The evocation of mood fits well with the previous three songs. The rhythmic motif is hauntingly effective; melodic digression results in long phrases. Schumann has clearly given attention to the *singing* aspects of the poem: *singing* of the woods, *songs* in grief and regret, and *melodies* of Autumn. Performers find themselves in an advancing Romantic musical idiom. Gracious vocalism, not lyric declamation, is the aim. They should bring warmth and color to each phrase. One could hypothesize a young Brahms as the composer of this Lied.

Ins Freie, #5, is in very different mood. There is a freshness about the melodic and harmonic language that calls for direct, uninhibited vocal timbre and strong keyboard articulation. Great energy is sustained in the Lied, perhaps somewhat overstated at the close. (Certainly a surprising composition from a "deteriorating" spirit!) For its period, this song is another groundbreaker; it is also the forerunner, unfortunately, of a number of late-nineteenth-century potboilers based on animated vocalism and pianism.

The final Lied, #6, is a masterpiece in miniature. The imaginative unaccompanied beginning of *Röselein, Röselein!* leads to a perfect questioning inflection in keyboard and voice at "müssen denn Dornen sein?" What follows is charming invention. With this song one would be willing to risk to an impartial jury the reputation of Robert Schumann as a major contributor to the Lied. Pianistic filigree between the gracious vocal phrases suggests Chopinesque or Bellinian fioriture. These embellishments function as effective commentary on the brief vocal statements among which they are dispersed and act as unifying configurations for the entire composition. A remarkably inventive questioning insertion at bars 20 and 21 is based on the opening vocal query (Ex. 21.1).

If this poetry is claptrap (Sams, p. 236), what is to be said of some of the less-than-stellar German translations of Burns that attracted Schumann in 1840 and continue to please critics? *Röselein, Röselein!* is a typical ribbon of Romantic verse that need not apologize for being worn; it has been brought to an exquisite level of musical realization by Robert Schumann. The serene, unhurried questioning, with its humorous philosophizing, will provide great joy for performers and their audiences. The song is suited to light male and female instruments and, if excerpted, is appropriate in a group of Schumann miniatures.

Opus 89 stands well as a set. Despite their seeming disparity, there is a unity of compositional adventuresomeness that binds the six Lieder together. A singer and a pianist who have courage to venture beyond the boundaries of the "forty favorites" will find here a rich source of wonderful music.

Example 21.1.   *Röselein, Röselein!*, bars 1–12.

Opus 90

Lied eines Schmiedes, #1, is the first of the six Nikolaus Lenau Lieder that comprise op. 90. It was composed in August of 1850 and is remarkable in its Florestan energy. The piano becomes an anvil. The Schumann Lied is at a more restrained level of intensity than is Brahms's treatment of a related subject, yet Brahms's strategy in *Der Schmied* is not unlike that of Schumann. Schumann chooses to give the poem (from Lenau's *Faust*) a folklike framework, in keeping with the smith's occupation. Through the use of heavy chords that form a firm harmonic base, the composer describes the shoeing of the horse and its forthcoming return to trotting. This is a delightful characterization of both horse and smith, and there is an underlying reminder of the brevity of life ("Trag auf dem Ritt mit jedem Tritt den Reiter du dem Himmel zu!"). *Lied eines Schmiedes* is not a bravura expression; it deserves immediacy and direct communication from both performers.

Sams (p. 250), remaining true to his frequently expressed skepticism regarding Schumann's 1850 abilities, presents the possibility that "some of these Lenau songs . . . and their arrangement by keys suggest the 1840 style; indeed, these may have been earlier sketches now refurbished, since all the poems had been published by 1838. But for the most part Schumann responds in his typical 1850 chromatic style."

There is a distinctly new attitude on Schumann's part toward the Lied in his last creative period. Yet, considering all songs of the 1840–50 decade, there is no internal evidence that Schumann at any period composed in a single style. It is true that the Lieder of the well-known cycles dating from 1840 mostly have a common idiomatic flavor, but even during those years Schumann's song output displays many facets. (Recall the Lieder he removed from *Dichterliebe*.)

For anyone who has long loved Schumann's setting of Lenau's *Meine Rose*, #2, it is difficult not to wax effusive. The keyboard writing hints of Chopin, and the melodic contour partakes of nearly full-blown Romantic vocalism. Schumann weaves a rich harmonic tapestry and constructs a soaring vocal melody above it. Yet with it all, he avoids heavy-handed Romantic posturing. The rose, sad and drooping under the sun's hot rays, is effectively depicted by the falling vocal lines ("der Rose, meiner Freude," bars 5–6, for example); the Chopinesque/ Bellinian element enters the vocal line with an embellishment at "vom heissen Strahl der Sonnen" (bars 8–10). (Brahms will often make use of this kind of "Neapolitan" fioritura in his Lieder, as will Strauss.) The song unites vocal and pianistic elements in a musical language that points toward Lieder to come later in the century (Ex. 21.2). The mosaic interplay of voice and piano at "reich ich den Becher Wasser aus dunklem, tiefen Bronnen" (bars 11–14) must be treated as an echoing duet between voice and piano. The subsequent "Du Rose meines Herzens" is a speech-inflection interjection that not only brings intimacy of expression but also sets off even more markedly the soaring, though restrained, vocalism it interrupts.

Moore (p. 210) comments:

> A continual dialogue between singer and the pianoforte's soprano voice is a feature of this delicate song. Too heavy for its stem the flower droops and in intimate sympathy voice and accompaniment follow each other in gentle falling drops. Sensitivity is demanded of the singer; the falling line has to be handled with care.

Moore (p. 211) also remarks that the singer "must be as elastic as a pianist in a Chopin Nocturne." He adds: "To me the song is not so much Chopinesque in spirit as Wolfian. It is in the same family as *Bedeckt mich mit Blumen* [Wolf] though as compositions they do not bear the faintest resemblance. . . . Schumann's is justifiably to scale, infinitely lighter in texture."

This Lied, though Wolfian in spirit, is not representative of the synthesis of voice and keyboard so characteristic of Wolf and evident in Schumann's own *Der Nussbaum* or *Zwielicht*. In *Meine Rose*, pianist and singer are equal solo partners, dialoguing but not conjoining. Does Schumann choose this route because his mental state makes him forget synthesis? Certainly not. He is branching beyond his earlier horizons, expanding his musical idiom, and in the pro-

Example 21.2.   *Meine Rose*, bars 1–10.

cess he will influence much late-nineteenth-century and early-twentieth-century Lieder composition.

Meine Rose is a wonderful bit of keyboard/vocal composing that every singer and pianist should know. The song is perhaps most appropriate for light voices and is right for both genders if the singer can maintain a subtle dynamic level. The last strophe must be pianissimo. Nowhere within this Lied is there room for visceral intrusion.

Kommen und Scheiden, #3, has dueting between voice and piano (as opposed to synthesis of the two instruments), as does *Meine Rose*. The piano sings a fragment in the opening two bars, to which the voice responds with its own segment; this small figure, which requires an arching phrase shape, acts as the unifying motif. Schumann's chromatic treatment from bar 17 onward to the conclusion of the song represents a remarkable expansion of form. Increased expressivity results precisely because of the abandonment of predictable formal elements. An unfavorable viewpoint (Sams, p. 253) should be cited: "The sense of the poem wavers and blurs into a rich confusion just as in the previous song; but here the musical outline is beginning to fade too, and what might have been a most beautiful song is vague and inarticulate."

For Fischer-Dieskau (p. 181):

Having reveled in beautiful melody [here Fischer-Dieskau is referring to *Meine Rose*, which he has just discussed], Schumann now reverts to his psychologically conditioned late style. *Kommen und Scheiden* . . . displays this clear abandonment of coherent melody. Fragments of text are treated in an impressionistic manner, memories of the beloved's appearance are loosely strung together. Such an impressionistic treatment has precedents in Schubert's *Der Doppelgänger* and *Die Stadt*.

Fischer-Dieskau is precisely on target with his evaluation of the composer's intentions. Despite Schumann's enriched harmonic palette, there are psychological and technical relationships between the late Schubert Lieder and some of the late Schumann Lieder. Schubert is the germinating source for the rest of the century.

The formal structure of *Kommen und Scheiden* is actually of tight construction, but its psychological insight is the keynote to the performance of this notably progressive Lied. The timbres of both pianoforte and voice must mark the nostalgia when the beloved, for some unrevealed reason, departs, leaving the poet to feel that "als Lebwohl sie winkte mit der Hand, war's ob der letzte Jugendtraum mir schwand." The "vague" and "inarticulate" character of the song is proof of the composer's keen penetration into his poetic source and of his success in achieving a proper musical translation. The postlude commentary may appear as a sweet bonbon to ears accustomed to what became a commonplace idiom by the close of the century, but it illustrates Schumann's capability of weaving melodic fragments into a harmonically enriched fabric.

It is natural to think of *Des Sennen Abschied* when turning to #4, *Die Sennin*. (The title of Lenau's poem is best translated as "The Cowgirl.") But the parallels, aside from the subject matter and the angular Tyrolean melody, are not remarkable. Whereas a continuous drone is the main distinguishing keyboard feature of *Des Sennen Abschied*, the mountaineer melody of *Die Sennin* moves over bright triplet figures doubled by both pianistic hands. Schumann is able to catch in the opening verses the changing moods of the poet, adroitly finding a theme for the echoing voice of the singing girl; he is equally successful in moving in later verses to somber philosophizing on the brevity of existence. He retains structural unity. Sams (p. 254) approves the first ten bars and predictably says: "The clear harmonies of the first ten bars suggest an earlier Schumann."

Die Sennin certainly bears favorable comparison to Lieder from Schumann's early years, including many from 1840. The opening keyboard passages, marked *pp*, must give a sense of carefree, winging song, in support of a somewhat angular vocal line. An inherent danger when encountering this keyboard rhythmic formula is that the pianist may treat it too dryly, with a misguided imitative harpsichord sound. Note that Schumann's marking is *mit Pedal*. Plainly a young woman's song, *Die Sennin* can best be sung by a light, clear soubrette whose opening timbre should bespeak joyful mountain singing and its echoing return.

Example 21.3. *Einsamkeit*, bars 1–12.

Her altered sentiment is mirrored in more subdued vocal timbre: "Aber einst, wie alles flieht, scheidest du mit deinem Lied, wenn dich Liebe fortbewogen, oder dich der Tod entzogen."

What a pleasure to sing and play *Einsamkeit*, #5 of the Lenau opus! Here we return to Schumann's successful technique involving a chromatically descending figure so effectively used in such Lieder as *Aus den hebräischen Gesängen* and *Zwielicht* (Ex. 21.3). The improvisatory figure moves through a number of keys, and the tonal center is often left in doubt. Fischer-Dieskau (p. 182) notes the change in Schumann's orientation:

Einsamkeit (Solitude, Opus 90, No. 5) demonstrates how Schumann in his middle and late periods had found new musical ways to interpret a poetic text. Gushing waves, the sound of wind, rustling leaves; all were part of Schubert's language which was adopted by Schumann and given his own, distinctive impressions as though seen through the prism of his "beautiful sadness" . . . emphasized by non-functional harmony in an impressionistic vein that shows no concern for traditional modulations nor the representation of specific emotions.

A quite different viewpoint comes from Sams (p. 255): "Schumann has no inspiration to express the healing spirit of love, and the chromatic taint of hopelessness persists to the end." On the contrary, to have abandoned the chromatic motif somewhere in midsong would have destroyed the "prism of his 'beautiful sadness'" so accurately described by Fischer-Dieskau. Schumann is willing to take a variety of risks regarding how best to interpret a poetic text.

Both pianist and singer must make much of the improvisatory nature of the harmonic permutations that move this Lied forward through chromatic keyboard configurations. A physical stage attitude that conveys quietude must prevail for both performers.

This may be an appropriate moment at which to interject a general comment regarding performance mannerisms. Swinging and swaying from the waist while singing, and visibly emoting at the keyboard when collaborating with singers in introspective Lieder is a mark of amateurism. Singers who mistake physical movement for freedom and who indulge in weaving and rocking, gesticulating, and "mugging" in the hope of increasing communication do a great disservice to the Lied and to themselves. Ceaseless motion is not a substitute for honest emotion. Constant body movement from pianist or singer reveals rhythmic enslavement, not freedom. Above all, following the song's final chord pianists should refrain from bowing the head over the keys for what seems an eternity and singers should resist remaining in prolonged statuesque awe at what they have created.

Einsamkeit is a penetrating expression, and it must have had special appeal for Brahms, who would become master of the "soulful" Lied. When performed with an understanding of the impressionistic goals of the composer, this Lied has the capacity to lift performers and listeners into a world of psychological insights realized through musical means. *Einsamkeit* goes far beyond the occasional heart-on-the-sleeve ambience of *Dichterliebe*. Perhaps it is this that elicits the comment from a number of authors that Schumann becomes less subjective (more objective) in the late Lieder. Objectivity versus subjectivity is not the question; the point lies in the conscious expansion on Schumann's part of the traditional boundaries of the Lied.

In the interest of salvaging a marvelous song from the critical dustbin, the conflicting evaluations of Sams and Fischer-Dieskau regarding *Der schwere Abend*, #6, must be considered. First, Sams (p. 255): "A song as oppressive as the night it describes. But the congruence with Lenau seems coincidental, as if the deathwish were Schumann's own rather than the poem's; and inside this lifeless music all expression lies stifled." Now Fischer-Dieskau (p. 184):

To realize how closely Schumann identified himself with a text one should compare his setting of *Der schwere Abend* . . . with that by Robert Franz. Schumann realizes an intimate dialogue between singer and pianist in the key of Eb minor —a key that seems to accentuate the oppressive mood. The dotted-rhythm motif in the piano part . . . is closely related to *Dichterliebe*, where we find it in No. 13; here a darker color suggesting wind instruments prevails. Once more

Example 21.4.   *Der schwere Abend*, bars 1–18.

the voice part ends in a deceptive cadence while the piano, with sweeping, syncopated chords, dwells to the end on the nearness of death. The rhythm of funeral bells provides the basic pattern; its musical interpretation resulted in one of Schumann's most glorious songs.

This truly magnificent Lied could not have been conceived without Schubert as precursor. The harmonic stateliness of the keyboard in Schubert's favorite octave for the portrayal of tragedy and reflection, the use of silence to heighten emotion, the slow, rhythmic progression of the melody, the profundity of the compositional means, and the resultant psychological impact all owe a debt to Franz Schubert (Ex. 21.4).

Viewing *Der schwere Abend* in the context of the entire opus, while recognizing his debt to the late Schubertian idiom, one can but stand in awe of the creative genius of Robert Schumann. Both singer and pianist must use colors of as dark a hue as the functioning of their instruments permits. An extreme legato (excepting the accented keyboard chords, of course) is called for from both performers. Any temptation on the part of the singer to do individual word painting or syllabic detailing is to be strongly resisted.

The duplets of the melody should be well defined over the steady $\frac{3}{4}$ rhythm, and the dotted notes and the eighth-note patterns that follow must be sung through to their full duration. The long notes (half notes and dotted halves) should not be rushed but filled with vocal sound leading to the next syllable, so that the harmonic intensity of the slow-moving pianoforte chording is not lost. Any attempt to "artistically underscore" individual syllables through crescendo-ing and decrescendoing (touching and retreating on individual notes, i.e., "sausaging") will destroy what Schumann has so courageously constructed.

In *Requiem*, #7, Schumann truncates to three the nine verses of an old Catholic text, no doubt to make it more manageable. Sams provides useful information regarding the genesis of this song, which was appended to the opus by Schumann when he mistakenly thought the terminally ill Lenau had already succumbed. Sams (p. 256) suggests that syphilis was the cause of the poet's demise and, as earlier noted, of Schumann's own deterioration and eventual death:

> Perhaps there is a clue in Schumann's revealing *Tagebücher* (Diaries) published in Leipzig in 1971. They record in May 1831 the symptoms of what seems to have been a syphilitic infection. . . . In the following month a diary note reads "Abälard, Abälard!" Peter Abelard was punished (by castration) for his forbidden love for Heloïse. Lenau's insanity and death were attributable to syphilis.

It is undeniable that during all of his creative life matters of physical and mental health seriously affected Schumann's ability to function. (See Ostwald's comments on this subject.) What is questioned here is the notion that the Lieder of the late period are "sickly" products of syphilis and are therefore inferior to songs written earlier.

Wie Harfenton is Schumann's instruction for the arpeggiated sixteenth-note harmonic filler that runs consistently through *Requiem*. The pietistic anonymous German translation comes from a Latin text. There is nothing sticky or patently sentimental in the setting.

Requiem is a big song; it demands rich vocal and pianistic sound at such moments (bars 36–45) as "hörst du? Jubelsang erklingt, Feiertöne, darein die schöne Engelsharfe singt" (hence the harplike keyboard configurations). This is not a particularly forward-looking Lied, nor does it reach heights of profound religious expression. There is little room for piety, a great deal for drama.

Because *Requiem* was something of a last-minute addition to op. 90 and exhibits different orientation, there may be reason to omit it from the Lenau songs when they are considered as a recital group. The Lenau Lieder are of high merit and are a good source for singers and pianists looking for fresh recital material.

22

Drei Gesänge (Byron), Opus 95, and Opus 96

Opus 95

The three Byron poems set in December 1849 to German translations by Theodor Körner were originally conceived for voice and harp. Schumann altered that scheme, recasting them for voice and pianoforte. They were published as appropriate for either harp or pianoforte. Experimental in nature, the pianoforte scoring of *Die Tochter Jephthas*, #1, sounds not far removed from a Stephen Heller etude. It cannot be considered one of Schumann's best successes at a new form of song. Yet a soprano will find it vocally gratifying.

The second Lied of the opus, *An den Mond*, is another matter. If it did not follow *Die Tochter Jephthas*, it might strike the ear as fresh and original. However, this second essay on harp arpeggios is rather overwhelming when heard in sequence to the first, though *An den Mond* is more imaginative and the total effect is pleasing.

The third Byron setting, *Dem Helden*, is worthy of performance as an example of Schumann trying his hand in a style remote from that of 1840. Sams (p. 227) considers these Byron settings "depressing" and "the product of a mind torpid in its idea of more harp songs, slack in its choice of verses, pedantic in its alterations, dull in its setting. These songs have as their only comment the sad one that they may contain further evidence of deterioration."

Dem Helden is to be sung *mit Begeisterung* (with rapture, inspiration, and enthusiasm), and the only possible way to perform it is rapturously, inspired, and enthusiastically. This strange Lied is packed with energy. It has an impetuous drive about it that seems difficult to equate with Sams's "torpor." There is nothing to suggest that it grows out of a state of depression. *Dem Helden* requires swiftly moving fingers and heavy *sf* chords from the pianoforte and a strong heroic sound from the voice. Dynamics of *ff* and *f* are indicated throughout. Does it bluster? Does it assume a monumental stance? Does it sound like an extended fanfare? All of these. Its sweeping energy points to many an equally noisy and posturing "heroic" Lied to come from later composers. Schumann's experiment of turning the pianoforte into a harp (not a new event in Lied history or for Schumann himself) was yet another step in his furthering of compositional style. Harpists who look for voice/harp literature should explore adapting these songs. Vocal instruments of small dimension will be lost. Perhaps a dramatic soprano, a *spinto* tenor, or a *Heldentenor* might find interesting programming in *Dem Helden*. Though they may not be great, it is hard to assess the Byron songs as "inert."

Opus 96

Opus 96, written in July of 1850, draws on a mixture of sources, including Goethe, August von Platen, von der Neun, and an unknown poet.

It is inevitable that any setting of Goethe's *Wanderers Nachtlied*, #1, will be measured against the incomparable Schubert masterpiece, which none will supersede. However, the Schumann setting (which he tactfully calls *Nachtlied*) has within it commendable quietude and peace. Schumann's slow diatonic harmonic progressions become enriched at bars 13 and 14 to express "kaum einen Hauch." The "Vöglein" are afforded a doubled inner-voice chromatic keyboard duet and may also be responsible for the thirds that move inward on each other in contrary motion at bars 19 and 21 (although Goethe's verse at that point has the birds hushed). Schumann's single "Warte nur" (on the interval of a minor sixth) and his major-second interval on "balde" catch the essence of Goethe's verse. "Ruhest du auch" appears above restless harmonic progressions and is finally realized by the subsequent consonance of the last chord that seems to say rest is not *now* possible but will come soon.

The singer and pianist should hold faithfully to the indicated *pp* dynamic; there must be not a ripple of variation from it except where marked in the keyboard score. Vocalism here comes as close to a state of immobility as it is possible for the singing voice to achieve. Schumann's vision seems to be a *personal*, not a *universal*, search for quietude, unlike the setting by Schubert. ("To see a world in a grain of sand, and a heaven in a wild flower," suggests Capell [p. 183], quoting William Blake.) Just because the Schubert setting stands alone ("It was all something that no one before Schubert had done—this compact, epigrammatic style of musical composition," says Capell) is no reason to ignore Schumann's beautiful Lied. Moore's highly personal response (p. 215) is right: "Schubert's immortal *Wanderers Nachtlied* is so loved and so indelibly imprinted on our hearts, that other settings are overshadowed by it and in consequence unheard. To my sorrow, and so far as I am aware, this [Schumann] song is never performed, yet it is very beautiful." When performers and their advisers have been told that a song violates the poetry, it is understandable that it is "never performed." Moore's judgment that *Nachtlied* is a beautiful song worthy of performance is the correct evaluation.

Even the most devoted apologist for the late Schumann Lieder will question Schumann's intentions in the setting of *Schneeglöckchen*, #2. (This song is to verse by an anonymous poet and not to be confused with the setting of the Rückert poem of the same title in op. 79.) Following thirty-two bars of arpeggiation, there is pianistic filler for which it is difficult to recognize musical or textual motivation. The structure is unorthodox, and *Schneeglöckchen's* vocal demands are considerable.

Sams's evaluation (p. 244) may not be too harsh, but his explanation is questionable: "The creative mind of a great composer is here heard in decline." During this same period and subsequently, Schumann was writing first-class Lieder. Were this *Schneeglöckchen* the product of a deteriorating mind, the rest of his oeuvre from that period would be equally "confused." It is logical to view *Schneeglöckchen* as an experiment, perhaps undertaken when the spark of genius was not at its peak. The song, in any event, may best rest as a curiosity on the printed page, without transference to the recital hall.

The third Lied of op. 96, to Platen's *Ihre Stimme*, could have come from the hand of any skilled mid-century composer. (If one didn't know the Lied's source, an educated guess might fall on Mendelssohn.) *Ihre Stimme* is traditional in its melodic sweep and in its arpeggiated accompaniment, highly singable, and rewarding to play. Here is no indication of artistic deterioration but, rather, of artistic choice. Were mental deterioration responsible for Schumann's late Lieder, one would expect to find songs badly written in the style of *Dichterliebe*, not in a totally different idiom. A decade after 1840, Schumann may have lacked some of the white-heat inspiration of the Lieder Year, but he could hardly have forgotten the style in which he had written earlier. He was looking for new modes of expression. In this particular case, however, *Ihre Stimme* emerges vocally and pianistically as a respectable, nonexperimental Lied, worthy of performance.

When he turns to von der Neun as a source, Schumann is faulted by critics for choosing less-than-first-rate poetry. A more appropriate assessment might be that Schumann has successfully enhanced second-rate verse. (Müller was a better poet than von der Neun, but one of Schubert's accomplishments is to have ennobled Müller's melodramatic stanzas.)

Composed in July of 1850 and remarkable for its youthful energy, *Gesungen!*, #4, is unfairly neglected. The unifying element is the aggressive masculinity produced by the octave bass figure that is introduced in the first bars of the song and continues to function as an ostinato. Additional agitation comes from a traditional sixteenth-note *tremolando* pattern, which Sams (p. 241) pejoratively calls "ominous automatism." (Should Schubert be condemned for what Richard Capell approvingly calls "calculated rhythmic monotony," for example, with *Gretchen am Spinnrade, Rastlose Liebe,* and *Der Erlkönig*?) Sams finds the use of unexpected harmonic progressions "the curious trick of composing in several minor keys at once." In point of fact, Schumann finds non-conventional harmonic means to depict the unpredictable driving storm as it snaps the tree branches.

Gesungen! is a fine song for a singer who can pour out vocal sound and for a pianist who can dig into the sonority of the keyboard. Florestan's energy permeates every bar; singer and pianist are called on to fight against wickedness. Schumann does not deal directly with the pious "Hear therein the sweet throats of the birds commending themselves to the love of God!" because to do so would interrupt his thematic figure and his musical design. He does, however, give token attention to the winged songsters in bars 8–10 by an ascending countermelody in the soprano keyboard line and through chromatic harmonic variation interwoven with the driving ostinato. Despite a certain trepidation in the face of other critical evaluations, one is emboldened to rate *Gesungen!* as a Lied of considerable value.

Some of the same Florestan energy characterizes *Himmel und Erde,* #5. Like *Gesungen!*, it is set to a poem by von der Neun. Another compelling bassline ostinato builds a foundation for the reiterated triplet figures and the thrusting melody. The key change from A♭ major to B major achieves a joyous realization of the month of May, and the whole section of tripping countermelody in the keyboard soprano voice is full of the breath of Spring. The coming of Autumn is mirrored in the descent of the vocal line and in the transition bars that lead back to A♭ major. With its thick keyboard texture—full chords at *f* dynamic, and a winging voice line—*Himmel und Erde* calls for a sizable vocal instrument, and sturdy pianism. A mood of exaltation is required of both performers. Brahms must have known this Lied; Schumann's approach prefigures some aspects of Brahms's more exuberant songs. (There are not a great number of them; many Brahms Lieder are elegiac in character.)

23

Lieder und Gesänge aus Wilhelm Meister (Goethe), Opus 98a

The *Wilhelm Meister* Lieder were written in 1849. As was remarked earlier, *Mignon* (*Kennst du das Land*) was originally published as the concluding song of *Liederalbum für die Jugend,* op. 27, #28, then judiciously relocated to become #1 of op. 98a, with songs based on poetry from Goethe's monumental novel. The degree of maturity given Mignon in the disparate conceptions in which she is portrayed by Schubert, Schumann, and Wolf makes an interesting study in itself. For Schubert, Mignon is still Goethe's young maiden. With Schumann and Wolf the listener is encountering not the dreams of youth but those of a mature woman. Wolf's Mignon assumes opera-diva dimensions, her songs lending themselves to full orchestration. Schumann's Mignon lodges between the Schubertian and Wolfian protagonists. Although Schumann originally included the song in his instructional book for the young, he remarked that he saw Mignon "on the threshold of adult life."

Walsh (p. 84) compares settings of *Kennst du das Land* (*Mignon*) from several major composers:

Wolf's frenziedly grandiloquent version and the more straightforward settings by Beethoven and Schubert are all better known than Schumann's song, which perhaps more nearly captures that blend of adult passion and childish bewilderment which lie[s] at the heart of Goethe's great lyric. The setting of the words shows Schumann at his best.

What a magnificent Lied for voice and pianoforte *Kennst du das Land* is! Its initial improvisatory keyboard figure speaks of nostalgia and longing; chromatic excursions move downward and upward over augmented harmonies. The singer begins with language-inflection patterns in semirecitative style, which shortly thereafter soar into unconstrained ecstatic melody. The first nine bars speak directly to the heart, and they serve as an impressive vestibule to this great Lied.

Beginning with bar 10, the triplet agitation in the keyboard leaps forward and is perfect for lifting the mounting vocal line to its first intense moment at "ein sanfter Wind vom blauen Himmel weht." At bar 20, "Dahin!" (and its subsequent repetitions) is of great impact. Then at bars 25–27, vocal and pianistic intensity moves to low range and dynamic level at the text repetition "dahin mit dir, o mein Geliebter, ziehn."

For transitional material between the first and second strophes, the opening pianoforte introduction is recalled, as though to pull Mignon back from her outburst to continue her recollections. It serves the same structural and emotive purposes before strophe 3. In *Kennst du das Land*, the pianoforte acts not as a keyboard instrument but as an orchestra (Ex. 23.1). (This is true of the Wolf setting as well.)

Schumann, in *Kennst du das Land*, has found a harmonic keyboard language and a vocal melody that, without alteration for each changing strophe, is adaptable to the words and to their deeper meanings. Sams (p. 211) rates this Lied quite differently: "As always, Schumann adapts the poems to his own expressive ends, here a child's song-book. Despite its charm the result is incongruous in its inadequacy, relying too much on the composer's instruction 'with enhanced expression in the second and third verses.'"

The intrinsic beauty of the setting makes comprehensible the strophic confines Schumann has selected (chosen perhaps because of his original intention to have *Kennst du das Land* conclude the *Liederalbum für die Jugend*). Moore (p. 198) comments: "Into this restrictive strophic mould Schumann has poured all his own hunger of soul." The vocal performer must be willing to bare *her* soul as well. The soprano or mezzo-soprano who sings this Lied will need to make use of sumptuous vocal timbre. As Moore suggests, Schumann discovers Mignon to be a conduit for his own soulfulness.

Ballade des Harfners, #2, for low male voice, in the published opus follows Mignon's *Kennst du das Land*. The songs that belong to Mignon herself will be considered first, because they form a logical performance group for female voice.

Nur wer die Sehnsucht kennt, #3, one of the most famous poems in German literature, has been set by numerous composers. In all the Mignon Lieder, Schumann relies on an expanded chromatic language to express intense emotion, specifically that of longing. Such harmonic expansion would have seemed

Example 23.1.   *Kennst du das Land*, bars 1–13.

much fresher at the time of its composition than after later extensive use by Liszt, Wagner, Wolf, and numerous late-nineteenth-century and twentieth-century composers. Schumann (and Liszt as well) made use of chromatic harmony, with enduring impact on Lieder construction, far in advance of most composers. Goethe's verses are emotionally compelling; Schumann's chromatic idiom provides musical language for their fullest realization (Ex. 23.2).

The contour of Schumann's melody conveys the subjective content of the text without following exactly the niceties of syntax and word inflection. For example, the *f* tied note on E♭ at "seh" in bar 7 is a perfect match for both language inflection and the long German vowel; the same rhythmic duration that occurs on "nach" (short-voweled and not an important part of the sentence) in bar 9 does not match. Examples of this sort can be found in the songs of every composer from Schubert to Strauss, but the charge is often brought against Schumann, and specifically here, that he distorts Goethe's verses. Schumann's handling of this great Goethe poem causes Sams to despair (p. 220):

In order to realize it [the general structure of the song] Schumann has to repeat nearly all the poem, which is not long enough for his purposes, and this is managed with curious ineptitude. As the [climactic] wave recedes it takes with it much of the sense of Goethe's beautiful lyric, like flotsam. Worse still, the musical quality is at a low ebb all the time.

Stein (pp. 124–25), who at least at times supports Goethe's dictum that music should serve as a frame to the poem, has this favorable report on Schumann's handling of *Nur wer die Sehnsucht kennt*:

> The finest of Schumann's *Wilhelm Meister* songs is surely the little-known "Nur wer die Sehnsucht kennt." For this poem, the most congenial to his temperament, he captures the true pathos of the words better than either Schubert or Wolf, or Tchaikovsky for that matter. Rich dark harmonies and a stunning vocal line set the mood at the outset, and it is sustained throughout the song. The texture is uniform.

Singers and pianists may be surprised that Stein considers Schumann's much-beloved Lied "little-known," but the quoted passages furnish telling comparisons between Stein's and Sams's critical assessments.

In his evaluation of *Nur wer die Sehnsucht kennt*, Moore (p. 216) remarks that "'es schwindelt mir, es brennt mein Eingeweide' is a scorching passage. . . . Bars 12 to 17 must make a telling impression on the hearer. . . . With the *crescendo* growing bitingly, 'brennt' is made momentous, provided the singer sees to it that the agony is protracted." The practical Moore (p. 217), recalling the settings of Schubert (there are six), Wolf, and Tchaikovsky, says:

Example 23.2.   *Nur wer die Sehnsucht kennt*, bars 1–8.

Example 23.3. *Heiss' mich nicht reden, heiss' mich schweigen!*, bars 1–7.

The most popular setting of all is Tchaikowsky's. Should it be condemned on this account? The writer confesses he loves it, though he is almost afraid to admit it. . . . Schumann's comes into the reckoning, for the first page of his song and the sweeping "Es brennt mein Eingeweide" are reason enough for allowing us to hear it.

Heiss' mich nicht reden, heiss' mich schweigen!, #5, is a remarkable composition in its union of contrasting elements. Because of the strength of its intrinsic musical and emotional merit, it holds a unique position in the song literature of the period. Beginning with the aggressively marching opening chords in bars 2 and 3, the listener is dramatically propelled into a new world of the Lied. Mignon's pronouncement "Heiss' mich nicht reden, heiss' mich schweigen!" traces its lineage to the *opera scena*. The *recitativo-accompagnato* of the opening four bars is strikingly altered at the word "schweigen" by a musical motif that displays an uncommon power of invention. Motivic fragments, harmonic language, melodic line, and vocal registration factors are amalgamated into one rare tapestry. The verse "denn mein Geheimnis ist mir Pflicht!," with its tortured arrival at Db on "Pflicht!" (bars 5–7), contains all the mystery and pain of which musical language is capable. At bar 7, the new repetitious eighth-note pattern (at *schneller*) is introduced by an expressive embellishment, as the left hand moves to the treble octave. These musical tesserae fall into forms as striking as the rearrangement of geometric patterns in a kaleidoscope (Ex. 23.3).

A reflective section with a cantabile vocal melody begins to unfold at bar 15. This grows in intensity until, at the *nach und nach schneller*, Mignon's agitation is greatly increased. The reiterated chordal movement under the vocal melody (an old habit with Schumann for producing movement and excitement) surges to the climactic point on the word "Schwur" at the *sf* marking (bar 38), for both voice and pianoforte.

There follow some of the most remarkable measures in the history of the Lied. Uncannily Schumann translates into musical notation the emotional content of "But my lips are sealed by an oath, and only a god may unlock them, only a god!" (bars 47–48). Schumann's harmonies at "nur ein Gott" and in the subsequent bars are Wagnerian *before* Wagner (Ex. 23.4).

This page of music is astonishing in that it comes from 1849. (Liszt also shows some "pre-Wagnerian" harmonies in his Lieder.) Fischer-Dieskau (p. 163) remarks: "Schumann goes beyond what he knew from *Tannhäuser,* appropriating a thematic technique pointing to the as yet unwritten Wagnerian music dramas." Sams (p. 222) summarizes his assessment of *Heiss' mich nicht reden, heiss' mich schweigen!* as follows: "This disjointed and willful music must be among the strangest examples ever offered of an art that is essentially unitary, intimate and responsive to language. . . . The impression is overwhelming that this song is about some tragic secret of Schumann's own."

Sams's final note concludes with: "Now the mental turmoil subsides exhausted; the music's spirit is broken. A few mumbled words are recalled from the previous excitement . . . and all is over."

To counterbalance Sams's usual negative assessment of the late Lieder, an extended quotation (pp. 123–24) from Stein is apropos:

> "Heiss' mich nicht reden" is a passionate outburst of great power. The music conveys a tense urgency in its opening chords and throughout the entire first stanza. . . . When the poem is over, Schumann is not ready to stop but pulls out the phrase "nur ein Gott" for a separate, impressive repetition. . . . The whole composition is a tour de force (like Schubert's "Erlkönig") exploiting emotional potentialities in the poem in a way that Goethe would never have dreamed possible. The song is so compelling, except for the second stanza, that one cannot help wishing he had simply left that stanza out. Schumann took even greater liberties elsewhere.

The pianoforte once more becomes an orchestra, and the changes of color required of the voice for the fluctuating moods must be mirrored in the keyboard. Schumann places the pianoforte largely in the lower-middle octave, in a sonorous region with a timbre receptive to tragic expression and reflection. The final text repetition comprises not "a few mumbled words" but some of the most emotive composing ever to come from the hand of Robert Schumann or any other composer.

The last of the songs for young Mignon, #9, *So lasst mich scheinen,* receives low marks from critics, even from those who see value in the other Mignon Lieder. Desmond (p. 50) comments: "A good beginning becomes disjointed; awkward leaps in the vocal line and some unfortunate word stress disturb the atmosphere."

Another criticism is that the melody takes on "hysterical" characteristics

Example 23.4. *Heiss' mich nicht reden, heiss' mich schweigen!*, bars 39–61.

not intended by Goethe (Fischer-Dieskau, p. 164). It is just this character of melodic "hysteria" that marks *So lasst mich scheinen* as another success in Schumann's conscious expansion of the boundaries of the traditional Lied.

The interweaving of fantasy and reality (Mignon as actress, Mignon as young woman aware of death) is already caught in Schumann's opening ambivalent rhythmic and harmonic figuration in bars 1, 2, and 4. The attempts of Mignon to maintain emotional control at "Dort ruh' ich eine kleine Stille" are totally abandoned as she cries out, "Dann öffnet sich der frische Blick" and "ich lasse dann die reine Hülle." It is true that false accentuation in setting the sounds of the German language results, but for good reason. Schumann adds more tragedy to Goethe's poetry than was the poet's intention. It is not true that Schumann did not understand Goethe or was unable to scan poetic meter; the composer augmented Goethe's voice with his own.

So lasst mich scheinen does not represent traditional melodic invention. Its melodies move tortuously. Moments of attempted self-control and outbursts of turmoil are expressed, not from the role she is playing but directly out of Mignon's own emotional state: "I felt deep pain enough. With sorrow I grew old too early; make me forever young again." Schumann himself, fully aware of the ravages of time, speaks through youthful Mignon. Sams (p. 223) feels strongly that this Lied is the result of "confusion and contrivance." His judgment, when faced with Schumann's new emotional and musical creativity, is expressed this way (pp. 226–27):

> But Schumann's setting seems to reflect only his own mental state. . . . There are seemingly endless shifts of rhythm; hardly any two bars are even analogous. In the voice part there is no longer even a rudimentary sense of scansion; in the music as a whole not a flicker of life, despite the palpably intense effort of creation.

The singer and pianist must allow themselves to be transported by Schumann's own creative imaginings into the composer's personal world of pain and its resolution. *So lasst mich scheinen* demands the most lyric and the most dramatic capabilities of both voice and pianoforte. This concluding song of the four Mignon Lieder sums up universal longing: Mignon's, Schumann's, that of its performers, and that of those who hear it.

These great Lieder deserve to be freed from the narrow aesthetic confinement in which they have long been held. They must be allowed to communicate the depth of human emotion that Schumann marvelously expressed in the style of his mature period. The songs of Mignon are well suited to a sizable soprano voice, but a dramatic mezzo-soprano instrument is equally fitting.

It would not be wise to program Philine's lighthearted *Singet nicht in Trauertönen*, #7, with the tragic Lieder of Mignon. Schumann rightly chooses a note of gaiety in this Lied to match the character of Philine. The soubrette Philine should be sung by a soubrette soprano. The vocal idiom (quickly moving melismatic arpeggiations and rapid syllabification) calls for a flexible instrument of bright timbre. *Singet nicht in Trauertönen* trips along with a lightness of heart that could scarcely have come from a state of depression. This Lied is from June 1849, a moderately manic period for Schumann, the same month in which *Kennst du das Land* and *Nur wer die Sehnsucht kennt* were composed. Sams (p. 224) initially ranks this Lied favorably:

> Here Schumann is doubly relaxed. The light verse relieves him for a while of the crushing responsibility of matching some of the greatest poems of his country's greatest poet. Better still, the main subject of the verse appeals to him. We hear the music being captivated by the charms of the vivacious young soubrette from *Wilhelm Meister*. The prelude is all gaiety and grace, changing in the accompaniment to a pizzicato guitar serenade; and the vocal melody is straight from the heart of Schumann's, or anyone's, lost youth. This memorable strain brings out counter-melodies from the piano, until all the music is alive with singing.

Yet Sams's disapproval of middle and late Schumann Lieder faithfully surfaces when Schumann sets the poet's description of the night: "The music seems duller than required." Sams does not like the last page. He suggests (p. 225): "Perhaps the song was finished amid the June melancholia which suited the Mignon songs." But Moore (p. 217) finds that "the humor and sparkle of it are admirably caught by Schumann."

This song is not, of course, in 1840 vein. It is written as a display aria for light soprano voice and goes much further with vocalization than one is accustomed to finding in early Schumann Lieder for female voice. The staccato pianoforte writing is crisp and must be played in virtuosic fashion. There is a frivolousness about *Singet nicht in Trauertönen* seldom found in Schumann, not even in *Aufträge*. Its charm is contagious; it has direct audience appeal. Here is the sort of song with which sopranos can successfully close a Lieder group. But the greatest Lied of 1849–50 it is not.

The remaining *Wilhelm Meister* Lieder should now be considered.

The Songs of the Harper are #2, #4, #6, and #8 of op. 98a. They make a plausible concert grouping, particularly in an all-Schumann concert, fitting well between *Dichterliebe* and a concluding set of three or four ballads. Such a selection alternates styles, allowing the singer and pianist to rise to Schumann's diverse challenges, which extend from Romantic introspection to flamboyant mid-nineteenth-century bravura.

There may be a certain reckless abandon about *Ballade des Harfners*, #2, composed in June 1849, but not a trace of depression. Once again Schumann breaks ground in free ballad style. His marking is *mit freiem deklamatorischen Vortrag*, and his musical ideas have the ring of artistic liberty delivered over initial harp strummings that begin at *f* level.

Ballade des Harfners is one of the most vigorous songs Schumann wrote. Any composer choosing to set this verse (as did Schubert and later Wolf) must be faced with the challenge of its length, its many characters, and its descriptive language. On the whole, Schumann manages all of it well. Critics complain that Schumann invented six different harp themes to help him out, but inasmuch as these musical figures are not unrelated and grow in intensity, there seems good reason for his having devised them. It is true that formal structure appears to have been thrown to the wind. Given the drama of the poetry, one might say, "All the better!"

Offensive to some Schumann Lieder watchers is the nature of the writing itself: vigorous vocalism and high tessitura. *Ballade des Harfners* has more the dimensions of an operatic aria than of a Lied. The range is slightly more than two octaves, from low G♭ to high G, one of the most extensive for male low voice in the Schumann song oeuvre. *Ballade des Harfners* is light-years removed from *Ich hab' im Traum geweinet*.

What has happened to the usually sweet singer of songs from 1840? Schumann is now successfully exploring new vistas for the Lied. Sams (p. 218) finds Schumann's musical ideas to be in turmoil and discovers within this late Lied a change from effortless singing to laborious ariosos half-remembered from earlier years. (Indeed not! Schumann's approach is new and fresh.) Sams concludes: "In such ways the song's many fine moments are all lost in a welter of irrelevance and confusion."

Ballade des Harfners is a grand improvisatory composition that allows singer and pianist to present a second, more dramatic Robert Schumann. One cannot claim that the Lied ranks at the top of ballad writing, but it can be confidently stated that this song is an adventurous exercise in the realization of hitherto-unexplored potentials (surpassing even Loewe's efforts) in ballad writing. A well-schooled baritone (only an accomplished singer dare undertake it), assisted by a skillful pianist who knows how to use the pianoforte for achieving instrumental color, should have a marvelous time with this declamatory, operatic scene.

In *Wer nie sein Brot mit Tränen ass,* #4, Schumann selects a noble, broadly constructed melody that lies in the most advantageous range of the baritone voice, maintaining a relatively high tessitura and requiring a commensurate level of energy. Schumann catches perfectly the inner meaning of the text by relying on the expressive possibilities of the male voice in this register. The vocal line is generous, as must be the vocal timbre. This is a singer's song and requires a voice of ample proportions. C minor harmonies are moved forward with a conventional keyboard triplet figure, no doubt to depict the strumming of the harp; the chromatic play of the triplets, while providing the necessary harmonic filler, well expresses the melancholy and guilt felt by the harper.

Schumann retains the triplet figure during the opening fourteen bars, then suddenly gives us sweeping harp arpeggios at *ff* level as the harper's thoughts become more impassioned. Equally ardent must be the singer's passion, continuing to increase up to "every guilt is punished on earth," after which the vocal line descends for the text repetition that terminates in anguish on the *p* low G. The keyboard postlude consists of harp arpeggios in gradually diminishing amplitude, concluding with a rolled *sf* C minor tonic chord. This is yet another work that indicates the new direction in which Schumann is taking the Lied.

Other viewpoints should be considered. Fischer-Dieskau (p. 162), after discussing the intensity of the harplike broken chords, comments: "The voice part remains tied to the muffled bass notes of the piano, relentlessly expressing the heavy burden of fate. The accompaniment displays a magical, almost impressionistic quality." Stein (p. 122) offers this opinion:

> In "Wer nie sein Brot mit Tränen ass" he [Schumann] introduces awe-inspiring arpeggios in the accompaniment to the lines "Ihr führt ins Leben uns hinein / Ihr lässt den Armen schuldig werden," while the vocal line is highlighted by two minor seventh leaps to a high C [actually the upper-middle-range C for the baritone voice] on the words "Leben" and "Armen." It is difficult to see what the composer had in mind. If he was depicting the mystery of the relationship between God and man, this is foreign to the poem.

Stein may have missed the composer's intent. Schumann purposely transcends his poetic source by translating into musical terms his understanding of the poet's deeper meaning. Stein, although often flexible in his views, generally does not approve when musicians tamper with poetic concept.

Sams (pp. 220–21) evaluates this significant 1849 Lied negatively:

> This structure cannot bear the emotional weight with which it is charged. The treading bass, the well-known triplet accompaniment rhythm, the obsessive harmony, the unmotivated introduction of prodigious harp-flourishes, as if the instrument had suddenly been remembered; all these things create an agony of frustration for the listener who can hear both the nobility and originality of the conception and the confusion and banality of its execution.

When objectively viewed, without being measured by criteria that do not pertain, *Wer nie sein Brot mit Tränen ass* comes across as one of the most interesting Lieder of 1849.

Wer sich der Einsamkeit ergibt, #6, is another song for a baritone voice of substance, a vocal instrument capable of producing fully vibrant and resonant sound and an unrelenting legato. The triplet figure, a descriptive harp pattern that Schumann used in *Wer nie sein Brot mit Tränen ass,* appears again in *Wer sich der Einsamkeit ergibt*. Schumann's rolled chords grow logically out of the triplet figures; they imitate the harp and underscore the emotion of "Ach! der ist bald allein" with remarkable appropriateness.

The vocal melody itself has a flow that follows declamatory word inflection yet achieves a noble contour. This is a facet of the new Schumann, by which he develops a style that unites what was later to be known as bel canto (to which he was opposed in 1840) with the Germanic penchant for integration of words and music. At bar 27, Schumann turns from the arpeggiated triplet figure to a chordal progression based on changing harmonies; then at bar 35, he inserts harp arpeggios. Shortly thereafter, he comes back to his rolled chords, which are clearly imitative of harp striking. Schumann concludes with a keyboard postlude built on previous material. This is programmatic music with roots in the eighteenth-century *Melodram*, here imaginatively reintroduced into the Lied in expanded Romantic garb.

The final Harper song, *An die Türen will ich schleichen*, #8, continues the fluent vocalism of the previous two Lieder. It frequently hovers in the singer's *zona di passaggio,* the passage zone between lower and upper ranges— Bb–Eb—of the dramatic-baritone voice. The slow-moving melody must be delivered at low dynamic level, yet completeness of vocal timbre is called for. The harp arpeggios ought to be unhurried. Poignancy and nobility of expression should be joined in the interpretative realizations of both singer and pianist.

Cooper, in his influential chapter in *Schumann: A Symposium* (p. 110), makes the customary negative case against the late Schumann Lieder, which has been paraphrased from critic to critic:

> The *Wilhelm Meister* songs . . . are among Schumann's most conspicuous failures as a song writer. Painfully oppressed by the philosophic significance of Mignon and the old harp-player, he rambles on in a portentous, pseudosymphonic style, with frequent modulations and unnatural vocal phrases, losing the thread of the poem and of his own musical design, and sometimes, as in No. 6 [*Wer sich der Einsamkeit ergibt*], visibly at a loss how to continue. . . . Only Philine's *Singet nicht in Trauertönen* is at least half successful, though here again the repetitions of the last line, and then again of the last phrase, are unforgivable.

Musicians who live with this music will have quite an opposing viewpoint. John Daverio's recent study (p. 428–29) reinforces this author's long-held viewpoint regarding the *Wilhelm Meister* Lieder:

> The *Meister* lieder no doubt number among Schumann's most powerful and affectively gripping creations, yet they have been neglected by all but a handful of performers and critics. The cycle seems to have succumbed to the caprices of history. . . . The work has often been judged a failed experiment. Many critics have remained insensitive to the fact that it is precisely in the dialectic between obviously lied-like qualities (cantabile melodic writing, foursquare syntax, strophic forms, discreet but expressive accompaniments) and dramatic, even operatic qualitites (declamatory vocal lines, proselike syntax, through-composed forms, quasi-orchestral accompaniments) that the raison d'être of the cycle resides. The interplay between lyricism and the drama reflects the tension between the inner world of the soul and the outer world of action so powerfully presented in Goethe's novel. No less than the literary operas of the late 1840s, Schumann's most emotionally charged song cycle is animated by a crucial theme of its literary source.

24

Sieben Lieder (Kulmann), Opus 104, Opus 107, and Vier Husarenlieder (Lenau), Opus 117

Opus 104

The neglected *Sieben Lieder*, op. 104, to poems by Elisabeth Kulmann, deserve performance. Schumann was in search of a musical idiom that would capture the yearnings of the poetess, who met death at age seventeen. His Kulmann settings have simplicity and childlike grace many removes from the expansive Mignon Lieder of the same period. These gentle Lieder prove that in his last creative years the composer flexibly bent an always intense sensibility to poetic sources by devising an aptly diverse compositional mode for each. Classification of these Lieder as the product of "a mind in deterioration" is unacceptable.

Schumann was not alone in admiring Kulmann's verses, as they generated much interest within literary circles of the time. Kulmann's works were widely disseminated, and Goethe praised the young writer's accomplishments. Her works were published in 1833 by the Russian Academy of Sciences. This brilliant young woman spoke Russian, German, and Italian. In addition to a prolific output of original poetry, she translated works of Anacreon and Alfieri. To dismiss her as a kind of curiosity is to denigrate a remarkable talent. Today there is the charge that Kulmann's verses are sentimental and saccharine. Sams (p. 266) grumbles: "More disconcerting still is the alacrity with which Schumann laps it all up, gravely commending its flavour." However, given the Romantic vineyard in which Schumann worked and recalling his early nearly ecstatic estimate of Jean-Paul as a major literary figure, it is not surprising that Robert Schumann in later years should turn to Elisabeth Kulmann.

In its simplicity and directness Schumann's op. 104 has charm. The songs are also important because the poetry comes from a female hand, a rarity in Lieder of the nineteenth century. (Even the poems later assumed to have been written by Marianne von Willemer set by Schubert were published as being by Goethe.) The entire brief opus offers an excellent introduction for a young singer to the Lied literature. Unpretentious vocalism and pianism are required.

Mond, meiner Seele Liebling!, #1, is as meritorious as a number of simple folk-oriented Lieder written earlier by Schumann. Projecting sadness as the cause of the moon's pale countenance and suggesting that the sun is the moon's ill consort may indeed be a naive poetic image, but Schumann catches the emotive implications. He remains true to the poetess's youthful need for comfort.

Viel Glück zur Reise, Schwalben!, #2, an engaging song, has a lilting melody and a jolly keyboard motif in $\frac{2}{4}$. The tight construction is momentarily interrupted by the quasi-recitative parlando passage: "I would like to go with you sometime." A jovial melodic figure then bounces forward. Although it may not be great poetry, *Viel Glück zur Reise, Schwalben!* is at least comparable to many verses set by any number of composers from Schubert through Strauss. There is no logical reason to demean this delightful little Lied. It is especially useful to a young soprano voice.

The third Lied of op. 104, *Du nennst mich armes Mädchen*, commences in G minor in melodic folklike idiom, then mounts upward to an E♭ major tonality supported in the keyboard by the familiar arpeggiated Schumann trademark, as the young girl describes the sun rising above her cottage at dawn. Harmonic progressions lead us back to G minor. Sams (p. 267) is disturbed by the number of rhythmic patterns within the brief Lied, which he sees as "total incoherence of the rhythms." Another viewpoint might be that the composer begins with simple harmonic and rhythmic progressions that correspond to the first two verses of poetry, then (as he had often done earlier) resorts to his favorite sixteenth-note arpeggiation for the mounting sentiment of the poetry, which figure he subsequently varies rhythmically with triplets before returning to the opening material. There is here no "incoherence."

Fischer-Dieskau (p. 195), who understands Schumann's admiration for Elisabeth Kulmann, finds *Der Zeisig* (The Finch), #4, the most successful song of the opus and he expresses particular appreciation for its two canonic lines. Sams (p. 267) comments that "the song is quite acceptable at its level; in op. 79 it might have made more of a name for itself." The composer has neatly caught Kulmann's joyful reaction to the finch's song contest. Again, fresh, unpretentious vocalism is appropriate, with clean, firm supportive pianism.

For *Reich mir die Hand, o Wolke*, #5, Schumann invents a sweeping vocal line that foreshadows early Brahms Lieder—traditional in general construction yet compelling in its unexpected development. Sams (p. 267) sees a relationship to *Gesungen!*: "The song recomposes the futile Op. 96, No. 4." This is unjustifiably harsh judgment on both songs. Fischer-Dieskau (p. 195) comments:

Example 24.1.   *Gekämpft hat meine Barke*, bars 1–3.

"There is something distinctive about 'Reich mir die Hand, o Wolke'. . . perhaps due to its likeness to Eichendorff's style."

Reich mir die Hand, o Wolke is one of two vocally demanding songs in the opus, the other being the concluding *Gekämpft hat meine Barke*, #7. A mood of urgency must be struck by singer and pianist, obtained through full vocal timbre and increased pianistic intensity.

Die letzten Blumen starben, #6, is a delicate Lied. It remains within the range of a tenth. Tessitura lies low. Schumann catches the young poetess's sighing through modest means. Unassuming vocalism and pianism are suitable to the portrayal of youthful *Weltschmerz*. Sams (p. 268) discovers that *Die letzten Blumen starben* "recomposes the hopeless Op. 104, no. 1 [*Mond, meiner Seele Liebling*] . . . a shadow's shadow." Playing and singing the two Lieder, one fails to find the shadow of a shadow or see either song as hopeless.

The last song of the opus, #7, *Gekämpft hat meine Barke*, takes musical generation from the nature of Kulmann's verse. Schumann strives with the angry sea not through wavelike motifs but by means of a firm rhythmic figure that creates the impression of relentless pounding. The pianist will need to mark well the syncopations and the dots that propel the mounting vocal line of the opening bars, just as the singer must. Full vocalism and supportive pianism make a fitting close to this group of seven songs (Ex. 24.1).

Even if not ostensibly a cycle, op. 104 is a worthy recital group for the vocalist who bonds with the sentiments of another young woman. The depth of Kulmann's verse moves it far beyond the mere rhyming of which the poetess has been accused (though she fared well among well-respected contemporaries). Could it be her gender? It might be that her youthfulness influences the evaluation her poetry has received in some current quarters. (Is Rimbaud dismissed because his poetic output is restricted to *his* adolescent years?)

Favorable assessment is often expressed for uncomplicated Lieder in similar vein from such a composer as Robert Franz. Schumann should not be made an exception. His venturing into a conventional realm reflects his ability to design a musical idiom befitting the poetry. There is little doubt that knowledge of Schumann's declining health has contributed to negative evaluation of his musical settings of the Kulmann poetry.

Opus 107

Opus 107, #1, *Herzeleid* (poem by Titus Ullrich) was composed in January 1851 in Düsseldorf. It is a song of intrinsic beauty. *Herzeleid* has a recurrent single motif to achieve musical cohesion (as in Schubert Lieder). The plaintive melody, which plays around the familiar conglomerate of B–C–D–A, recalls a technique repeatedly found in the songs of 1840. The close-intervalled texture portrays the helplessness and despondency of quiet madness, and the incessant keyboard water motif, prefiguring drowning, reinforces that mood. A descent into the low-middle register of the keyboard for the concluding four bars of the song may be associated with Ophelia's watery death.

It is, of course, tempting to suggest, as a number of commentators have, that Robert Schumann was drawn to the poetry because of the future tragedy caused by his own developing madness, but there is nothing to support such an assumption. In fact, medical records show that Schumann was in a moderately manic phase when composing *Herzeleid*. The song must be sung and played with a sense of detachment and resignation. No histrionics should be indulged. Madness here goes deeper than melodramatic presentations of that malady. Schumann catches to perfection Ophelia's psychological state.

Die Fensterscheibe, #2, is set to another Ullrich poem, whose verses, while they have much literary value, do not readily lend themselves to musical translation. The shattering of the windowpane, the bloody hand, the meeting of pairs of eyes, and the breaking of a heart all occur in rapid poetic flashes for which any composer would be hard pressed to find musical language. Schumann wisely avoids any literal attempt, choosing instead a jaunty dotted figure that concentrates on the festive scene of the opening line of verse ("As I was cleaning the windows for the feast day, so that they would mirror the sun's rays, thinking of many things, he went proudly by"). Schumann retains the basic motif while enriching it harmonically as the girl cuts her hand and the blood flows. The musical realization avoids dramatic excess but finds an appropriate character for the small tragedy of broken window pane and broken heart. The Lied begins in chipper mood and ends in sorrow. The last eight bars are a study in unexpected harmonic progressions. It is a woman's song and should be sung with simplicity yet with quiet intensity. Pianist and singer ought to observe carefully the *nicht schnell* marking. Subdued vocalism and pianism are expected.

There are rhythmic similarities between Schumann's setting of *Der Gärtner*, #3, and Wolf's later treatment of the same Mörike text. Wolf knew and respected the Schumann version. Wolf's "princess" is full of gaiety and charm. His young rider could be any spirited young woman. Schumann's princess is noble and elegant. Because Schumann varies his keyboard figures to produce some irregularity in the cantering, his princess rides less impetuously and more cautiously than does Wolf's. Granted, *Der Gärtner* as conceived by Wolf is delightfully radiant. The Schumann setting, mostly because of its rhythmic variations, is captivating in a quite different but no less striking manner.

The singer should use greater restraint in rendering Schumann's beautiful young rider than when defining the more exuberant Wolfian protagonist. The pianist is challenged to point up the rhythmic variations based on the dotted-quarter/sixteenth-note patterns and the alternating triplets. The diminished-seventh chords of the concluding phrase offer questioning commentary on the little drama. Schumann's *Der Gärtner* is neglected largely because of the popularity of the more aggressive Wolf setting, but there is a quality of propriety and refinement in the Schumann Lied that grows on one.

The Paul Heyse text of *Die Spinnerin*, #4, incites Schumann to invent the right musical figure for both the mechanical movements of spinning and the emotional state of the young spinner, a lesson he learned from Franz Schubert. Here, as so frequently, Schumann is particularly adept at capturing the personality of the character portrayed by the poet. His unrelenting sixteenth-note *gruppetto* pattern is built on semitones and harmonic shiftings that catch the underlying pain and longing of a young woman for whom no lover has spoken. This is another demonstration of the variety in compositional skills developed by Schumann in his last creative years.

The writing is exceptionally idiomatic (reminiscent of Mendelssohn?) for the pianist, who should follow carefully the dynamic shadings indicated by Schumann. The singer's task is to treat the melodic line as "accompaniment" to the keyboard figure while cleanly enunciating the text in a sorrowful, subdued legato. The young woman's despair is even more deeply expressed through five bars of gradual ritardando as she asks, "Why should I keep spinning? I cannot tell." Somehow she goes on. The pianist should play the rhythmic motif hesitatingly as the girl expresses her grief, then return at once to *im Tempo* for the concluding four bars. This is a subtle musical translation of a poetic vignette also successfully set by Brahms.

Wolfgang Müller's *Im Wald* is the poetic source for #5. There is a directness about its rhythms and harmonies that seems ill-adapted to describing butterflies, birds, and deer as they all flee from the wanderer. Schumann is attracted more to a walk in the woods than to what transpires there or to the poet's pain. Melodic invention is not of the highest order, nor is the keyboard writing exceptional.

Abendlied, #6 of op. 107, to a text by Johann Gottfried Kinkel, might seem unusually constructed to those familiar only with the Schumann songs of 1840. It makes use of consecutive keyboard triads in triplets (best perceived in two slow beats to the bar) over which the singer moves in $\frac{4}{4}$ time. Evening is artfully evoked at "it has become so still; in the silence one hears everywhere the footsteps of angels." Perhaps the triplet figure is the gentle moving of angel wings.

"Close to the keys" should be the pianistic aim, with a mild rubato for the opening rhythmic ostinato. Schumann gives the triplet ostinato to the keyboard bass voice at bar 12, then in bar 15 joins all pianistic voices in singing the motif in higher register. The melody is full of grace and flows tranquilly forward. Schumann has admirably caught the quietude of evening, the search for serenity, and the longing for freedom from despair and sickness expressed in the stanzas he selects from a longer poem. There is great beauty in both keyboard and vocal writing. *Abendlied* was influential on both Brahms and Wolf.

Opus 117

The *Vier Husarenlieder*, so far removed from the songs of 1840 as to appear from a different hand, are not easily understood by those who know only the popular early Lieder of Schumann. No matter who writes them, military and battle songs are seldom successful. But Schumann is highly effective in setting these four Lenau hussar poems. The songs of op. 117 are patently aggressive and militaristic. Only voices of good resonance balance, capable of both depth and brilliance (the traditional chiaroscuro vocal tone of the international professional), should take on this assignment. An understanding of vocal registers and the color possibilities in registration distinguishes the writing.

The judgment that the quality of the Lieder deteriorates as Schumann's illness advances comes partly from critics who object to Schumann's growing reliance on ample voices of professional dimensions. There is evidence within the song literature itself that as the years progress Schumann's lyric declamation tends to give way to expansive vocal writing. The premise that the composer was unable to compose effective Lieder beyond the Lieder Year (which is repeated by critic after critic without thorough examination of the songs themselves) is close to scandalous. That poetic meter suffers more at Schumann's hands in his later years, as has often been stated, is not true. There are numerous examples of songs from both 1840 and 1850 in which the poetry is purposely relegated to a secondary position, pianism and vocalism become professionally demanding, and synthesis is not the chief goal.

Mit wildfeurigem Ausdruck is Schumann's marking for #1, *Der Husar, trara!*, and wild and fiery it should be. There is purposeful blustering, masculine posturing, and competitive exuberance. The angular melodic lines with their leaping phrases are completely in keeping with Lenau's overdrawn portrait of the wild hussar.

Sams's assessment (p. 263): "The ostensible mood is one of bluff assurance. But the music, like the verse, bristles with short sharp phrases like sabres arranged in a compulsive pattern, and hectically overemphasized by repetition. Nevertheless this is an effective song; perhaps *too effective for comfort*" (My emphasis). Pianist and singer should give themselves unstintingly to the athletic parameters of fingers and vocal folds. No holds are barred.

Der leidige Frieden, #2 of the opus, is ballad-like and continues some of the spirit of #1, but at a lower degree of bravado for both instruments. (The tempo marking is *nicht schnell*.) Pianistic rhythm continues to be driving but sedate; the vocal line is less extensive than in *Der Husar, trara!* and demands especially good textual articulation from the singer. On the surface forthrightly soldierly, professing careless adventuring, and carrying forward the extroversion of #1, this Lied confesses to a deeper emotion through tonal ambiguities that remain unresolved to the final bar.

Den grünen Zeigern, #3, is to be performed *mit Lustigkeit*. A joyous, masculine medium it is. The rhythmic element is markedly swaggering, imitative of barracks songs, and the Lied exudes Hungarian fervor. Bass octaves give firmness and purposefulness to the keyboard, offering strong support to the inten-

Example 24.2. *Da liegt der Feinde gestreckte Schar*, bars 13–16.

wei - ter ruft der Trom-pe - ten-ruf,   er wischt an die Mäh-ne sein nas-ses Schwert,und

wei - ter springt sein lu - sti-ges Pferd,   mit ro -   - tem Huf.

tional brashness of the vocal line. The six concluding postlude bars are meant as bugle calls. Dynamic *f* markings occur repeatedly, indicating that Schumann was interested in big sound from both keyboard and voice.

Da liegt der Feinde gestreckte Schar concludes this cycle of four songs. (Schumann omitted a fifth poem.) While retaining an air of militarism, it displays a new facet of the hussar's character, sensibilities that momentarily go beyond the earlier soldier posturing. C minor provides an appropriate seriousness to the battlefield scene of fallen enemy soldiers. The low male voice tessitura adds to the solemnity. Schumann requires a low F from his dramatic baritone, who must then mount upward with powerful vocalism as the trumpets interrupt momentary reflection, calling him back to the battle. The Lied offers the singer a chance to portray a remarkable combination of exuberant warrior and sensitive human being. The return to the fray, with the hussar's blood-spattered horse charging onward, becomes a triumphant battle cry. Schumann concludes with two bars of *pp* that represent his own sentiment about the tragedy of battle. The song is one not of mere blustering but of considerable psychological insight (Ex. 24.2).

Although the pianist is not here the equal musical partner often required in Schumann Lieder, in this case he or she must deliver powerful, descriptive orchestral sound that catches the energy of the writing. In all probability, the galloping triplet octave figures depict the horse hooves so vividly described in the poem. Large low male voices (the dedication was to baritone Heinrich Behr) miss an opportunity for vigorous singing and emotive expression if they fail to program these Lieder. The songs of op. 117 provide excellent material for the bass-baritone and even for the rangy bass voice. Because they belong to the low male voice, the songs should not be transposed to higher keys.

Close association with the variety of compositional techniques used by Schumann in his late period leads one to believe that, regardless of the fluctuating physical and psychological conditions during all periods of his life, Schumann is here walking new paths of creativity.

25

Opus 119, Opus 125, and Maria Stuart Lieder, Opus 135

Opus 119

Die Hütte, composed in September 1851 together with two other poems from Gustav Pfarrius's *Waldlieder*, was published as op. 119. Schumann found the precise tone for this homey poetic expression of contentment that speaks of a cottage built in the woods. In spirit as well as in musical forthrightness, *Die Hütte* is related to Haydn's *Ein kleines Haus* (perhaps better known in its Italian translation, *Un tetto umil*). Happy domesticity and a love of nature are conveyed through simple harmonic means. Says Fischer-Dieskau (p. 196): "*Die Hütte* . . . is lively and attractive; not suffering from mannerisms such as suspensions to express languishing sentiment." Sams's evaluation (p. 269) is not in agreement: "It is sad to find the virile motif . . . in this reduced state." Further, Sams finds "inept" accentuation of the text.

Die Hütte is not among Schumann's most inventive Lieder, but it is a pleasant song, calling for honest vocalism and direct keyboard involvement. Appropriate for inclusion in a group of representative Schumann Lieder, *Die Hütte* is especially suitable as a studio or recital assignment for young singers and pianists. Its vocal and pianistic requirements are more modest than those of many other late-period Schumann Lieder.

Warnung, #2 of this opus, offers singer and pianist a lovely vignette that displays Schumann's remarkable creative diversity. The initial descending keyboard motif, moving from right to left hand, acts as a unifying element for the Lied and is compelling in itself. It dictates the shape of the vocal line that subtly mirrors the keyboard, signaling from Schumann yet another imaginative interplay between voice and pianoforte, an instrumental relationship quite removed from his most customary 1840 idiom. Its singability makes it an excellent item for the voice studio. The song lies exceedingly well for mezzo-soprano.

It is, of course, to the pianist that the task of phrase contouring is largely given. Portraying the unaware little bird who by singing faces death from the menacing owl is not the happiest assignment given a singer. There may be some justification in suggesting that it was not a warning of impending danger that was uppermost in Schumann's mind, regardless of the title of the poem, but evocation of night's onset. Singer and pianist may program this song with confidence in its intrinsic merit and the direct appeal it will make to the listener.

Der Bräutigam und die Birke, #3, is full of good cheer. The opening bars for both pianoforte and voice catch the gay, folklike elements of the dialogue between the birch tree and the bridegroom. If Schumann was suffering from depression, no evidence of that condition invades his creativity here.

The simple chordal accompaniment of the first four bars gives way at bars 5 and 6 to a dancing figure that anticipates wedding-day joy. Alternation of the motif of the opening four bars with the subsequent two bars, repeated several times, produces an appropriate "question and answer" structure between bridegroom and birch tree. The final eight bars are impelled forward in playful parlando fashion through a *lebhafter* tempo with tumbling syllabic triplets. Schumann did not intend to write a monumental song, and the outcome cannot be placed among his top-drawer Lieder. *Der Bräutigam und die Birke* is a pleasureful folklike Lied that has a viable role in both teaching and performance circumstances. Simplicity, forthrightness, nonchalance, and playfulness should be the goal of both pianist and singer.

Opus 125

Die Meerfee, #1, exhibits another facet of the diversity that Schumann brings to his late Lieder. It was composed in July of 1850 to the scintillating verse of Julius Buddeus. The opening seven semistaccato bars in the pianoforte, with their initial intriguing chromatic harmonies (bars 1–4), ring like the bright silver bells of the ensuing staccato vocal line. Once again, joy and colorful fantasy belie any invasion of morbidity. *Die Meerfee* is a song of great charm and surprising harmonic development. The leap from the original A major into momentary B♭ major color (bar 29) is appropriately abrupt as we turn from the sea fairy to the enchanted boy on shipboard. His dreaminess is signified by the sequence of harmonies that lead back to a concluding A major. *Die Meerfee* is a pearl taken from the coach of the sea fairy herself. In this brief composition, harmonic richness and inventiveness go beyond the poetic source, producing multicolored nuances that must be matched by both pianist and singer. *Die Meerfee* gives rich opportunities for interpretative and musical subtlety.

Inevitably, several authors have drawn comparisons between *Die Meerfee* and the Loewe and Mendelssohn settings of fairyland, but beyond sharing a generic poetic landscape there is little actual relationship between Schumann's treatment and that of the other two composers. Performers may be dismayed to read (Sams, p. 247) that "any creative spark is smothered by the smooth inanities of the verse, and Schumann's own matching mood." As well as being a charming song suitable for public performance, *Die Meerfee* is particularly useful in the training of young soprano and tenor voices.

In *Husarenabzug*, #2, Fischer-Dieskau (p. 187) finds that "we first encounter a technique later made use of by Hugo Wolf's songs: the expression of cockiness and high spirits by using eighth-note chords, staccato, with rapidly changing harmonies." Sams (p. 248) finds it fortunate that this is Schumann's only Carl Candidus song and adds: "Brahms inherited either Schumann's copy of the poems or his taste for them, and set several to music." Sams further comments: "The musical ideas, though jaded, are perhaps tolerable enough for one verse of this appalling poem; but they are already inept by the second, and the stolid repetitions of the drum and tucket [trumpet flourish or fanfare] effects soon become deadly." Fischer-Dieskau wonders (p. 180) "whether Brahms inherited the volume of poetry used by Schumann, his idol. While Schumann's setting is weak, the younger composer later was to create several magnificent songs based on these rather mediocre poems."

The poem does not represent the pinnacle of German poetic inspiration but is typical of—and no worse than—much military verse indigenous to German nineteenth-century poetry, especially that which romanticizes the figure of the dashing hussar.

The energy achieved by Schumann, beginning with the octave *sf* and continuing with the drumming of the eighth-note/sixteenth-note rhythmic patterns, is noteworthy. By using the fully resonant timbre of well-produced masculine vocalism, a tenor with flair can bring this Lied to life, much to his advantage. *Husarenabzug* is a practical alternative for the sizable young tenor voice not yet capable of the subtleties required by the Eichendorff *Liederkreis* or *Dichterliebe*. The pianist can have a happy moment playing at the drum and the bugle. Great Lied literature? Perhaps not, but certainly at a level comparable to some earlier songs by Robert Schumann. There is nothing "jaded" about the musical idiom, nothing "stolid," nothing "inept," nothing "deadly." It is, in short, an excellent song for a vital male vocal performer and an energetic pianist collaborator. This song points to many Lieder yet to come from the hands of other composers as the nineteenth century progressed, and to many twentieth-century songs as well.

The third song of op. 125, *Jung Volkers Lied*, is to verses by Mörike. Its opening figure has a freshness and vigor that make believable the roguish character about to be introduced, a role the singer must vocally enact. Scurrying sixteenth notes of the opening two bars, doubled at the octave, give way in the third and fourth bars to a dotted-eighth/sixteenth-note figure, a rhythmic pattern that frequently occurs within the song. These two keyboard motifs combine to permit the driving impetus Schumann brings to his Jung Volker portrayal. They must be played with flourish. The melody outlines a descending arpeggio, a pattern used dozens of times in other Schumann Lieder. Sams discovers (p. 261) that "the opening melody is borrowed from—of all things—*Mondnacht*, at 'die Erde still geküsst, etc.,' and is not only in the same notes and key but even has (bar 45) the added decoration. Perhaps the word 'Ehe' was a subconscious link." However, *Mondnacht* and *Jung Volkers Lied* are not related even remotely. They have little in common, either in spirit or in compositional concept. Performers who sing and play this Lied at the indicated *sehr lebhaft* metronomic marking of 100 (was Schumann's metronome slow, as has been reported?) to the quarter note and who recognize the character of the aggressive arpeggiated melody will be unable to associate *Jung Volkers Lied* with the mysterious melodic invocations of *Mondnacht*, the quintessential *Stimmungslied*.

Once again Schumann shows his ability for characterization, fully realizing Jung Volker's blustering about his questionable parenthood. The song is a fitting companion to the one that precedes it. Range and *tessitura* are somewhat lower than those of the previous two Lieder, but the whole opus could be suitable for a dramatic tenor or for a lyric baritone who manages an impressive upper range. These Lieder should be robustly sung and played.

Frühlingslied, #4, to a poem by Ferdinand Braun, is a delightful invitation to celebrate the joys of Spring. Octave doublings of the fifth of the scale introduce ornaments that seem to evoke a country dance. The trills and turns are mirthful. Schumann catches us up and involves us in his own ebullient energy. The vocal line is angular and often arpeggio-oriented, and calls for directness of expression. The inherent exuberance of this Lied could have come only from a vital spirit. It should be performed that way.

The verse is strophically set, and as is the case in nearly every strophic song ever written, it is up to performers to vary strophes through suitable changes in word and keyboard accents. Segments 4 and 5, with their warning advice, must be given an increased sense of urgency. Simplistically joyful, *Frühlingslied* can brighten up any Lieder group.

The next Lied, *Frühlingslust*, #5, on verses by Paul Heyse, represents Schumann's last love affair with Spring before the onset of his own personal Winter. It is the kind of exposition that, although traditional in its roots, had considerable influence on composers yet to come. There is about it both a flowing melodic contour in the conservative Mendelssohnian manner and a sweeping Brahmsian pianoforte structure. The pianist is given rich material built on a glittering right hand that happily surges over a lower-voiced melody; the singer is offered a gracious vocal exercise. Here is an evocation of the joys of Spring equal to many better-known Spring songs.

Maria Stuart Lieder, Opus 135

The five Maria Stuart Lieder (*Gedichte der Maria Stuart*) cannot be encountered without engendering great sympathy for the composer as well as their royal protagonist. The songs are to translations by Baron Gisbert Vincke from poetry attributed to Mary, Queen of Scots, and come from December 1852, when for the last time the debilitating illness that was to destroy that vital dual personality—Eusebius/Florestan—was held in abeyance. Schumann presented these Lieder to Clara as a Christmas present. A strange gift, it might seem, but understandable, given the circumstances under which they were written and Schumann's awareness of his own condition. Sams (p. 273) remarks:

> One of the saddest entries in Schumann's diary records his joy on completing *these last five dismal songs*. We can only conjecture what personal meaning he found in them. The first begins "I am going away." The last ends "Save me." Soon after their completion came his mental breakdown, his attempt to drown himself in the Rhine, and his incarceration in the asylum at Endenich, where in July 1856 he died. (Italics mine.)

We are grateful to Fischer-Dieskau for his power of discernment and objectivity regarding these last works (pp. 198–99):

> These poems . . . assume a key position in Schumann's life, constituting a terminal point: they are the composer's last songs. . . . The style of this small cycle does not allow for melodies in the manner that Schumann had initiated 13 years before. Language and its rhythm now govern form, including the manner of accompaniment. A style distantly related to what Wagner had fashioned now appears in the *Lied*. Relinquishing all oratory and emphasis, Schumann presents the spiritual condition of a woman under the shadow of death.

For #1 of the opus, *Abschied von Frankreich*, Schumann relies on a pianoforte procedure that served him well throughout his composing career—the arpeggiated *gruppetto* in sixteenth-note values, delineating changing harmonies. The basic formula allows Schumann to create a traditional melody, one that could have been from the hand of a number of his contemporaries.

This mode of composition changes immediately with #2, *Nach der Geburt ihres Sohnes*, whose "melody" is intoned over minimal keyboard motion that, through harmonic simplicity, achieves a devotional atmosphere. Schumann's sensitivity to the text is expressed in a musical idiom that resembles psalmody (Fischer-Dieskau, p. 199).

In *An die Königin Elisabeth*, #3, Schumann's abundantly diverse muse finds yet another idiom. Fischer-Dieskau (p. 199) offers an insightful evaluation: "*An die Königin Elisabeth* . . . also is governed by the accents of speech, resulting in a kind of accompanied recitative. An angular rhythmic pattern supports the melody which provides no rests for breathing. There is a hint of courtly ceremonial."

Example 25.1.   *Abschied von der Welt*, bars 1–9.

Despite the accompanied-recitative nature of this Lied, there is no need to resort to a detached parlando style for its performance. The intensity of the text, the well-founded consternation of Queen Mary, her appeal to her cousin, and her hearing voices of hope and fear are caught by Schumann in ways too subtle for analysis. His own realization of "the force of fate [that] often hurls down the sail in which we put our trust" jumps out from the page.

Mary Stuart's *Abschied von der Welt*, #4, becomes Robert Schumann's own farewell to the world. His setting of the text has little in common with conventional melody. The opening keyboard motif in various registers is a musically unifying element above which the voice chants. Emotional reserve is maintained (Ex. 25.1).

Gebet, the final song of this last cycle, is a testimonial to Schumann's ability to concentrate on musical construction, and to his sensitivity to the poetic source, until the very end of his deeply moving personal struggle (Ex. 25.2). The words of Fischer-Dieskau (p. 199) merit quotation:

In *Gebet* (Prayer, No. 5) Schumann succeeds in characterizing a moment of resignation, to a degree that Wagner, even with the greatest restraint, could not

Example 25.2. *Gebet*, bars 1–8.

have accomplished. Still, it is fascinating that at this moment in history, two composers, holding diametrically opposed positions, came close to each other through their declamatory styles. From their respective positions they were able to define a new kind of diction in German song. The Stuart songs mark the limit to which Schumann was able to restrict his vocal means of expression, reducing his musical language to a minimum. They stand at the end of a long, consistent development, from the fullness of unbridled fantasy to a soft, barely audible protest against the noisy music of his time.

Lorraine Gorrell, herself a singer, remarks (p. 151): "The Maria Stuart songs are highly effective in performance and appropriate to the mood of the poems on which they are based. Although not vocally difficult, they require a sensitive, intelligent interpretation."

The songs are uniquely for female voice, probably most suited to a mezzo-soprano. They require the emotive colors of warmth, human resignation, longing, fear, and devotion. In these five Lieder, the sophisticated performer has an opportunity to portray noble womanhood. Restraint, not remoteness, is the key for performers of the Maria Stuart Lieder. One could wish that this small cycle were given more frequent performance.

26

Solos and Duets from the Ensemble Collections: Opuses 29, 34, 37, 43, 74, 78, 79, 101, 103, 112, and 138

The duet literature is scattered among various opuses. The Friedländer edition of the Schumann duets (*Duette für zwei Singstimmen mit Pianoforte Begleitung* [C. F. Peters]; the most recent edition published as *Duette für Gesang und Klavier*) makes accessible under one mantle thirty-four duets. Duet opuses should be programmed in their entirety, when possible. Ideally, this is true of all the ensemble opuses, but it would be a pity to maintain a purist attitude that forbade selections being excerpted from any or all of them.

Before consideration of the duet Lieder, it may be worthwhile to quote from Schumann's collection of aphorisms regarding folk-song derivation and ensemble singing (p. 35): "You should early come to understand the compass of the human voice in its four principal sorts. Listen to it in the chorus; seek to discover in which intervals lies its principal strength and through which of them it best expresses softness and tenderness."

Opus 29

Ländliches Lied, op. 29, #1, for two sopranos, is marvelously fresh and exuberant. There is about it an irresistible charm and grace that enhances Geibel's poetry. With a cheerful V_7 arpeggio Schumann introduces the voices, which, entering in nearly canonic imitation of each other, often sing out in harmonious thirds.

Schumann's modulatory skill contributes to a delightful setting of the events of Nature. This passage is interrupted by "und denket still, ob der Liebste nicht kommen will" (bars 18–22) as the young girl thinks of her lover, singing now over halted motion in the keyboard, and the two voices become almost recitative-like. A return to the original vocal material is accomplished through repetition of the opening V_7 arpeggio, but this figure then becomes engagingly varied before the final strophe, and the keyboard strides in climactic sixths. The sopranos then continue their own duet in sixths at "O du selige Maienzeit, o du selige, selige Zeit!" A more successful joining of two female voices and pianoforte can scarcely be imagined.

(*Lied*, #2, is for three soprano voices; #3 is scored for S. A. T. B. with triangle and tambourine ad libitum. Neither is considered here.)

Opus 34

In op. 34 Schumann has given tenors and sopranos a joyous gift of song.

Liebesgarten, #1 (to a Reinick text), in gently flowing $\frac{6}{8}$, is best suited to the soubrette soprano and the *leggiero* tenor. The high tessitura for the tenor dictates the Lied's appropriateness to a light, lyric instrument; otherwise balance problems result between the two voices.

Liebhabers Ständchen, #2, to a translation of a Burns poem, is a gem! The little drama makes one think of Brahms's *VergeblichesStändchen*, with which *Liebhabers Ständchen* admirably holds its own. Agitated keyboard sixteenths introduce the tenor serenade as the boy stands outside in the rain and pleads for permission to enter. Schumann remarkably catches the humor of the text. The repetitions of "o lass mich ein die eine Nacht!" at various pitch levels grow in excitement. The girl's resounding "Nein, nein, ich öffne nicht!" and the keyboard conclusion must induce a smile and a chuckle from even the most jaded listener.

Unterm Fenster, #3, also to a Burns poem, continues the bantering between tenor and soprano of *Liebhabers Ständchen*. The urgent rapping in the keyboard introduces *her* annoyed question and *his* frantic reply. The demands for the tenor voice are great, with repeated interjections of high A at a relatively rapid tempo.

Unterm Fenster and *Liebhabers Ständchen* fit charmingly together, especially in contrast to the slower *Familien-Gemälde*, #4, to verse by Anastasius Grün, which follows them. In *Familien-Gemälde*, the tenor part is uncomfortably low for many light tenor voices. The soprano part also lies low for a soubrette, who would most probably be paired with a *leggiero* tenor in a group of these duet Lieder. Schumann concludes with an eighteen-bar postlude, perhaps in response to "und dachten der schönen Vergangenheit" and "und dachten von ferner, künftiger Zeit."

Opus 37

Robert wrote his publisher that *Zwölf Gedichte aus "Liebesfrühling"* was composed jointly with Clara. He hoped the set could be published in time to surprise Clara on her birthday, which wish was realized. Included in op. 37 are three duets, #6, #7, and #12, to texts by Rückert.

Liebste, was kann denn uns scheiden?, #6, is a sweet and happy song of limited vocal demands and sparse interjectory chordal accompaniment. Tenor and soprano have four questioning solo segments each, joining in thirds at the sixth bar in all four strophes with "Nein" and concluding each strophe with a charming two-bar duet. Diversification between the solo passages and the occasional unanticipated brief duet statements makes this a uniquely appealing Lied.

The mood of *Liebste, was kann denn uns scheiden?* changes with *Schön ist das Fest des Lenzes*, #7. Pianoforte collaboration occurs in the rich lower-middle keyboard octave. The two voices are treated in modified canonic manner at the remove of one bar, with engaging word repetitions. This leads to some unexpected melodic and harmonic sport that should be pointed up by the singers. (*Schön ist das Fest des Lenzes* is found in S. A. T. B. arrangement in *Minnespiel*, #5, op. 101.)

So wahr die Sonne scheinet, #12, is marked for soprano with *Tenor oder Bariton*. In chorale-like form, with traditional close harmonies, it lies low for both sopranos and tenors; more appropriately, it belongs to baritones and mezzo-sopranos. A pleasant and performance-worthy Lied, it does not rank among Schumann's most inventive creations. (*So wahr die Sonne scheinet* appears again as #8 in *Minnespiel* in S. A. T. B. form.)

This group of Lieder supports the criticism that Schumann (despite his advice about the need to be acquainted with the characteristics of each vocal category) seemed not always to take into account range and *tessitura* factors. *Zwölf Gedichte aus "Liebesfrühling,"* which includes both solos (#2, #4, and #11 are by Clara Schumann) and duets for soprano and tenor, makes a wonderfully complete set in a duet recital.

Opus 43

Opus 43 consists of three duets for soprano and *Alt* (mezzo-soprano or contralto). *Wenn ich ein Vöglein wär*, #1, is to a text by an unknown poet. Even though low-ranging for both voices, it pleases through traditional female part singing. Following the initial fourteen bars of running notes in the bass clef, Schumann gives the keyboard his reliable arpeggiated "filler." The pianoforte at times joins the two singers in thirds and sixths. This is probably the best known of the Schumann duets. The writing is so felicitous that it almost seems to sing and play itself (Ex. 26.1).

Herbstlied, #2, with text by August Mahlmann, combines the favorite

Example 26.1.   *Wenn ich ein Vöglein wär*, bars 1–6.

sixteenth-note *gruppetti* configuration with an irregularly occurring ostinato-like bass and creates polarity between the keyboard soprano and bass voices not unlike the luxuriant pianoforte texture on which Brahms would come to rely (Ex. 26.2). Thirds and sixths in the singing voices are doubled by the keyboard inner voices. At bar 25 and continuing through much of the duet, Schumann introduces a new rhythmic figure—harp arpeggios in sextolets—which, as was seen earlier, is considered in some quarters to indicate an inability to set a text imaginatively. The result is a flow of vocal and keyboard timbres in a happy composition for two voices and pianoforte.

Schön Blümelein, #3, is a setting of another Reinick poem. Sparkling *p* triplets, chiefly in patterns of harmonic sixths, set the stage for the morning walk, where flowers, butterflies, bees, and ladybugs are encountered. The folk character is embellished at the keyboard by quickly-moving fingers. Tender expression and good vocal legato from the singers and effervescent articulation from the pianist will realize the inherent charm of this little duet.

Spanisches Liederspiel, Opus 74

The songs of the *Spanisches Liederspiel*, op. 74, were composed in 1849. The title page carried this note from Schumann: "The texts are taken from folk songs and romances from the Spanish, translated by E. Geibel." The collection was published as *Spanisches Liederspiel. Eine Cyclus von Gesängen aus dem Spanischen für eine and mehrere Stimmen*. These exceptional Lieder were written for one, two, or four voices with pianoforte accompaniment. There are songs for solo tenor, solo soprano, and solo bass, duets for soprano and alto, tenor and bass, and soprano and tenor, and two vocal quartets. (Only the duets are considered here.) *Spanisches Liederspiel* should be heard in its entirety when the performance forces can be assembled. With good reason, Schumann himself was very happy with them.

Erste Begegnung (the title, "First Meeting," was aptly supplied by Schumann) is an appropriate #1 for the opus. Schumann finds precise ethnic rhythms for these Spanish Lieder. Over a marked guitarlike $\frac{3}{4}$ rhythmic pattern in the key of A minor, Schumann introduces brief vocal phrases in parallel thirds and sixths. He makes use of a small keyboard motif based on the opening vocal figure that injects a distinctive Spanish flavor. This pattern, passing back and forth between the keyboard and the female voices, is a unifying element. The modulation to momentary Bb major (bars 17–20) is assisted by the same figure that sees service in subsequent bars. The double entendre of the text (the youth picking many roses and the girl confessing to her mother her infatuation as he gave to her the most beautiful of the roses) is cleverly caught by Schumann. There is an excitation, a forward tumbling of emotion, perhaps some apprehension. The four final pianoforte measures sum it all up.

Available duet recital literature for tenor and bass voices is limited. *Intermezzo*, #2, is a welcome addition. The *tessitura* for each singer lies in the *zona di passaggio* (upper-middle range). The timbre of the two male voices in their respective registers is beautifully augmented by the lower-middle-octave keyboard, producing a sonority of warmth and richness from the two voices and the pianoforte. Both singers must be sufficiently skilled to maintain the relatively high *tessitura* with ease and gentleness and to preserve an extreme legato, remaining at *p* dynamic. Sustained, cumulative phrases require ability to renew breath rapidly. (There are no rests indicated in the first twenty-four bars.) Schumann retains the folk element to perfection while creating a sophisticated harmonic support in the keyboard.

Using two male voices to sing a personal *aubade* to a sleeping maiden is a novel idea. Probably Schumann's choice was prompted by his scheme to assign

Example 26.2.   *Herbstlied*, bars 1–4.

duets to diverse vocal categories, thereby achieving several vocal-timbre combinations within the opus.

Were the identity of the composer unknown, one might logically attribute this duet to Johannes Brahms.

Liebesgram, #3, is reflective yet fully emotive. No wonder Schumann assumed that op. 74 would be among his most successful songs! The first bars of *Liebesgram*, announced with a seventh-chord motif in the two female voices and in the keyboard, provide themes out of which the G minor sections develop in intricate detail. The later ten bars in G major offer relief with a more diatonic texture, making the return to the chromatic G minor harmonies emotionally telling. Soprano and contralto voices stay within ranges that permit resonance balances favorable to the lower harmonics of the spectrum of each singer. Schumann's *p* and *f* markings are to be religiously observed.

In der Nacht, #4, is yet another example of compositional diversity. A Baroque-like right-hand theme, wedded to nineteenth-century chromatic harmonies, occupies the opening five bars. Long vocal lines are suspended over starkly stated keyboard fragments. Interrupted vocal lines weave in and out above the pianoforte statement. Later harmonic progressions and momentary modulations blur tonality. The melodic and harmonic inventions are of the highest order.

The singers and the pianist must actualize within the long phrases the alternation of movement and repose engendered by Schumann's harmonic language. The composition makes remarkable use of interplay between chromatic and diatonic harmonies (which would become so characteristic of Wolf's art), thereby juxtaposing moments of stability and instability. Schumann brings a quality of emotional depth seldom surpassed in either his Lieder or those of any composer.

(*Es ist verraten*, #5, is a bolero for four voices. There is not a more endearing vocal quartet!)

Melancholie, #6, is a dramatic aria in miniature that transcends traditional Lied boundaries. Perhaps Schumann had in mind a voice like that of one of his favorite sopranos, diva Schröder-Devrient. Its melismatic patterns (bar 8) based on seventh-chord harmonies at the word "Leben," and its later leaps of tenths produce an effect not far removed from operatic vocalism. Seldom is so much vocal drama contained in so short a time span. One thinks of Mozart's *Als Luise die Briefe ihres ungetreuen Liebhabers verbrannte* (in spirit, not in harmonic language). The Lied form seems ready to burst its confines. Sams (p. 192) says: "The result is not without grandeur." Fischer-Dieskau (p. 153) finds the song "evocative of Southern temperament."

For the tenor voice, *Geständnis*, #7, as regards its vocal requirements, is a recognizable male sibling of *Melancholie*. The far removal of these Lieder from the style of most of the songs in opuses 25, 39, 42, and 48 is a testimonial to the evolution of Schumann's Lied concept. Aesthetic goals are no longer directed to lyric declamation, nor to synthesis of word and music; false syllabic accents, text repetitions, and vocal display are given free hand. Not surprisingly, given his

Example 26.3.   *Botschaft*, bars 84–90.

consistent aesthetic orientation, Sams (pp. 192–93) is not happy: "A strange middle-aged mixture of passion, caution and fustian . . . after this first sweetness the inside tastes woody. The harmonic tension slackens, the accompaniment figure lags . . . then the music begins to posture again; and the peroration is all too deliberate and familiar." On the contrary, what a blessing this highly vocal essay for tenor voice is!

Growing from its initial pianoforte trill, *Botschaft*, #8, erupts with spumescent Latin energy. Based on bolero rhythms, *Botschaft* is one of the most successful attempts from any composer to capture the flavor of Spanish dance. All through its extensive length, Schumann sustains a level of jocularity that captivates the ear and amazes with its rhythmic and melodic inventiveness.

The technical demands on both female singers and the pianist are high; in every bar, *Botschaft* requires performance competence at the most skillful professional level. The rapid arpeggios, splashing upward from low to high range, the harmonic permutations of the bolero theme as it is developed and embellished in the keyboard, and the contrary motion of the voices subsequently joining in pyrotechnical vocalization (bars 84–90) are quintessential elements. A superb duet Lied (Ex. 26.3).

(*Ich bin geliebt*, #9, is another vigorous vocal quartet, with which *Spanisches Liederspiel* terminates.)

Opus 78

Schumann's remarkable energy of 1849 is equally apparent in his setting of Rückert's *Tanzlied*, #1, op. 78. This *Liebeswalzer* need not take second place to any composition in that genre by any hand. Florestan is in good form, enjoying himself thoroughly, as can be seen in the opening keyboard figure (bars 1–7). Modulatory activity, as in bars 26–52, produces a blurring of the harmonic sense as pairs of *Mädchen* and *Bübchen* recklessly swirl through the dance. Bars 65–76 are illustrative of the pianistic verve that brings to life the strong Dionysian dance elements in *Tanzlied*. The singers must swoop through their alternating long phrases with vitality and vigor. Never will tenor and soprano find a more rewarding duet in waltz form (Ex. 26.4).

Er und Sie, with text by Kerner, is #2 of op. 78. The two soloists (tenor and soprano) dialogue independently for the first half of the duet, then join harmoniously as the Lied develops. At several points, the tessitura of the tenor voice could overpower the soprano voice, so that special care for ensemble balance must be taken. Easy vocalism from both singers is called for in this *bel canto* exercise.

In #3, *Ich denke dein*, soprano and tenor engage in pure lyricism, beautiful phrase shaping, and dynamic subtlety. Schumann's setting of this beloved Goethe text is one of the most successful it has ever been given. Vocal timbres and keyboard colors melt the listener's heart. Schumann's lyric response to *Ich denke dein* would have an influence on composers who were to write duet Lieder in the following decades.

Wiegenlied am Lager eines kranken Kindes, #4, is noteworthy for yet another device that Hugo Wolf would make use of: closely clustered dissonant notes—generally minor seconds—simultaneously struck to denote smallness. Schumann relies on this figure with great frequency in *Wiegenlied am Lager eines kranken Kindes*. The duet illustrates (as has been previously pointed out) that Schumann, contrary to what is often repeated, was not averse to using mechanical keyboard means to describe poetic events. It could be posited that the comforting of a sick child (are the small dissonant harmonic clusters its petulant cries?) is represented in the rocking rhythmic motifs. Soprano and tenor voices are comfortably scored, and a low dynamic

Example 26.4.   *Tanzlied*, bars 1–7.

level must be maintained. There are many lullabies and cradle songs in the nineteenth-century Lied literature, some being among the most popular of all Lieder. Schumann's *Wiegenlied am Lager eines Kranken Kindes* deserves a high ranking among them.

Opus 79

In the Spring of 1849, Schumann began his *Liederalbum fur die Jugend*, op. 79.

Mailied, #9 (#10 in the Friedländer numeration), is an optional duet. Soprano II is listed ad libitum, since the pianoforte mostly sings the same notes that are indicated for the second singing voice. The poetic source, indicated as "Fliegendes Blatt," is Christian Adolf Overbeck. (The poem should not be confused with the Kulmann *Mailied* of op. 103.) Folk-song elements predominate. Although it is not without charm, *Mailied* seems of lesser musical value than a number of remarkable duets from Schumann's hand.

Number 15 (Friedländer #16), marked *sehr schnell*, is a setting of *Das Glück*, a poem by Hebbel. Much of the pleasure it gives is derived from two singers pattering (*sehr schnell*) rapid texts at each other. *Das Glück* requires precise articulation from both sopranos; it must be performed playfully. Excited little phrases are tossed back and forth between the two singers while the keyboard intersperses detached chordal fragments until the surprising turn of events for the last seven bars, where a dashing right hand (bar 70) discovers a final resolution (bars 72–75).

For *Frühlingslied*, #18 (Friedländer #19), Schumann is back again with his broken-arpeggio harmonic filler, over which the sopranos sing a happy folk song. It is to the pianoforte that the composer directs his chief attention. Between strophes and at the conclusion, thematic material develops into a miniature keyboard etude. The challenges for the singers are superb enunciation and tonal exuberance.

Another study in rapid textual articulation for a pair of sopranos is to be found in *Die Schwalben*, #20 (Friedländer #21). Several strophes of swiftly flying swallows inhabit both voice and pianoforte scorings. Singers looking for lighthearted duets will be happy to become acquainted with these Lieder.

Minnespiel, Opus 101

Because of the success of *Spanisches Liederspiel*, Schumann felt encouraged to write a second group of songs for various combinations of voices and pianoforte. *Minnespiel aus Rückerts "Liebesfrühling,"* op. 101, was the result. *Minnespiel* includes solo Lieder for soprano and tenor and duets for alto and bass, alto and soprano, and alto and tenor, together with two S. A. T. B. scorings. When a vocal quartet is available, the entire opus should be performed as a unit.

In this opus, Schumann turns to another compositional mode, different from the gay atmosphere of the Spanish settings. This is immediately apparent

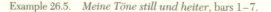

Example 26.5.   *Meine Töne still und heiter*, bars 1–7.

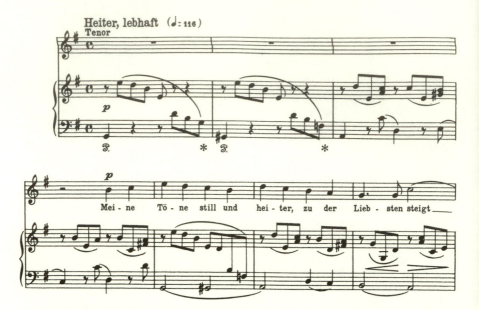

in *Meine Töne still und heiter*, #1, which in its first section displays a melodic breadth that points toward Johannes Brahms (Ex. 26.5). The yearning of the unrequited lover is expressed in soaring lines that later became a Brahmsian trademark. Schumann thereby writes superb vocalism for tenor voice, grateful in every way. He selects two separate poems from Rückert and combines them into the Lied *Meine Töne still und heiter*. It may be that Schumann chose the second section, in which the beloved opens her window and smiles at the lover, to counter the incompleteness of the lover's efforts in the first poem. In any event, the setting of the second poem does not directly segue from the first. It is in a swinging $\frac{6}{8}$ (the first is in a noble $\frac{4}{4}$) and ascends through quickly enunciated syllables to unexpected vocal heights that drastically alter the previous mood. If it is contrast the composer is intending, he achieves his aim. The second section has three strophes that conclude with a postlude that makes no musical reference back to the first section, leaving the two portions even more disjunct. Further, the lilting $\frac{6}{8}$, although pleasing, comes across as somewhat superficial when viewed in the context of the whole Lied.

The tenor who sings this Lied must have an instrument and technique sufficient to the generous nature of the melodic discourse of section A. In section B, an equalized vocal scale from lower to upper registers is essential. In the A portion, the pianist has the task of making the flowing arpeggios and their harmonic definition fit the vocal melody; in section B, played at a jolly $\frac{6}{8}$, he or she must strike skippingly with the right hand, while the left provides sufficiently firm support for the solo voice.

Liebster, deine Worte stehlen, #2, is given to the soprano. (It would lie equally well for a mezzo-soprano.) The first several bars are of special interest. As was to be the case in several other instances in the late Lieder, Schumann introduces a recitative statement before developing the melodic body of the Lied. This works exceedingly well, setting apart in pensive fashion the opening line of "Beloved, your words steal my heart from my bosom." The faster tempo and the new melody at "How can I hide my joy, my pain, from you!" increase excitement and exaltation. A well-conceived song for female voice, *Liebster, deine Worte stehlen* requires an inexorable legato and an opulent vocal timbre. The pianoforte score is fairly rich in texture as well. Schumann's admonition not to begin too *rasch* but to gradually become more impassioned ought to be followed.

Ich bin dein Baum, o Gärtner, #3, for contralto and bass, shows continued evidence of a more serious intention than is to be found in the Spanish songs. The Lied is of big conception. It has long vocal lines in registers that are full and resonant. A few brief imitative soloistic motifs comment in the upper-middle octave of the pianoforte, but Schumann mostly stays in the lower octaves. He thereby complements the low registers of the two singers (bars 38–42). Following a solo exposition from the contralto, the two voices proceed in interlocking fashion: *she* the tree, *he* the gardener. How could these Lieder be considered dark, depressing, and without vigor, as has been suggested? There is no morbidity here, only an idealized vision of love. In *Ich bin dein Baum, o Gärtner*, as in the other Lieder of this opus, Schumann reveals a depth of expression, an aura of love, that equals even that of Brahms (Ex. 26.6).

With *Mein schöner Stern!*, #4 of this 1849 opus, Schumann reaches a major peak of creativity. He returns to a compositional mode he had made frequent use of in 1840: the insistent reiterated chord in rhythmic eighth-note pattern (as in *Du bist wie eine Blume*, *Ich grolle nicht*, and many other Lieder previously considered). Schumann now spins over it one of his most memorable vocal lines. There is a depth of emotion through vocal and pianistic means that proves Schumann's continued growth as a Lied composer. He combines his earlier skill

Example 26.6.   *Ich bin dein Baum, o Gärtner*, bars 38–42.

with an expanded concept of the Lied as a medium for vocalization. Insupportable is Sams's statement (p. 5) that "the feelings of guilt and unworthiness which haunted him [Schumann] all of his life are also expressed in his songs (e.g., *Mein schöner Stern!*)." No one has the personal insight to determine that the continuously arching melodic phrases parallel the composer's personal need to seek, through love, rescue from the darkness into which he would eventually sink.

The combination of falling octaves and ascending vocal lines achieves an expansive dimension of vocal and keyboard timbres that holds the listener through its grandeur. The interplay of voice and keyboard is a new sort of synthesis, even for Schumann; there is total integration of keyboard sonority and vocal intensity. Schumann's younger contemporary, Johannes Brahms, with his penchant for phrases of long duration, would further expand the synthesis of vocal and pianistic sonorities. A pensive postlude concludes this magnificent Lied for tenor voice.

Transposition for low voice is perhaps irresistible, but much would be lost in the resultant muddiness of the keyboard octaves; baritone timbre is inappropriate to *Mein schöner Stern!* Let baritones make use of the wonderful songs and ballads Schumann has specifically written for them, and leave this paragon to their tenorial colleagues (Ex. 26.7).

Any musician thoroughly acquainted with the Schumann Lieder comes away in awe from #6, *O Freund, mein Schirm, mein Schutz!* Were there ever doubts as to Schumann's interest in taking the song into a number of exploratory directions, this song would dispel them. It is not just a case of Schumann putting his own harmonic stamp on an academic, imitative Baroque musical language; he takes that language and forges it into a highly intense new Romanticism. Through Baroque suspensions built over a ground bass, Schumann expresses the sentiment of a tortured soul who finds hope with "O friend, my shelter, my protection." The vocal line is moved from one level of intensity to another through chromatic harmonies that are in ceaseless motion. Longing, bitterness, and a cry of sorrow are seared into the sensibilities of the listener with each chordal progression. A hymnlike vocal melody evolves from an inventive harmonic texture. The totality of *O Freund, mein Schirm, mein Schutz!* is overwhelming (Ex. 26.8).

In the interest of balance, a commentary from Sams on *O Freund, mein Schirm, mein Schutz!* (pp. 215–16) follows:

> Here is nothing to express. Instead, the fustian text, with its quaint overtones of Biblical imagery done into botched verse, seems to put him in mind of the church cantatas of Bach. But he also modernizes the musical language, giving it a new insistence and angularity to match Rückert's short lines in rhymed triplets. The result must have sounded very singular in 1849 and is still without parallel in Schumann's work.

This neglected song, indicated for *Alt oder Sopran*, shows one aspect of the long road Schumann had taken from his first days of exploration with the Lied at age eighteen, when he confided in a letter (Fischer-Dieskau, p. 25) to Gottlob Wiedebein:

Example 26.7. *Mein schöner Stern!*, bars 1–17.

In my previous letter I failed to tell you that I am knowledgeable in neither harmony, thorough-bass, nor counterpoint, but am instead a simple student of nature, following a blind and vain instinct, wanting to cast off my shackles. But now I will begin to study composition earnestly!

Still present within the mature Schumann is the youth who sought to cast off his shackles. Long since, Schumann had mastered traditional harmony and the uses of thoroughbass, but what is most important is his putting them to use by breaking new ground in his perpetual search to expand the perimeters of the Lied.

Die tausend Grüsse, die wir dir senden, #7, is a fiery duet for tenor and so-

Example 26.8.   *O Freund, mein Schirm, mein Schutz!*, bars 1–9.

prano, full of exuberance, much of it at *f* dynamic. Keyboard arpeggios in a resilient $\frac{6}{8}$ lead the singers in; they thrust themselves upon the scene. For both singers the vocal tessitura and the melodic excursions call for a number of high A's; this is the kind of vocalism sturdy dramatic voices can deliver best. The unmitigated joy of *Die tausend Grüsse, die wir dir senden* is infectious.

(As previously mentioned, *Minnespiel* concludes with a quartet for S. A. T. B., *So wahr die Sonne scheinet*, #8, which also appears in the Rückert Lieder, op. 37, #12, as a soprano and baritone duet, already considered.)

Opus 103

Elisabeth Kulmann is the source for a set of four duets, *Mädchenlieder*, op. 103, for two female voices. In *Mailied*, #1, Schumann again uses a compact dissonant harmony that denotes smallness. A bright and sunny D major, with lively staccatos for voice and keyboard parts, generates a bouncing folk-dance melody in keeping with "dann zu frohen Tänzen!" The musical texture of *Mailied* is slight. A certain elegance is joined to the folk element. Delightfully jovial, it must be sung and played with a light touch and with complete rhythmic steadiness.

Frühlingslied, #2, is not an example of Schumann's most imaginative reply to the call of Spring. The unison triplets in the pianoforte and the somewhat undistinguished melodies for the two sopranos offer at best a contrast to other styles encountered in the opus. (The same title occurs as a solo Lied, #4 of op. 125, and as a duet ad libitum, #18, op. 79.) These verses of Kulmann have a youthful charm about them. It would seem that Schumann, for that reason, treated them with becoming simplicity.

An die Nachtigall, #3, like *Mailied*, is an ennobled folk Lied, here with off-beat dancing rhythms. Schumann does not musically imitate nightingale calls. Rather, nightingale warbling ("Dein Gesang erklinge schmetternd überall") is indicated through a wide range of dynamics (*sf, ff, f, p*, and *pp*) and relatively little use of descriptive motivic patterns. The brook appears at *pp* level without the motion Schubert might have invented. Two soprano voices and keyboard can achieve an appealing ensemble with *An die Nachtigall*.

The fourth and final song of the Kulmann duet Lieder is *An den Abendstern*. Melodious, gentle, with relatively long phrases deployed over swaying keyboard triplets, *An den Abendstern* is a pleasant exercise. Legato singing and playing are essential to its success. Warmth and completeness of timbre will lift it beyond the mundane. The composer is aware of the possibilities of vocal quality resulting from the tessitura of each of the female voices. Schumann offers intimate ensemble singing.

Opus 112

Ei Mühle, liebe Mühle, #20 of op. 112, to a text by Moritz Horn, was originally intended as the final chorus of *Der Rose Pilgerfahrt*, a work for solo voices, chorus, and piano (later scored for orchestra). It appears here as a duet, and it is of interest precisely because on this occasion the composer makes use of a musical figure to render the mill. The directness of the melody in an aggressive C major and the prominent keyboard embellishments catch both the mill's mechanical work and a Sunday's festivities. Straightforward singing and playing invigorate this duet Lied.

(*Drei Lieder*, op. 114, for three female voices, is not considered here.)

Opus 138

Opus 138, which relies on Geibel translations from the Spanish and Portuguese, was published posthumously as *Spanische Liebeslieder* and was originally for four-hand accompaniment. Number 1 of the opus is a pianoforte prelude. In #2, *Tief im Herzen trag' ich Pein* (the original poem by Vaz de Camões), a solo melody of great beauty slowly unfolds over harplike chords in G minor. There is integration of voice and keyboard motifs, with mounting and descending intervals destined to sigh together. Contrary to criticism that there are so many themes and fragmentary ideas in this song that they lead to confusion (Sams, p. 194), the motifs complement each other, producing a highly emotive and compact expression of grief. The singer and pianist should savor this interplay (as in the first ten bars—even more fully realized in the remaining bars). Schumann indicated *Tief im Herzen trag' ich Pein* was for soprano voice, most probably because he wished to give each of the ensemble singers solo opportunities. The Lied could be equally advantageous to other vocal categories.

O wie lieblich ist das Mädchen, #3 (the original poem is by Gil Vicente), is designated by Schumann for tenor voice. Grace, wit, and charm have seldom been so neatly translated into musical terms. There is a folk flavor about the melody, but *O wie lieblich ist das Mädchen* in its musical sophistication goes beyond folk-song writing. In strophic repetition, the seaman, the knight, and the shepherd boy are each questioned about the beautiful, charming, sweet girl. A pianistic motif, first appearing in bars 11–13, poses the lover's rhetorical questions. *O wie lieblich ist das Mädchen* must be played and sung with brilliance and humor. It is essential to observe the keyboard staccato markings designed to achieve lightness; excessive pedaling is to be avoided. Tessitura and range indicate a technically skilled light tenor voice (preferably a *leggiero*). The sustained high B♭ should be sung fully and with joy. Tenorial lyricism and playfulness are keys to this Lied.

Bedeckt mich mit Blumen, #4 (poet anonymous), is a passionate song. (Wolf's well-known version from his *Spanisches Liederbuch* is another great setting.) The opening rhythmic motif in the keyboard urgently propels the soprano and mezzo-soprano (*Alt*) melodies as they soar from low to high ranges, distanced from each other at the interval of a third, and sometimes in canonic fashion. Interplay between pianoforte and voices is exciting and disquieting. The initial G minor turns to G major at "Von Jasmin und weissen Lilien sollt' ihr hier mein Grab bereiten," and the duet remains in major tonality for bars 14 through 21. Sixteenth-note chromatic configurations in the pianoforte express agitation, while at the same time the vocal line assumes an attitude of serenity. At the return to G minor, intensity begins to grow; the voices and pianoforte interweave brief textual repetitions. Emotional peaking, developed from the chromatic harmonies of the previous measures, comes for the two singers at bar 35. The pianist concludes with an extended version of the impassioned initial figure. Skillful singers and an accomplished pianist are clearly needed. *Bedeckt mich mit Blumen* stands at the forefront of the Lieder duet literature.

Young (p. 121), in tune with the twentieth-century conformist English-language criticism of the late Schumann Lieder, makes the following assessment of the duet literature: "Almost without exception his duets, lacking the grace of those of Mendelssohn, are without point or even charm. *Liebste, was kann denn uns scheiden?*, *Ei Mühle*, *Bedeckt mich mit Blumen*, *Blaue Augen*, are among the most alarming headstones in the graveyard of Romanticism."

The fifth Lied of op. 138, *Flutenreicher Ebro*, to an anonymous text, has met with such high critical acclaim that one breathes a sigh of relief that even its date of composition is insufficient reason for skeptics of the late Schumann to ignore its intrinsic value. Frequently in this study pejorative critique directed at the late songs has been quoted unfavorably. It is only fair to acknowledge a thoughtful evaluation of this late composition from an oft-quoted critic. Sams (p. 195) comments that Schumann writes a gay song, cheerfully unconcerned by the poem's suggesting the beloved does *not* think of her admirer; Sams believes Schumann mistakes the joys of Nature and the lover's condition for compar-

Example 26.9.   *Flutenreicher Ebro*, bars 1–5.

isons not contrasts: "We may be glad that he did; for this brief but welcome return to his earlier manner has an added maturity of craftsmanship, and the result is a masterpiece of unsullied and radiant charm." The keyboard's task is to imitate a guitar accompaniment. Above it must float, in graceful fashion, the lyric tenor voice. The text is a male expression, but a soprano should not be denied the opportunity to program such a jewel (Ex. 26.9).

Fischer-Dieskau (p. 168) finds that this Lied "stands out above the other songs in the group with its abundance of melody." He relates that Stephen Heller's *Improvisata* (op. 98) for pianoforte is titled *Über die Romanze Flutenreicher Ebro*, and in it Heller quotes the melody of Schumann's *Flutenreicher Ebro*.

(Number 6 is a pianoforte intermezzo for four hands.)

Weh, wie zornig ist das Mädchen, #7 (to another Vicente poem), is pure musical delight. The verses speak of the maiden's anger as she walks the hills with her flocks, but Schumann is in frolicsome mood. He cannot take her anger seriously but suspects that her display has a motive that is understood by her observer. As is true of so many of these late Lieder, the internal evidence is that Schumann's artistry was not affected by any prevailing psychological or pathological condition that might have been ravaging mind and body.

A light tenor voice is called for here. Short vocal phrases that consist of a single bar alternate with a similar keyboard figure. Singer and pianist must execute each of these phrases by direct statement. To deliver the right tone of skepticism regarding the girl's anger, the singer should use an exaggerated legato (with the exception of the indicated staccato passage). The keyboard trill in bars 25 and 26 ought to be saucily executed. These effects characterize the petulance of *das Mädchen*, not her deep anger. Schumann offers kindly understanding of the situation with his text repetitions. During the course of his career, he interpreted poetry in his own way. In this instance, he brings to the Lied more humor and sympathy for the young woman than are inherent in the poem itself.

With #8, Pedro de Padilla's poem *Hoch, hoch sind die Berge*, the mezzo-soprano (the Lied is designated for *Alt*) is given her solo moment. It is an "art song" in the folk idiom. Not plumbing the sense of loss experienced by the young woman when her disappearing mountaineer lover does not answer her call, *Hoch, hoch sind die Berge* instead becomes a pleasant narration. The Lied deals in understatement, as do most traditional folk-song settings; it should be performed without intensity, as the telling of a simple tale, just as it might have been sung and played by a raconteur to an intimate circle of listeners. This is not to say that it is not a worthy song. In fact, it is a forerunner of Lieder by later composers, including Brahms and Mahler, who repeatedly turned to folk sources. Harmonically and melodically *Hoch, hoch sind die Berge* is traditional; Schumann's elevation of the folk idiom to an artistic level without loss of *volkstümlich* simplicity is indicative of his perceptive handling of diverse literary subjects. (Schubert is the main source of this genre, of course, but Schumann completely transcends the folk idiom, producing an enriched art form.)

As has already been stated, it is not easy to find nonoperatic duet material for tenor and bass voices. *Blaue Augen hat das Mädchen*, #9, is a cheerful duet. Introductory chords announce forthright vocal statements. Soon the squareness of the vocal setting is offset by a dancing keyboard figure that at first seems not closely related but later integrates with the voices. The vocal demands of *Blaue Augen hat das Mädchen* are not insignificant. The duet certainly is not "an alarming headstone in the graveyard of Romanticism."

(The tenth and concluding song of this cycle is the vocal quartet *Dunkler Lichtglanz, blinder Blick*.)

The complete *Spanische Liebeslieder*, with its *Vorspiel* for four hands, its duets, and its final quartet, makes a captivating set. Negative twentieth-century criticism is largely responsible for its performance neglect.

Sommerruh, to a text by Christian Schad, has no opus number. It first appeared in *Deutscher Musenalmanach* in 1850 and reappeared in 1857. The musical setting, for soprano and mezzo-soprano, is slight but charming. It begins in the upper keyboard range while the singing voices begin in low registers. The juxtaposition of diverse voice and keyboard registers, and the placid character of the vocal lines as they are moved along by the pianoforte's rhythmic patterns, remarkably evoke the peace of a Summer's day. Even if not of great genius, this gentle music has much beauty.

27

Provenzalisches Lied, #4, *Ballade*, #7, Opus 139, and *Der Contrabandiste*, Opus 74, App.

I had considered concluding this manual on style and interpretation in the Lieder of Robert Schumann with Robert's December 1852 farewell to the Lied and to his creative life as expressed by the *Gedichte der Maria Stuart*, op. 135. In that case, the final salute would have been directed to Eusebius. But I want to call again on Florestan to keep in focus the two equal lifelong partners of Schumann's creative genius.

Provenzalisches Lied, #4, and *Ballade*, #7, op. 139, come from January 1852 and are settings of poems by Uhland. (Other parts of the opus are for soli, chorus, and orchestra, the whole dedicated to Brahms.) There is an astounding energy present in *Provenzalisches Lied*, with additional indications of the new directions in which Schumann was taking the Lied; he unites traditional and forward-looking elements into a challenging composition for both singer and pianist. *Provenzalisches Lied* takes its inspiration from the troubadour origins of the solo Lied. Yet it is far from academic; it is performers' music and should be sung and played with joy and gusto.

Both *Provenzalisches Lied* and *Ballade* were written with the harp in mind as the accompanying instrument, and the pianist must tackle Schumann's somewhat exaggerated imitations of a virtuosic harp. It is the duty of the singer (a tenor is indicated for *Provenzalisches Lied*) to adopt a noble vocal attitude.

Sams (p. 271), writing of *Provenzalisches Lied* and *Ballade*, remarks: "The two songs . . . are the last flowers of Schumann's genius as a song writer, and they make a good end."

Ballade is indicated for baritone voice. Schumann's highly successful ballad writing began in early 1840. His mastery continued into the late ballads and is clearly demonstrated here. Uhland, a powerful poet of the ballad, provides excellent material for Schumann's dramatic instincts.

The strong effect of *Ballade* is achieved by an alerting initial announcement in the keyboard of a rhythmic pattern constructed in fanfare fashion, introducing the broad, dignified, recitative-like narrative statement of the vocal line. Just as Wagner, in *Die Meistersinger von Nürnberg*, created a form of Lied previously unheard, so here Schumann takes the ancient ballade form and raises it to new declamatory dimensions. There are several brief moments in this ballad when the diatonic (not the chromatic) Wagner seems not far removed. The grand narrative style of Uhland's verse demands a new concept of vocal melody, just as Wagnerian prose dictated a new melodic approach. Schumann is drawn to the harplike keyboard configurations used with such frequency in the late Lieder. However, he does not merely rely on descriptive harp music; he introduces a remarkable key change in bar 12 and harmonic developments over the next nine measures that are some of the most interesting progressions to be found in his Lieder.

A baritone voice of ample size and range is essential to the performance of *Ballade*. Schumann's indication is *mit grosser Kraft* (with great strength). Dynamic markings are *f* and *ff*, and numerous sforzandos are interspersed. This song is among the most useful Lieder for the operatic baritone in search of dramatic concert literature. The singer is given opportunity to portray "three songs" sung out by the young challenger, each with its own theatrical flavor, the last ending in the slaying of King Sifrid. *Ballade* obviously fits into a group of Schumann ballads where dignity, power, and strong vocal and dramatic display are required. It is one of the great ballads of the nineteenth century. One marvels at the neglect it has suffered.

Several early songs have greater musicological interest than programmable appropriateness. As has been mentioned, Schumann, at age eighteen, first tried his hand at several Justinus Kerner poems, *Kurzes Erwachen*, *Gesanges Erwachen*, and *An Anna*. Thematic material from these songs was later incorporated into works for piano.

Der Contrabandiste, Opus 74, App.

Der Contrabandiste (*Kontrabandiste*), written as an annex to op. 74 in March of 1849, is additional evidence of Schumann's continuing creativity during that year. A display Lied for low male voice, *Der Contrabandiste* has the ring of a buffo opera aria, with roots in Mozart and Rossini. This is not the same Robert Schumann who wrote (p. 236): "And here you still speak of Italy, of Bellini and the land of song. When will we have done with the naive superstition that we could learn something about song from them?" It is not that Schumann has forgotten how to compose Lieder with a sensitive synthesis of word and music, how to make use of lyric declamation, or how to interweave keyboard and voice; he makes a decision to write a bravura aria, and he does it well.

Schumann's lack of mindfulness for word coloration in this Lied upsets some observers: "There is little attention to individual words here, but the prevailing virtuoso quality led Carl Tausig and later Sergei Rachmaninoff to arrange the piece for solo piano" (Fischer-Dieskau, p. 153); "Schumann's music derives directly from the text; but he is still unconcerned about individual words" (Sams, p. 193). These comments again impose a misplaced aesthetic ideal on Schumann's intention. With some frequency in his late Lieder Schumann goes south of the Alps for his inspiration, no longer disdaining the vocal display he had considered offensive earlier. Yet he runs this Italianate source through a Germanic filter. He is now quite content to place one foot on a southern Alp and the other in a German meadow. Unique in its *buffo* aspects, *Der Contrabandiste* still partly reveals the Robert Schumann of the early ballads, who enjoys sketching and sculpting literary characters of an exotic nature, clothing them with musical vestments. Regardless of what period of his life they come from, such characterizations are at a consistently high level.

A baritone who sings this Lied must have command of a two-octave (short of one note) performance range. He needs a strong sense of drama and should possess the technical means to execute high-lying agility figures. In order to retain the character of the protagonist, these configurations are to be sung vibrantly, with clean articulation at *f* dynamic level. The *ossia* passages that begin at bar 48 and again at bar 79 are inserted as an alternative solely for a baritone unable to execute the velocity patterns. Much of the bravura flavor of the Lied is lost if the *ossia* passages (whatever their history) are substituted. As is the case in other late Lieder for low male voice, Schumann writes for an instrument of operatic dimensions (bars 77–84).

While here the baritone is the smuggler, the pianist is the horse who prances and gallops. The sixteenth notes must be crystal clear, the grace notes fresh and crisp, the staccatos sharp and insolent. Both horse and rider, as they defiantly dash away, are motivated by a devil-may-care attitude. What a wonderful medium for the dramatic baritone or for the agile bass-baritone looking for recital material that will display skillful use of his instrument (Ex. 27.1)!

Brief mention must be made regarding the three Schumann compositions in *Melodram* form: *Schön Hedwig*, op. 106, #1, *Die Ballade vom Haideknaben*, op. 122, #1, and *Die Flüchtlinge*, op. 122, #2. Because they are not within the Lied genre, they are mentioned only in passing. Textual recitation using the spoken voice, not the singing voice, over descriptive orchestration was a popular compositional mode of the eighteenth century carried over into the nineteenth, evident even in the grave-digging episode from Beethoven's *Fidelio* and the Wolf's Glen scene from *Der Freischütz*. (Strauss's *Enoch Arden* [1897] and his *Das Schloss am Meere* [1899] are late examples of the *Melodram*.)

Eighteenth-century composers, notably Zumsteeg (1769–1802), transferred descriptive music from the orchestra to the keyboard. Zumsteeg's ballad style exercised a direct influence on young Schubert. It is not surprising, then, that

Example 27.1.   *Der Contrabandiste*, bars 47–56.

Robert Schumann, who explored so many facets of the Lied, should try his hand at the *Melodram* form, producing three of them. None are rated highly, partly because the idiom itself seems to modern listeners old-fashioned and naive. However, *Sprechstimme*, as well as the Lied genre, are indebted to the *Melodram*.

Yet these experiments with the *Melodram* reveal Schumann's long and continuing quest to solve the problem of the relationship of song to speech, of poetry to music. His early disdain for the then internationally reigning Rossinian style of vocal writing, the quite sudden discovery of his own musical language of lyric declamation, his attempt to elevate the joining of word and music, and voice and keyboard, beyond the Schubertian model while avoiding the excesses of the emerging Wagnerian declamatory style—all explain the wide diversity within the Lied oeuvre of Robert Schumann. Ivey (p. 198, paraphrasing Rudolf Felber) comments:

> The second period, from 1847 to 1851 . . . [is] intensively subjective in terms of an increased harmonic complexity, a melodic pursuit of more realistic declamation through the use of larger intervals, changes of register, and a more chromatic line which often exploits augmented and diminished intervals. There is also an inclination to place great reliance upon rhythmic elements in the search for greater control of declamation. At the same time, there is even more re-

sponsibility assigned to the piano and the demands upon the accompanist become almost virtuosic.

Ivey (p. 204) summarizes Schumann's position in the historical development of the Lied:

> In his command of suitably lyric declamatory devices, then, he was one of the leading figures of the nineteenth century in accomplishing still another synthesis—a close approximation of the best features of song and poetic recitation. And in addition there is his absorption into song style of such operatic devices as dramatic vocal lines and pseudo-recitative, which could serve the purposes of a shorter, more concise lyrical style without at the same time becoming infected with operatic excesses.

What has been described by some commentators as a loss of direction was actually an indication of the ongoing creative process of the ever-searching artist. Thilo Reinhard (p. 23) evaluates Schumann's diverse approaches to the Lied as follows: "Schumann was one of the few who dared to leave repeatedly the well-proven path and experiment with new means of expression; he thereby reveals his significance as a transitional figure whose life-work reaches from the heart of the Romantic movement to a new era of realism."

The contribution of Robert Schumann to the Lied goes beyond the composition of some beloved Lieder. He was in many respects a synthesizer of an extensive range of cultural philosophies, including those of Herder and Goethe, and the impulsive, groundbreaking musical instincts of Franz Schubert. The evolution of virtuosic pianism, eminently displayed in the works of Chopin and Liszt, was not ignored in Schumann's late songs, as he assimilated and expanded these elements. Standing midway within the history of the modern Lied, from its eighteenth-century inception to its twentieth-century development, Schumann joins Schubert, Brahms, Wolf, and Strauss to form the great quintet of Lied composers.

REFERENCES

Abraham, Gerald. "Robert Schumann," *The New Grove Dictionary of Music and Musicians*, ed. Stanley Sadie. Vol. 16. London: Macmillan, 1980.

Capell, Richard. *Schubert's Songs*. London: Duckworth, 1928.

Chissell, Joan. *Schumann*. New York: Collier, 1962.

Cooper, Martin. "The Songs," *Schumann: A Symposium,* ed. Gerald Abraham. London: Oxford University Press, 1952.

Dale, Kathleen. "The Piano Music," *Schumann: A Symposium,* ed. Gerald Abraham. London: Oxford University Press, 1952.

Daverio, John. *Robert Schumann: Herald of a New Poetic Age*. New York: Oxford University Press, 1997.

Desmond, Astra. *Schumann Songs, BBC Music Guides*. Seattle: University of Washington Press, 1972.

Einstein, Alfred. *Music in the Romantic Era*. New York: Norton, 1947.

Fischer-Dieskau, Dietrich. *Robert Schumann: Words and Music: The Vocal Compositions,* transl. by Richard G. Pauley. Portland, Oregon: Amadeus Press, 1981.

Gorrell, Lorraine. *The Nineteenth-Century German Lied*. Portland, Oregon: Amadeus Press, 1993.

Grieg, Edvard. "Robert Schumann," *Century Magazine*, 47, 1894.

Hallmark, Rufus. *The Genesis of Schumann's "Dichterliebe": A Source Study*, ed. George Buelow. Ann Arbor: UMI Research Press, University Microfilms International, 1979.

Hallmark, Rufus. "The Poet Sings," *German Lieder in the Nineteenth Century*. New York: Schirmer, 1996.

Heine, Heinrich. *Sämtliche Werke I/1: Buch der Lieder*, ed. Pierre Grappin. Hamburg: Hoffmann und Campe, 1975.

Ivey, Donald. *Song: Anatomy, Imagery, and Styles*. New York: Free Press, 1970.

Komar, Arthur, ed. *Schumann: "Dichterliebe": An Authoritative Score*. New York: Norton, 1971.

Moore, Gerald. *Poet's Love*. New York: Taplinger, 1981.

Nauhaus, Gerd, ed. *The Marriage Diaries of Robert and Clara Schumann*, transl. Peter Ostwald. Boston: Northeastern University Press, 1993.

Ostwald, Peter. *The Inner Voices of a Musical Genius*. Boston: Northeastern University Press, 1985.

Prawer, S. S. *The Penguin Book of Lieder*. New York: Penguin, 1964.

Reich, Nancy B. *Clara Schumann: The Artist and the Woman*. Ithaca, N.Y.: Cornell University Press, 1985.

Reinhard, Thilo. *The Singer's Schumann*. New York: Pelion Press, 1989.

Sammons, Jeffrey L. *Heinrich Heine*. Princeton: Princeton University Press, 1979.

Sams, Eric. *The Songs of Robert Schumann*. Bloomington: Indiana University Press, 1993.

Sams, Eric. *The Songs of Hugo Wolf*. London: Methuen, 1961.

Schumann, Robert. *On Music and Musicians*, ed. Konrad Wolff, transl. Paul Rosenfeld. New York: Pantheon, 1946.

Slater, E., and Meyer, A. "Contributions to a Pathography of the Musicians," *Confinia Psychiatrica*, 1959. 2 : 65–94.

Stein, Jack M. "Robert Schumann," *Poem and Music in the German Lied*. Cambridge: Harvard University Press, 1971.

Turchin, Barbara. *Robert Schumann's Song Cycles in the Context of the Early Nineteenth-Century "Liederkreis."* Ann Arbor: University Microfilms International, 1981.

Walsh, Stephen. *The Lieder of Robert Schumann*. London: Cassell, 1971.

Warrack, John. "Wilhemine Schröder-Devrient," *The New Grove Dictionary of Music and Musicians*, ed. Stanley Sadie. Vol. 16. New York: Macmillan, 1980.

Whitton, Kenneth. *An Introduction to German Song*. London: Julia McRae, 1984.

Young, Percy. *Tragic Muse: The Life and Works of Robert Schumann*. London: Hutchinson, 1957.

INDEX